Datalog and Logic Databases

Synthesis Lectures on Data Management

Editor
Z. Meral Özsoyoğlu, *Case Western Reserve University*
Founding Editor
M. Tamer Özsu, *University of Waterloo*

Synthesis Lectures on Data Management is edited by Meral Özsoyoğlu of Case Western Reserve University. The series publishes 80- to 150-page publications on topics pertaining to data management. Topics include query languages, database system architectures, transaction management, data warehousing, XML and databases, data stream systems, wide scale data distribution, multimedia data management, data mining, and related subjects.

Datalog and Logic Databases
Sergio Greco and Cristian Molinaro
2015

Big Data Integration
Xin Luna Dong and Divesh Srivastava
2015

Instant Recovery with Write-Ahead Logging: Page Repair, System Restart, and Media Restore
Goetz Graefe, Wey Guy, and Caetano Sauer
2014

Similarity Joins in Relational Database Systems
Nikolaus Augsten and Michael H. Böhlen
2013

Information and Influence Propagation in Social Networks
Wei Chen, Laks V.S. Lakshmanan, and Carlos Castillo
2013

Data Cleaning: A Practical Perspective
Venkatesh Ganti and Anish Das Sarma
2013

Datalog and Logic Databases

Sergio Greco and Cristian Molinaro

ISBN: 978-3-031-00726-2   paperback
ISBN: 978-3-031-01854-1   ebook

DOI 10.1007/978-3-031-01854-1

A Publication in the Springer series
SYNTHESIS LECTURES ON DATA MANAGEMENT

Lecture #41
Series Editor: Z. Meral Özsoyoğlu, *Case Western Reserve University*
Founding Editor: M. Tamer Özsu, *University of Waterloo*
Series ISSN
Print 2153-5418   Electronic 2153-5426

Datalog and Logic Databases

Sergio Greco and Cristian Molinaro
DIMES, Università della Calabria

SYNTHESIS LECTURES ON DATA MANAGEMENT #41

ABSTRACT

The use of logic in databases started in the late 1960s. In the early 1970s Codd formalized databases in terms of the relational calculus and the relational algebra. A major influence on the use of logic in databases was the development of the field of logic programming. Logic provides a convenient formalism for studying classical database problems and has the important property of being *declarative*, that is, it allows one to express *what* she wants rather than *how* to get it.

For a long time, relational calculus and algebra were considered the relational database languages. However, there are simple operations, such as computing the transitive closure of a graph, which cannot be expressed with these languages. Datalog is a declarative query language for relational databases based on the logic programming paradigm. One of the peculiarities that distinguishes Datalog from query languages like relational algebra and calculus is *recursion*, which gives Datalog the capability to express queries like computing a graph transitive closure.

Recent years have witnessed a revival of interest in Datalog in a variety of emerging application domains such as data integration, information extraction, networking, program analysis, security, cloud computing, ontology reasoning, and many others. The aim of this book is to present the basics of Datalog, some of its extensions, and recent applications to different domains.

KEYWORDS

relational databases, logic programs, datalog, recursion, negation, function symbols, aggregates, query optimization

Contents

Acknowledgments

We are very grateful to Leo Bertossi for his valuable comments, and to Tamer Özsu for the opportunity to write this book.

We would also like to express our thanks to Diane Cerra at Morgan & Claypool for her constant support and assistance.

Sergio Greco and Cristian Molinaro
October 2015

CHAPTER 1

Introduction

The use of logic in databases started in the late 1960s. In the early 1970s, Codd formalized databases in terms of the relational calculus and the relational algebra. A major influence on the use of logic in databases was the development of the field of logic programming. Logic provides a convenient formalism for studying classical database problems.

For a long time, relational calculus and algebra were considered the relational database languages. However, there are simple operations, such as computing the transitive closure of a graph, which cannot be expressed with these languages. Datalog is a declarative query language for relational databases based on the logic programming paradigm. From a syntactical standpoint, an important difference between Datalog and logic programs is that function symbols are not allowed in Datalog. One of the peculiarities that distinguishes Datalog from query languages like relational algebra and calculus is *recursion*, which gives Datalog the capability to express queries like computing a graph transitive closure.

Recent years have witnessed a revival of interest in Datalog in a variety of emerging application domains such as data integration, information extraction, networking, program analysis, security, cloud computing, ontology reasoning, and many others.

The aim of this book is to present the basics of Datalog, its extensions, and recent applications to different domains.

This book starts with a brief review of first-order logic, the relational model, and complexity classes in Chapter 2.

Chapter 3 introduces the syntax and different (equivalent) semantics of the Datalog language. Moreover, simple algorithms for the evaluation of Datalog queries are presented. Complexity and expressive power are analyzed as well.

Then, different extensions are considered, namely negation, functions symbols, and aggregates. Each of them is addressed in a separate chapter.

In Chapter 4, we first consider negation, which is an important feature to formalize common sense reasoning in knowledge representation, as it enables us to express nonmonotonic queries. Different increasingly liberal restrictions on the use of negation are considered, starting from different notions of "stratification" and ending with an arbitrary, or "unstratified," use of negation. For the latter, two different well-known semantics are presented, namely the stable model and the well-founded semantics. Then, we consider Datalog extended with a limited form a negation embedded in the *choice* construct. We also briefly discuss the extension of Datalog with disjunction.

In Chapter 5, Datalog is extended to include function symbols. Function symbols are widely acknowledged as an important feature, as they often make modeling easier and the resulting encodings more readable and concise. Unfortunately, the main problem with their introduction in Datalog is that the least model of a program can be infinite and thus the bottom-up program evaluation might not terminate. The chapter reports on recent research on identifying classes of programs allowing only a restricted use of function symbols while ensuring finiteness and computability of the least model.

In Chapter 6, another important feature of query languages is considered, namely aggregates. The most common aggregate operators are considered and we show how they help express optimization problems.

In Chapter 7, we report techniques that take advantage of the information in Datalog queries to make their evaluation more efficient. The first technique is the well-known *magic-sets rewriting* method, which consists of rewriting a Datalog query into an equivalent one that combines the advantages of the bottom-up and top-down evaluation strategies. The second technique applies to a special class of Datalog queries, called *chain queries*.

Finally, Chapter 8 briefly illustrates the use of Datalog in different current database applications.

CHAPTER 2

Logic and Relational Databases

A database is a collection of data organized to model relevant aspects of reality and to support processes requiring this information.

A database model is a formalism to describe how data are structured and used. It provides the means for specifying particular data structures, for constraining the data associated with these structures, and for manipulating the data. The most popular example of a database model is the *relational model*, although several other data models have been proposed and are currently used. The relational model was introduced by E. F. Codd in 1970 [Codd, 1970] as a way to make Database Management Systems (DBMSs) independent of any particular application.

Logic and databases have gone a long way together since the beginning of the relational data model itself. One of the first relational database query language, namely the relational calculus, is a fragment of first-order logic. Logic provides a convenient formalism for studying classical database problems.

In this chapter, we report the basics of first-order logic, relational model, relational query languages, data dependencies, and complexity classes.

2.1 FIRST-ORDER LOGIC

In this section, we report syntax and the Herbrand semantics of classical first-order predicate logic.

2.1.1 SYNTAX

A *first-order language* consists of an alphabet and all formulas that can be built from it. An *alphabet* consists of the following classes of symbols:

- a set of *variables*;

- a set of *constants*;

- a set of *function symbols*;

- a set of *predicate symbols*;

- the *connectives* ¬ (negation), ∨ (disjunction), ∧ (conjunction), → (implication), and ↔ (equivalence);

- the *quantifiers* ∃ (there exists) and ∀ (for all); and

- the parentheses "(" and ")", and the comma ",".

Each predicate and function symbol is associated with a fixed *arity* (i.e., the number of arguments), which is a non-negative integer for predicate symbols and a positive integer for function symbols (the role of function symbols with arity 0 is played by the constants). Thus, the sets of connectives, quantifiers, and parentheses are fixed. We also assume that the set of variables is infinite and fixed. The sets of constants, function symbols, and predicate symbols may vary and determine different first-order languages.

Terms are recursively defined as follows:

- a constant is a term;

- a variable is a term;

- if f is a function symbol of arity m and $t_1, \ldots, t_m$ are terms, then $f(t_1, \ldots, t_m)$ is a term.

Formulas are recursively defined as follows:

- if p is a predicate symbol of arity n and $t_1, \ldots, t_n$ are terms, then $p(t_1, \ldots, t_n)$ is a formula (also-called *atom*);

- if F and G are formulas, then so are $\neg F$, $(F \wedge G)$, $(F \vee G)$, $(F \to G)$, and $(F \leftrightarrow G)$; and

- if F is a formula and X is a variable, then $\exists X F$ and $\forall X F$ are formulas.

An atom of the form $p(t_1, \ldots, t_n)$ will be also-called a *p-atom*. In the following, a formula $(F \to G)$ will be written also as $(G \leftarrow F)$. Some well-known binary function symbols (e.g., $+$) and predicate symbols (e.g., $=$) are written in infix notation, that is, the symbol is written between the arguments. In order to avoid an excessive use of parentheses, we introduce a *binding order* among the connectives and the quantifiers: we assume that $\neg$, $\exists$, and $\forall$ bind stronger than $\wedge$ which in turns binds stronger than $\vee$ which binds stronger than $\to$ and $\leftrightarrow$. We also assume that $\vee$, $\wedge$, $\to$, and $\leftrightarrow$ *associate to the right*. A formula of the form $\forall X_1 \ldots \forall X_n F$ will be also written as $\forall X_1, \ldots, X_n F$, and likewise for the existential quantifier $\exists$. Thus, for instance, the formula[1]

$$\forall X \forall Y ((p(X) \wedge \neg r(Y)) \to (\neg q(X) \vee (q(X) \vee s(Y))))$$

can be rewritten as

$$\forall X, Y (p(X) \wedge \neg r(Y) \to \neg q(X) \vee (q(X) \vee s(Y)))$$

which can be in turn rewritten as the following formula because we are assuming that $\vee$ associates to the right

$$\forall X, Y (p(X) \wedge \neg r(Y) \to \neg q(X) \vee q(X) \vee s(Y)).$$

---

[1]Here p, q, r, and s are predicate symbols.

A term or formula is *ground* if no variables appear in it.

The *scope* of $\forall X$ (resp. $\exists X$) in the formula $\forall X F$ (resp. $\exists X F$) is F. A *bound* occurrence of a variable in a formula is an occurrence immediately following a quantifier, or an occurrence within the scope of a quantifier of the variable immediately after the quantifier. Any other occurrence of a variable is *free*. A formula without free variable occurrences is called a *sentence*. Thus, for instance, in the formula

$$\exists X p(X, Y) \wedge q(X)$$

the first two occurrences of X are bound, while the third one is free, because the scope of $\exists X$ is $p(X, Y)$. The occurrence of Y is free. In the formula

$$\exists X(p(X, Y) \wedge q(X))$$

all occurrences of X are bound because the scope of $\exists X$ is $p(X, Y) \wedge q(X)$. The occurrence of Y is free. Neither of the previous two formulas is a sentence as they have a free variable occurrence. The formula

$$\exists X(p(X, X) \wedge q(X))$$

is a sentence because it does not have free variable occurrences (the only variable in the formula is X and all its occurrences are bound).

Logic Programs.   Logic programs are sets of certain formulas of a first-order language. A *rule* is a formula of the following form:

$$\forall X_1 \ldots \forall X_m \, A_1 \vee \cdots \vee A_k \vee \neg L_1 \vee \cdots \vee \neg L_n,$$

where the A_i's are atoms, the L_j's are literals, and $X_1, \ldots, X_m$ are all the variables occurring in the formula's atoms and literals. The rule above can be written in the following special form (where all variables are implicitly assumed to be universally quantified at the front of the rule):

$$A_1 \vee \cdots \vee A_k \leftarrow L_1 \wedge \ldots \wedge L_n.$$

A *logic program* is a finite set of rules. With any logic program P we can associate a first-order language L_P whose constants, function symbols, and predicate symbols are exactly those occurring in P.

A *fact* is a ground rule with $k = 1$ and $n = 0$, that is, a rule of the form

$$p(t_1, \ldots, t_k) \leftarrow,$$

where the t_i's are ground terms. For notational simplicity, we will often write this fact simply as

$$p(t_1, \ldots, t_k);$$

that is, we drop the symbol $\leftarrow$.

2.1.2   HERBRAND SEMANTICS

Let L be a first-order language whose set of constants is not empty. The *Herbrand universe U_L* of L is the possibly infinite set of ground terms which can be built using constants and function symbols of L. The *Herbrand base B_L* of L is the (possibly infinite) set of ground atoms which can be built using predicate symbols of L and ground terms in U_L. A *Herbrand interpretation* (or simply *interpretation* in the following) for L is a subset of the Herbrand base B_L.

In order to define the notion of satisfaction of a formula by an interpretation, we need the notion of variable assignment to accommodate variables occurring free in formulas. A *variable assignment* is a function assigning each variable to an element of U_L and each element of U_L to itself. Given a variable assignment σ, a variable X, and a ground term t in U_L, we use $\sigma[X/t]$ to denote the variable assignment that is the same as σ except that $\sigma(X) = t$. Below we define when an interpretation I *satisfies* a formula F w.r.t. a variable assignment σ, denoted $I \models_\sigma F$. Let I be an interpretation, σ a variable assignment, F and G formulas. Then,

- if F is an atom $p(t_1, \ldots, t_n)$, then $I \models_\sigma F$ iff $p(\sigma(t_1), \ldots, \sigma(t_n)) \in I$;

- $I \models_\sigma \neg F$ iff $I \models_\sigma F$ does not hold;

- $I \models_\sigma F \vee G$ iff $I \models_\sigma F$ or $I \models_\sigma G$; and

- $I \models_\sigma \forall X F$ iff $I \models_{\sigma[X/t]} F$ for every $t \in U_L$.

We now define when I satisfies other kinds of formulas not mentioned above w.r.t. σ by expressing the remaining connectives and the quantifier $\exists$ in terms of $\neg$, $\vee$, and $\forall$:

- $F \wedge G$ is rewritten as $\neg(\neg F \vee \neg G)$;

- $F \rightarrow G$ is rewritten as $\neg F \vee G$;

- $F \leftrightarrow G$ is rewritten as $(F \rightarrow G) \wedge (G \rightarrow F)$, which is rewritten as $(\neg F \vee G) \wedge (\neg G \vee F)$; and

- $\exists X F$ is rewritten as $\neg \forall X \neg F$.

The difference between variables occurring free (for which the considered variable assignment is relevant) and those which are not is important. When interpreting a formula, the only bindings we need to know are those of free variables; we can change any of other bindings and still get the same result.

More formally, given an interpretation I, a formula F, and two variable assignments σ_1 and σ_2 agreeing on the variables occurring free in F, the following holds: $I \models_{\sigma_1} F$ iff $I \models_{\sigma_2} F$. As a consequence, if F is a sentence, then $I \models_{\sigma_1} F$ iff $I \models_{\sigma_2} F$ for any two variable assignments σ_1 and σ_2. Thus, when F is a sentence, we use $I \models F$ to denote that $I \models_\sigma F$ for any variable assignment σ. In such a case, we also say that I is a *model* for F (or F is *true* in I). Given a set S of sentences and an interpretation I, we say that I is a *model* of S iff I is a model of every sentence in S. We say that S is *satisfiable* if there exists a model for it, otherwise it is *unsatisfiable* or *inconsistent*. If every interpretation is a model of S then S is *valid*.

Given another set of sentences S', we say that S *semantically implies* S', denoted $S \models S'$, iff every model of S is also a model of S'. Finally, S and S' are *semantically equivalent* iff $S \models S'$ and $S' \models S$.

2.2   RELATIONAL MODEL

We assume the existence of the following pairwise disjoint sets: a set of *constants*, a set of *attributes*, and a set of *relation names*. The set of constants is called *database domain* and will be denoted as C. Each attribute A is associated with a set of constants called the *attribute domain* and denoted as $dom(A)$. Each relation name r has an *arity* n, which is a natural number, and is associated with a finite sequence of n attributes $A_1, \ldots, A_n$. A *relation schema* is of the form $r(A_1, \ldots, A_n)$. A *relation* R over $r(A_1, \ldots, A_n)$ is a finite subset of $dom(A_1) \times \cdots \times dom(A_n)$. Each element of R is called a *tuple*. Given a tuple $t = (a_1, \ldots, a_n)$ in R, we use $t[A_i]$ to denote a_i. Likewise, for a sequence X of attributes $A_{i_1}, \ldots, A_{i_m}$, $t[X]$ denotes the tuple $(t[A_{i_1}], \ldots, t[A_{i_m}])$. Intuitively, R can be seen as a table where each row is a tuple of R, each column refers to an attribute A_i and the values contained in the i-th column are taken from the attribute domain $dom(A_i)$.

A *database schema* is a set $\{S_1, \ldots, S_m\}$ of relation schemas; a *database instance* (or simply database) D over such a schema is a finite set of relations $\{R_1, \ldots, R_m\}$ where each R_i is a relation over schema S_i. If schema S_i is of the form $r_i(A_1, \ldots, A_n)$, the *extension* or *instance* of relation name r_i in D is R_i.

Query languages are introduced to derive information from databases. A *query* is a function that takes as input a database (over a fixed input schema) and gives as output another database (over a fixed output schema). Queries can be expressed by means of a given query language, such as the *relational algebra*, the *relational calculus*, *SQL* (Structured Query Language), or Datalog. The expressive power of a language is measured in terms of the set of queries that can be expressed using the language—for this purpose, queries have to be *generic*, that is, invariant under renamings of the database domain.

Next, we present the relational algebra and the relational calculus.

2.2.1   RELATIONAL ALGEBRA

The relational algebra extends the algebra of sets and consists of five primitive operators defined below. Consider two relation schemas $r(A_1, \ldots, A_n)$ and $s(B_1, \ldots, B_m)$ and let R and S be two relations over the first and second schema, respectively. The primitive relational algebra operators are defined as follows:

- *Cartesian product*: $R \times S = \{(r_1, \ldots, r_n, s_1, \ldots, s_m) \mid (r_1, \ldots, r_n) \in R \wedge (s_1, \ldots, s_m) \in S\}$;

- *Union*: $R \cup S = \{t \mid t \in R \vee t \in S\}$;

- *Difference*: $R - S = \{t \mid t \in R \wedge t \notin S\}$;

- *Projection*: $\pi_X(R) = \{t[X] \mid t \in R\}$, where X is a sequence of attributes among $A_1, \ldots, A_n$; and

- *Selection*: $\sigma_F(R) = \{t \mid t \in R \wedge F(t)\}$. Here F is an expression built using the logical connectives $\vee, \wedge, \neg$, and atomic expressions of the form $E_1 \ op \ E_2$ where op is a comparison operator, whereas E_1 and E_2 are constants or attributes names. $F(t)$ denotes the true/false value given by evaluating expression F over tuple t.

The relational algebra defined above is also-called *named*, since attribute names are used in the relational algebra operators. In the *unnamed* relational algebra attributes are referred to by their positions in the relation schema. So, in the projection and selection operators, we can refer to an attribute A_i of a relation R over schema $r(A_1, \ldots, A_n)$ using the expression $\$i$ instead of A_i.

Several derived operators have been defined as well. Derived operators do not increase the expressive power of the language (i.e., they do not allow us to express more queries), but are introduced to make expressions more comprehensible and their evaluation more efficient. For instance, the derived operators *intersection* and *join* are defined as follows:

- *Intersection*: $R \cap S = \{t \mid t \in R \wedge t \in S\} = R - (R - S) = S - (S - R)$; and

- *Join*: $R \bowtie_F S = \{(r_1, \ldots, r_n, s_1, \ldots, s_m) \mid (r_1, \ldots, r_n) \in R \wedge (s_1, \ldots, s_m) \in S \wedge F(r_1, \ldots, r_n, s_1, \ldots, s_m)\} = \sigma_F(R \times S)$, where F is a selection expression (here we are assuming that the schemas of R and S have no common attribute).

In the unnamed relational algebra, the atomic expressions of F are of the form $\$i \ op \ \$j$, with $1 \leq i \leq n$ and $1 \leq j \leq m$, that is, $\$i$ refers to an attribute of R and $\$j$ refers to an attribute of S. Thus, $R \bowtie_F S = \sigma_{F'}(R \times S)$ where F' is obtained from F by replacing each atomic expression $\$i \ op \ \$j$ with $\$i \ op \ \$(n + j)$.

Example 2.1   Suppose to have two relations *Employee* and *Department* over relation schemas *employee*(*EmpId*, *EmpName*, *Dept*) and *department*(*DeptId*, *DeptName*), respectively. The query asking for the names of the employees who work in the department *physics* can be expressed in the named relational algebra as:

$$\pi_{EmpName}\big(Employee \bowtie_{Dept=DeptId} (\sigma_{DeptName=physics}(Department))\big).$$

In the unnamed relational algebra, the same query can be expressed as follows:

$$\pi_{\$2}\big(Employee \bowtie_{\$3=\$1} (\sigma_{\$2=physics}(Department))\big).$$

Notice that in the join condition, $\$3$ refers to the third attribute of *Employee* whereas $\$1$ refers to the first attribute of *Department*.

2.2.2 RELATIONAL CALCULUS

The *relational calculus*, introduced below, is another formalism to express queries in the relational model and can be viewed as a specialization of first-order logic. More precisely, the language we present in this subsection is sometimes called *domain calculus*, because variables range over the underlying database domain; in *tuple calculus*, which we do not consider, variables range over tuples.

Consider the first-order language L whose set of constants is the database domain C, the set of function symbols is empty, and the set of predicate symbols consists of the set of relation names and comparison predicate symbols. Notice that the Herbrand universe U_L is equal to C. An atom of the form $p(t_1, \ldots, t_n)$, where p is a relation name and the t_i's are terms, is called *relation atom*; an atom of the form $t_1 \ op \ t_2$, where op is a comparison predicate symbol and t_1, t_2 are terms, is called *comparison atom*—here the infix notation has been used for op. When op is $=$, we call the atom *equality atom*.

Notice that a database D can be seen as a set of facts: if $(a_1, \ldots, a_n)$ is a tuple belonging to the extension of a relation name r in D, then we have a fact $r(a_1, \ldots, a_n)$. Thus, in the following we will look at databases as finite sets of facts. This also means that a database D can be seen as a (finite) Herbrand interpretation for L. As a consequence, we can define when a database D *satisfies* a formula F w.r.t. a variable assignment σ, denoted $D \models_\sigma F$, in the same way as defined for interpretations in Section 2.1.2—in this regard, notice that if F is a comparison atom $t_1 \ op \ t_2$, then $D \models_\sigma F$ iff $\sigma(t_1) \ op \ \sigma(t_2)$ holds.

A *relational calculus query* is an expression of the form:

$$\{(u_1, \ldots, u_n) \mid F\},$$

where the u_i's are terms of L, F is a formula of L, and the variables in $(u_1, \ldots, u_n)$ are exactly the variables occurring free in F. Notice that each u_i is either a constant or a variable (as L does not have function symbols) and the same term can be repeated in $(u_1, \ldots, u_n)$.

Example 2.2 Consider again the database schema consisting of the two relation schemas *employee*(*EmpId*, *EmpName*, *Dept*) and *department*(*DeptId*, *DeptName*). The query asking for the names of the employees working in the *physics* department can be expressed with the following relational calculus query:

$$\{(Y) \mid \exists X \, \exists Z \; employee(X, Y, Z) \wedge department(Z, physics)\}.$$

Given a database D and a relational calculus query Q of the form $\{(u_1, \ldots, u_n) \mid F\}$, the semantics of Q over D is

$$Q(D) = \{(\sigma(u_1), \ldots, \sigma(u_n)) \mid \sigma \text{ is a variable assignment and } D \models_\sigma F\}.$$

We also say that tuples in $Q(D)$ are the *answers* to Q over D.

In the first-order language L considered so far, the set of constants is equal to the database domain C. The semantics above can be generalized to allow explicit specification of the underlying domain to use (i.e., the set of constants over which variables may range). The *active domain* of a database D, denoted $adom(D)$, is the set of constants appearing in D. Likewise, we use $adom(Q)$ and $adom(F)$ to denote the set of constants appearing in a relational calculus query Q and formula F, respectively. The semantics of a relational calculus query over a database with respect to a particular domain C', called *evaluation domain*, is defined as seen before except that the underlying set of constants of the language is C' and the range of variable assignment is C' rather than C. Notice that the supersets of $adom(D) \cup adom(Q)$ are the only domains with respect to which it makes sense to evaluate Q over D, so we assume $(adom(D) \cup adom(Q)) \subseteq C' \subseteq C$. In order to specify the evaluation domain C' w.r.t. which a query is evaluated we use the notation $Q_{C'}(D)$. Note that if C' is infinite, then $Q_{C'}(D)$ can be an infinite set of tuples.

Domain Independent and Safe Relational Calculus Queries.   A relational calculus query Q is *domain independent* if for every database D, and every pair C', C'' such that $(adom(D) \cup adom(Q)) \subseteq C', C'' \subseteq C$, it is the case that $Q_{C'}(D) = Q_{C''}(D)$. Thus, for an arbitrary database, a domain independent relational calculus query gives the same result regardless of the domain with respect to which is evaluated. In other words, if Q is domain independent, then $Q_{C'}(D)$ does not change when C' changes. This means that $Q_{C'}(D)$ can be computed for $C' = adom(D) \cup adom(Q)$.

Example 2.3   Consider the relation schema $r(A, B)$ and the following relational calculus queries:

$$Q^1 = \{(X, Y) \mid \exists U\, \exists Z\, (r(U, Z) \vee r(X, Y))\},$$

$$Q^2 = \{(X, Y) \mid \neg r(X, Y)\},$$

$$Q^3 = \{(X) \mid \forall Y\, r(X, Y)\}.$$

All the queries above are not domain independent. To see why, consider a relation $R = \{(a, a), (a, b)\}$ and let C' be a domain. It is easy to check that $Q^1_{C'}(\{R\}) = \{(x, y) \mid x \in C' \wedge y \in C'\}$ and $Q^2_{C'}(\{R\}) = \{(x, y) \mid x \in C' \wedge y \in C' \wedge (x, y) \notin R\}$.

As the results of Q^1 and Q^2 contain values of C', then their results clearly depend on C'. It is easy to see that Q^3 will always contain values taken from the input relation; nevertheless, it is not domain independent. In fact, it is easy to see that if C' is infinite, then $Q^3_{C'}(\{R\})$ is empty. The same holds if, for instance, $C' = \{a, b, c\}$. However, if $C' = \{a, b\}$, then $Q^3_{C'}(\{R\}) = \{(a)\}$. Hence, Q^3 can give different results over the same relation when different evaluation domains are considered.

On the other hand, it is easy to see that the following queries are domain independent, as the query answers depend only on the content of the input database:

$$Q^4 = \{(X, Y) \mid \exists Z(r(X, Z) \wedge r(Z, Y))\},$$

$$Q^5 = \{(X, Y) \mid r(X, Y))\}.$$

The problem of deciding whether a relational calculus query is domain independent is undecidable [Abiteboul et al., 1995, Ullman, 1988]. It is important to observe that the fact that we can express relational calculus queries that are not domain independent is not a positive aspect as, in the presence of an infinite database domain, we can get query answers that have an infinite number of tuples.

We now present some syntactical restrictions that lead to a class of relational calculus queries, called *safe*, that are guaranteed to be domain independent. Safe relational calculus queries are a subset of the domain independent relational calculus queries [Abiteboul et al., 1995, Ullman, 1988].

Safe relational calculus is derived from relational calculus by imposing the following restrictions on formulas.

1. The universal quantifier $\forall$ is not used. This does not affect the expressiveness of the language as expressions of the form $\forall X F$ can be rewritten as $\neg(\exists X \neg F)$.

2. The disjunction operator is applied only to formulas having the same set of free variables.

3. For any maximal sub-formula F of the form $F_1 \wedge \cdots \wedge F_n$, all the free variables of F must be *limited* in the following sense:

   - a variable is limited if it is free in some F_i and F_i is not a comparison atom and is not negated;

   - if F_i is of the form $X = c$ or $c = X$, where X is a variable and c is a constant, then X is limited; and

   - if F_i is of the form $X = Y$ or $Y = X$, where X, Y are variables and Y is limited, then X is limited.

4. Negation is applied only to an F_i in a maximal sub-formula F of the form $F_1 \wedge \cdots \wedge F_n$ where all free variables are limited.

The safe relational calculus and the relational algebra have the same expressive power, that is, the set of queries that can be expressed by them is the same.

Example 2.4   The relational calculus queries Q^4 and Q^5 of Example 2.3, which are domain independent, are also safe. The relational calculus query $Q = \{(X, Y, Z) \mid F\}$, where F is the following formula

$$r(X, Y, Z) \wedge \neg(p(X, Y) \vee q(Y, Z)),$$

is domain independent but is not safe because F violates Condition 2—specifically, Condition 2 is violated by the subformula $p(X, Y) \vee q(Y, Z)$. On the other hand, if F is the formula below, then the relational calulus query is safe

$$r(X, Y, Z) \wedge \neg p(X, Y) \wedge \neg q(Y, Z).$$

2.2.3 CONJUNCTIVE QUERIES

Conjunctive queries (first introduced in Chandra and Merlin, 1977) are a natural class of commonly arising queries that enjoy different desirable properties (e.g., checking for equivalence and containment of conjunctive queries is decidable). They can be expressed in the languages seen so far as follows.

- Relational calculus: relational calculus queries of the form $\{\overline{Y} \mid \exists \overline{X} \, r_1(\overline{U}_1) \wedge \cdots \wedge r_k(\overline{U}_k)\}$ where $\overline{Y}$ is a tuple of variables (that must appear in the conjunction) and constants, $\overline{X}$ is the tuple of variables in the conjunction that are not in $\overline{Y}$, the r_i's are relation names, and the $\overline{U}_i$'s are tuples of terms (i.e., variables and constants). Notice that relational calculus queries of this form are safe, and thus, domain independent.

- Relational algebra: relational algebra queries using only positive selection (i.e., selection conditions are restricted to be conjunctions of equalities), projection, and Cartesian product.

Example 2.5 The relational calculus query of Example 2.2 is conjunctive. The relational algebra query of Example 2.1 can be rewritten into the following equivalent conjunctive query (recall that the join operator is a derived operator that can be expressed by means of Cartesian product and selection):

$$\pi_{EmpName}\left(\sigma_{Dept=DeptId}\left(Employee \times (\sigma_{DeptName=physics}(Department))\right)\right).$$

2.2.4 DATA DEPENDENCIES

Data dependencies are used to express integrity constraints on data, that is semantic properties that database instances should satisfy to properly reflect the real state of the world. Data dependencies are also used in database schema design to define *normal forms*, that is, conditions that a "good" relational database schema has to satisfy in order to reduce or eliminate redundant information. Recent years have seen a renewed interest in data dependencies since they play a central role in several current database applications such as data exchange and integration [Fagin et al., 2005, Lenzerini, 2002] and ontology management [Calì et al., 2009a,b]. For a more complete treatment of the subject we refer to Abiteboul et al. [1995] and Greco et al. [2012a].

An *embedded dependency* is a first-order logic sentence of the form:

$$\forall \overline{X}, \forall \overline{Y} \, (\phi(\overline{X}, \overline{Y}) \rightarrow \exists \overline{Z} \, \psi(\overline{X}, \overline{Z})),$$

where $\overline{X}$, $\overline{Y}$, and $\overline{Z}$ are tuple of variables, $\phi(\overline{X}, \overline{Y})$ and $\psi(\overline{X}, \overline{Z})$ are conjunctions of relation and equality atoms, called the *body* and the *head* of the dependency, respectively. Without loss of generality we can assume that equality atoms may appear only in the head of the dependency and there is no existentially quantified variable involved in an equality atom.

Subclasses of embedded dependencies are:

- *unirelational* dependencies: only one relational symbol is used in ϕ and ψ;

- *1-head* dependencies: only a single atom in the head;

- *tuple generating* dependencies (TGDs): no equality atoms;

- *full* dependencies: no existentially quantified variables $\overline{Z}$; and

- *equality generating* dependencies (EGDs): full, 1-head with an equality atom in the head.

Example 2.6   Consider the database schema consisting of the two relation schemas *employee(EmpId, EmpName, Dept)* and *department(DeptId, DeptName)*. The following equality generating dependency states that, given a database D over the schema above, the instance of *department* in D cannot contain two distinct tuples with the same value on *DeptId*.

$$\forall D, N_1, N_2 \ (department(D, N_1) \wedge department(D, N_2) \rightarrow N_1 = N_2)$$

The previous dependency is a *functional dependency* (in particular, a *key dependency*) and *DeptId* is a *key* of *department* [Abiteboul et al., 1995, Greco et al., 2012a].

In general, a functional dependency is an equality generating dependency of the form

$$\forall \overline{X}, \overline{Y}_1, \overline{Y}_2, \overline{Z}_1, \overline{Z}_2 \ (p(\overline{X}, \overline{Y}_1, \overline{Z}_1) \wedge p(\overline{X}, \overline{Y}_2, \overline{Z}_2) \rightarrow \overline{Z}_1 = \overline{Z}_2),$$

where $p(\overline{X}, \overline{Y}_1, \overline{Z}_1)$ and $p(\overline{X}, \overline{Y}_2, \overline{Z}_2)$ are relation atoms with $\overline{X}, \overline{Y}_1, \overline{Y}_2, \overline{Z}_1$, and $\overline{Z}_2$ being lists of variables. This functional dependency can be expressed also as $A \rightarrow B$, where A is the set of attributes of p corresponding to $\overline{X}$ and B is the set of attributes of p corresponding to $\overline{Z}_1$ (and $\overline{Z}_2$). A relation R over the schema of p *satisfies* such a functional dependency if, for every two tuples $t_1, t_2 \in R$, if $t_1[A] = t_2[A]$ then $t_1[B] = t_2[B]$.

The following tuple generating dependency states that, given a database D over the schema above, for every tuple t in the instance of *employee* in D, there must be a tuple t' in the instance of *department* in D s.t. $t[Dept] = t'[DeptId]$

$$\forall E, N, D \ (employee(E, N, D) \rightarrow \exists M \ department(D, M)).$$

The previous dependency is also called *inclusion dependency*.

Dependency Skolemization.   Given a TGD d of the form

$$\forall \overline{X}, \forall \overline{Y} \, (\phi(\overline{X}, \overline{Y}) \rightarrow \exists Z_1, \ldots, Z_n \, \psi(\overline{X}, Z_1, \ldots, Z_n))$$

the *skolemized version* of d, denoted $sk(d)$, is the following sentence

$$\forall \overline{X}, \forall \overline{Y} \, (\phi(\overline{X}, \overline{Y}) \rightarrow \psi(\overline{X}, f_{Z_1}^d(\overline{X}, \overline{Y}), \ldots, f_{Z_n}^d(\overline{X}, \overline{Y}))),$$

where each $f_{Z_i}^d$ is a fresh function symbol of arity $|\overline{X}| + |\overline{Y}|$. Thus, existentially quantified variables in the head of d are replaced by *skolemized terms*. For a full data dependency d (including EGDs), $sk(d) = d$.

2.3   COMPLEXITY CLASSES

Let Σ be a finite alphabet and $L \subseteq \Sigma^*$ be a *language* in Σ, that is, a set of finite strings over Σ. Let T be a Deterministic Turing Machine (DTM) or a Nondeterministic Turing Machine (NDTM), such that *(i)* if $x \in L$, then T accepts x, and *(ii)* if $x \notin L$, then T rejects x. In this case, we say that T *decides* L. In addition, if T halts in time $O(f(n))$, we say that T decides L *in time* $O(f(n))$. Similarly, if T halts within space $O(f(n))$, we say that T decides L *within space* $O(f(n))$ (for details on DTM and NDTM, see Johnson [1990] and Papadimitriou [1994]).

We define the following sets of languages:

$$
\begin{aligned}
\text{TIME}(f(n)) &= \{L \mid L \text{ is a language decided by some DTM in time } O(f(n))\} \\
\text{NTIME}(f(n)) &= \{L \mid L \text{ is a language decided by some NDTM in time } O(f(n))\} \\
\text{SPACE}(f(n)) &= \{L \mid L \text{ is a language decided by some DTM within space } O(f(n))\} \\
\text{NSPACE}(f(n)) &= \{L \mid L \text{ is a language decided by some NDTM within space } O(f(n))\}.
\end{aligned}
$$

All these sets are examples of *complexity classes*. Complexity classes of most interest are not classes corresponding to particular functions but their unions such as, for example, the union $\cup_{d>0}\text{TIME}(n^d)$ taken over all polynomials of the form n^d. Some common complexity classes are:

$$
\begin{aligned}
\text{P} &= \bigcup_{d>0} \text{TIME}(n^d) \\
\text{NP} &= \bigcup_{d>0} \text{NTIME}(n^d) \\
\text{EXPTIME} &= \bigcup_{d>0} \text{TIME}(2^{n^d}) \\
\text{NEXPTIME} &= \bigcup_{d>0} \text{NTIME}(2^{n^d}) \\
\text{PSPACE} &= \bigcup_{d>0} \text{SPACE}(n^d) \\
\text{EXPSPACE} &= \bigcup_{d>0} \text{SPACE}(2^{n^d}) \\
\text{L} &= \text{SPACE}(\log n) \\
\text{NL} &= \text{NSPACE}(\log n).
\end{aligned}
$$

The list does not contain the nondeterministic counterparts of PSPACE and EXPSPACE because $\bigcup_{d>0} \text{NSPACE}(n^d)$ coincides with the class PSPACE and $\bigcup_{d>0} \text{NSPACE}(2^{n^d})$ coincides with the class EXPSPACE.

The *complementary class* of a complexity class $\mathcal{C}$, denoted co-$\mathcal{C}$, is defined as follows. For every language L in Σ, let $\overline{L}$ denote its *complement*, that is, the set $\Sigma^* \backslash L$. Then, co-$\mathcal{C}$ is $\{\overline{L} \mid L \in \mathcal{C}\}$.

Below we define the *polynomial hierarchy classes*. In order to do it, we first need to introduce *oracle Turing machines*. Let A be a language. An *oracle DTM* T^A, also-called a DTM *with oracle A*, can be thought of as an ordinary DTM augmented by an additional *write-only* query tape and additional three states *query*, $\in$, and $\notin$. When T^A is not in the state *query*, the computation proceeds as usual (in addition, T^A can write on the query tape). When T^A is in *query*, T^A changes this state to $\in$ or $\notin$ depending on whether the string written on the query tape belongs to A; furthermore, the query tape is instantaneously erased. As in the case of an ordinary DTM, the expended time is the number of steps and the required space is the number of cells used on the tape and the query tape. The oracle replies to a query in unit time, and thus, roughly speaking, models a call to a subroutine that is evaluated in unit time. An *oracle* NDTM is defined as the same augmentation of a NDTM.

Let $\mathcal{C}$ be a set of languages. The complexity classes $\mathsf{P}^{\mathcal{C}}$ and $\mathsf{NP}^{\mathcal{C}}$ are defined as follows. Given a language L, we have $L \in \mathsf{P}^{\mathcal{C}}$ (resp. $L \in \mathsf{NP}^{\mathcal{C}}$) if and only if there is some language $A \in \mathcal{C}$ and some oracle DTM (resp. NDTM) T^A such that T^A decides L in polynomial-time. The *polynomial hierarchy* consists of classes Δ_i^p, Σ_i^p, and Π_i^p defined as follows:

$$\Delta_0^p = \Sigma_0^p = \Pi_0^p = \mathsf{P}$$
$$\Delta_{i+1}^p = \mathsf{P}^{\Sigma_i^p} \qquad \text{for } i \geq 0$$
$$\Sigma_{i+1}^p = \mathsf{NP}^{\Sigma_i^p} \qquad \text{for } i \geq 0$$
$$\Pi_{i+1}^p = \text{co-}\Sigma_{i+1}^p \qquad \text{for } i \geq 0.$$

The class PH is defined as $\bigcup_{i \geq 0} \Sigma_i^p$. Notice that $\mathsf{NP} = \Sigma_1^p$, co-NP $= \Pi_1^p$, and $\Delta_2^p = \mathsf{P}^{\mathsf{NP}}$.

Let L_1 and L_2 be languages. Assume that there is a DTM R such that *(i)* for all input strings x, we have $x \in L_1$ if and only if $R(x) \in L_2$, where $R(x)$ denotes the output of R on input x; and *(ii)* R halts within space $O(\log n)$. Then, R is called a *logarithmic-space reduction* from L_1 to L_2 and we say that L_1 is *reducible* to L_2. Let $\mathcal{C}$ be a set of languages. A language L is called $\mathcal{C}$-*hard* if any language L' in $\mathcal{C}$ is reducible to L. If L is $\mathcal{C}$-hard and $L \in \mathcal{C}$, then L is called $\mathcal{C}$-*complete* or *complete for* $\mathcal{C}$.

BIBLIOGRAPHIC NOTES

Relational model and relational algebra were introduced by Codd [1970]. Codd [1972] introduced relational calculus showing its equivalence with relational algebra. For a more complete treatment of relational databases the reader is referred to Abiteboul et al. [1995], Date [2000], Elmasri and Navathe [2000], Garcia-Molina et al. [2009], Maier [1983], Ramakrishnan and Gehrke [2003], Silberschatz et al. [2010], Ullman [1988]. For a more complete treatment of logic programming we refer to Apt [1991], Lloyd [1987], while for a detailed exposition of complexity notions we refer to Johnson [1990] and Papadimitriou [1994].

CHAPTER 3

Datalog

Datalog is a declarative query language for relational databases based on the logic programming paradigm. From a syntactical standpoint, an important difference between Datalog and logic programs is that function symbols are not allowed in Datalog. For a long time, relational calculus and algebra were considered the relational database languages. However, there are simple operations, such as computing the transitive closure of a graph, which cannot be accomplished with those languages. One of the peculiarities that distinguishes Datalog from the query languages presented in the previous chapter is *recursion*, which gives Datalog the capability to express queries like computing a graph transitive closure.

3.1 SYNTAX

A *Datalog rule r* is (a logic program rule) of the form:

$$A_0 \leftarrow A_1, \ldots, A_n,$$

where $n \geq 0$, the A_i's are atoms where no function symbol appears, and every variable appearing in A_0 also appears in at least one of $A_1, \ldots, A_n$. The last requirement is called *safety* and is used to avoid rules yielding infinite relations from finite ones. Comparison operators are not allowed in a Datalog rule. A_0 is called the *head* of r and is denoted by *head*(r); the conjunction $A_1, \ldots, A_n$ is called the *body* of r and is denoted by *body*(r). With a slight abuse of notation, *body*(r) will be also used to denote the *set* of atoms appearing in the body of r. The intuitive meaning of the Datalog rule above is that if $A_1, \ldots, A_n$ are all true, then A_0 has to be true. A *fact* is a ground rule with empty body; we call it a *p-fact* if p is the predicate symbol in the head. For notational simplicity, we will often write a fact simply as A_0. rather than $A_0 \leftarrow$., that is, we drop the symbol $\leftarrow$.

A *Datalog program* is a finite set of Datalog rules. The *definition* of a predicate symbol p in a program P, denoted *def*(p, P), is the set of rules of P having p in the head atom. Recall that a database can be seen as a finite set of facts. In the context of logic programming all the knowledge (facts and general rules) is usually contained in a single logic program. As Datalog has been developed for database applications, we will consider two sets of Datalog rules:

1. a set of facts D representing tuples of a database; and

2. a Datalog program P whose rules define new relations (or "views") from the database.

D is called the *Extensional Database* (EDB) and P is called the *Intensional Database* (IDB). We will refer to D simply as database and refer to P as Datalog program. Thus, predicate symbols are partitioned into two disjoint sets: *base* (or EDB or *extensional*) and *derived* (or IDB or *intensional*) predicate symbols. The definition of base predicate symbols is stored in D. Base predicate symbols can appear in the body of rules in P but not in the head. Derived predicate symbols cannot appear in D and their definition is in P. We will use P_D to denote $P \cup D$. An atom whose predicate symbol is base (resp. derived) is also-called a *base* (resp. *derived*) *atom*.

Example 3.1   The following database stores the edges of a directed graph by means of facts of the form $edge(v_1, v_2)$, meaning that there is an edge from vertex v_1 to vertex v_2 in the graph:

$$edge(a, b).$$
$$edge(b, c).$$
$$edge(c, d).$$

Below is a Datalog program to compute the transitive closure of a graph stored by means of *edge*-facts:

$$tc(X, Y) \leftarrow edge(X, Y).$$
$$tc(X, Y) \leftarrow edge(X, Z), tc(Z, Y).$$

Intuitively, the first rule above says that if there is an edge from a vertex X to a vertex Y, then (X, Y) belongs to the transitive closure of the graph. The second rule says that if there is an edge from a vertex X to a vertex Z and there exists a vertex Y such that (Z, Y) belongs to the transitive closure, then (X, Y) belongs to the transitive closure as well.

It is worth noting that the transitive closure of a graph cannot be expressed using the relational algebra and calculus [Aho and Ullman, 1979].

The *dependency graph* $\mathcal{G}_P$ of a Datalog program P is a directed graph defined as follows: the set of vertices is the set of derived predicate symbols appearing in P; for each pair of derived predicate symbols p and p' (not necessarily distinct) appearing in P, there is an edge from p' to p iff P contains a rule where p' appears in the body and p appears in the head. Program P is said to be *recursive* if the dependency graph $\mathcal{G}_P$ is cyclic. A derived predicate symbol p is said to be *recursive* if it occurs in a cycle of $\mathcal{G}_P$; two predicate symbols p and p' are *mutually recursive* if they occur in the same cycle. As an example, the Datalog program of Example 3.1 is recursive as its dependency graph has an edge from tc to tc. A predicate symbol p *depends on* a predicate symbol p', denoted $p' \leq p$, if there is a path from p' to p in $\mathcal{G}_P$; $leq(p)$ denotes the set of all predicate symbols p' for which $p' \leq p$.

Given a Datalog program P, a rule in P with head predicate symbol p is *linear* if there is at most one atom in the body of the rule whose predicate symbol is mutually recursive with p. If each rule in P is linear, then P is *linear*. Clearly, the Datalog program of Example 3.1 is linear.

Conjunctive queries can be expressed by non-recursive Datalog programs with only base predicate symbols occurring in the body. More precisely, a conjunctive query can be expressed by means of a Datalog rule of the form

$$ans(\overline{X}) \leftarrow r_1(\overline{X}_1), \ldots, r_n(\overline{X}_n),$$

where *ans* is a derived predicate symbol, $\overline{X}$ is a tuple of variables (that must appear in the rule body) and constants, the r_i's are base predicate symbols, and the $\overline{X}_i$'s are tuples of terms (i.e., variables and constants).

Example 3.2 Consider again the database schema consisting of the two relation schemas *employee*(*EmpId*, *EmpName*, *Dept*) and *department*(*DeptId*, *DeptName*). The query asking for the names of the employees working in the *physics* department can be expressed with the following Datalog rule:

$$ans(Y) \leftarrow employee(X, Y, Z), department(Z, physics).$$

3.2 SEMANTICS

In this section, we report three semantics for Datalog programs. These semantics are "equivalent" in that they give the same extensions to derived predicate symbols.

3.2.1 MODEL-THEORETIC SEMANTICS

Let P be a Datalog program and D a database. The *Herbrand universe* H_{P_D} of P_D is the set of constants appearing in P_D. The *Herbrand base* B_{P_D} of P_D is the set of ground atoms which can be built using predicate symbols appearing in P_D and constants of H_{P_D}.

A (ground) atom A' is a *ground instance* of an atom A if A' can be obtained from A by substituting every variable in A with some constant in H_{P_D}—with multiple occurrences of the same variable being replaced with the same constant. We use *ground*(A) to denote the set of all ground instances of A. Likewise, a (ground) rule r' is a *ground instance* of a rule r in P_D if r' can be obtained from r by substituting every variable in r with some constant in H_{P_D}. The *ground instantiation* of r, denoted *ground*(r), is the set of all ground instances of r. The *ground instantiation* of P_D, denoted *ground*(P_D), is the set of all ground instances of the rules in P_D, that is, *ground*(P_D) $= \cup_{r \in P_D}$ *ground*(r).

An *interpretation* of P_D is any subset I of B_{P_D}. The truth value of a ground atom A w.r.t. I, denoted *value$_I$*(A), is *true* if $A \in I$, *false* otherwise. The truth value of a conjunction of ground atoms $A_1, \ldots, A_n$ w.r.t. I is *true* if every A_i ($1 \leq i \leq n$) is *true* w.r.t. I; otherwise, the truth value of the conjunction w.r.t. I is *false*. Notice that if $n = 0$, the conjunction is empty and its truth value w.r.t. I is *true*. A ground rule r is *satisfied* by I, denoted $I \models r$, if the conjunction in the body is *false* w.r.t. I or the head atom is *true* w.r.t. I; we write $I \not\models r$ if r is not satisfied by I. Thus, a ground rule r with empty body is satisfied by I if *value$_I$*(*head*(r)) = *true*.

An interpretation of P_D is a *model* of P_D if it satisfies every ground rule in *ground*(P_D). A model M of P_D is minimal if no proper subset of M is a model of P_D.

It is well known that P_D has a unique minimal model, which coincides with the intersection of all models of P_D, and thus is the least (under set inclusion) model of P_D. The model-theoretic semantics of P_D is given by its (unique) least model.

Thus, the model-theoretic semantics for a Datalog program is given by a minimal set of ground atoms satisfying the ground instantiation of the program. The minimality requirement is because the model should not contain more ground atoms than necessary to satisfy the ground rules in $ground(P_D)$. In this way, the least model contains exactly the atoms in D plus those that are semantically implied by $D \cup P$ as a first-order theory.

Example 3.3   Let D be the database and P the Datalog program of Example 3.1. It is easy to see that an interpretation of P_D satisfies all ground rules of P_D iff it contains at least the following set M of ground atoms:

$$edge(a,b).\quad tc(a,b).\quad tc(a,c).$$
$$edge(b,c).\quad tc(b,c).\quad tc(b,d).$$
$$edge(c,d).\quad tc(c,d).\quad tc(a,d).$$

Indeed, M is the least model of P_D. Notice that M is a model of P_D and no proper subset of it is a model of P_D.

3.2.2   FIXPOINT SEMANTICS

The fixpoint semantics is an operational semantics given in terms of an operator called the *immediate consequence operator*. Intuitively, this operator derives new ground atoms starting from known ground atoms, using the rules of a Datalog program.

Let P be a Datalog program and D a database. The *immediate consequence operator* $\mathcal{T}_{P_D}$ of P_D is defined as follows. Given a set I of ground atoms, then

$$\mathcal{T}_{P_D}(I) = \{A_0 \mid A_0 \leftarrow A_1, \ldots, A_n \text{ is a ground rule in } ground(P_D) \text{ and } \\ A_i \in I \text{ for every } 1 \leq i \leq n\}.$$

Thus, $\mathcal{T}_{P_D}$ takes as input a set of ground atoms I and returns as output a set of ground atoms $\mathcal{T}_{P_D}(I)$, called the *immediate consequences* of I w.r.t. P_D. Clearly, for every fact in D, its head is an immediate consequence of any set I of ground atoms as the fact body is empty. We say that a set of ground atoms I is a *fixpoint* of $\mathcal{T}_{P_D}$ if $\mathcal{T}_{P_D}(I) = I$.

It is easy to see that $\mathcal{T}_{P_D}$ is monotonic, that is, if $I_1 \subseteq I_2$, then $\mathcal{T}_{P_D}(I_1) \subseteq \mathcal{T}_{P_D}(I_2)$, for any sets of ground atoms I_1 and I_2. By the Knaster-Tarski theorem, since $\mathcal{T}_{P_D}$ is monotonic it has a least fixpoint (that is, a fixpoint that is included in any other fixpoint), which we denote as $lfp(\mathcal{T}_{P_D})$. The fixpoint semantics of P_D is given by the least fixpoint $lfp(\mathcal{T}_{P_D})$.

The least fixpoint can be computed as follows. The i-th iteration of $\mathcal{T}_{P_D}$ $(i \geq 1)$ w.r.t. I is defined as follows: $\mathcal{T}_{P_D}^1(I) = \mathcal{T}_{P_D}(I)$ and $\mathcal{T}_{P_D}^i(I) = \mathcal{T}_{P_D}(\mathcal{T}_{P_D}^{i-1}(I))$ for $i > 1$. By iteratively applying $\mathcal{T}_{P_D}$ we always reach a fixpoint in a finite number of iterations, that is, there always exists a finite n such $\mathcal{T}_{P_D}^i(I) = \mathcal{T}_{P_D}^n(I)$ for any $i \geq n$. Such a fixpoint is denoted as $\mathcal{T}_{P_D}^\infty(I)$. The least fixpoint of $\mathcal{T}_{P_D}$ can be computed by iteratively applying $\mathcal{T}_{P_D}$ starting from the empty set, that is, $lfp(\mathcal{T}_{P_D}) = \mathcal{T}_{P_D}^{\infty}(\emptyset)$.

The least model of P_D, discussed in the previous section, is equal to $lfp(\mathcal{T}_{P_D})$. Thus, this approach provides an alternative constructive definition of the semantics of a Datalog program.

Example 3.4   Let D be the database and P the Datalog program of Example 3.1.

$$
\begin{aligned}
\mathcal{T}_{P_D}^1(\emptyset) = & \ I_1 = & \mathcal{T}_{P_D}(\emptyset) = & \ \{edge(a,b), edge(b,c), edge(c,d)\} \\
\mathcal{T}_{P_D}^2(\emptyset) = & \ I_2 = & \mathcal{T}_{P_D}(I_1) = & \ I_1 \cup \{tc(a,b), tc(b,c), tc(c,d)\} \\
\mathcal{T}_{P_D}^3(\emptyset) = & \ I_3 = & \mathcal{T}_{P_D}(I_2) = & \ I_2 \cup \{tc(a,c), tc(b,d)\} \\
\mathcal{T}_{P_D}^4(\emptyset) = & \ I_4 = & \mathcal{T}_{P_D}(I_3) = & \ I_3 \cup \{tc(a,d)\} \\
\mathcal{T}_{P_D}^5(\emptyset) = & \ I_5 = & \mathcal{T}_{P_D}(I_4) = & \ I_4.
\end{aligned}
$$

Thus, I_4 is the least fixpoint of $\mathcal{T}_{P_D}$, and, indeed, it is equal to the least model of P_D (cf. Example 3.3).

3.2.3   PROOF-THEORETIC SEMANTICS

The last semantics for Datalog programs is based on proofs. Specifically, the proof-theoretic semantics defines the semantics of a Datalog program P and a database D in terms of the set of ground atoms that can be proven from D using the Datalog rules of P as proof rules.

First of all, we need to define a *proof*. A *proof tree* of a ground atom A from a database D and a Datalog program P is a labeled tree where:

- each vertex of the tree is labeled with a ground atom;

- each leaf is labeled with a ground atom for which there is a fact in D;

- the root is labeled by A;

- for each internal vertex labeled with A_0, there exists a ground rule $A_0 \leftarrow A_1, \ldots, A_n$ in *ground*(P) such that the vertex children are $A_1, \ldots, A_n$.

Proof trees provide proofs of ground atoms. Given a ground atom A to prove, one can look for a proof either in a *bottom-up* or in a *top-down* fashion. The bottom-up approach is an alternative way of looking at the fixpoint semantics. One begins with the ground atoms in facts of D and then uses rules of P to infer new ground atoms as done by the immediate consequence operator. This is iteratively done until no new facts can be derived.

The top-down approach searches for a proof starting from a particular atom or set of atoms. In a sense, the top-down approach tries to avoid the inference of atoms that are irrelevant for proving the atoms of interest. Before presenting the details of a top-down procedure called *SLD resolution*, we introduce some additional notions.

A *goal clause* in an expression of the form

$$\leftarrow B_1, \ldots, B_m,$$

where $m \geq 0$ and the B_i's are atoms (with no function symbols). When $m = 0$ the goal clause is called *empty goal clause* and is denoted as $\square$.

A *substitution* θ is a finite mapping from variables to terms and is written as $\theta = \{X_1/t_1, \ldots, X_n/t_n\}$ where the X_i's are distinct variables and the t_i's are terms. We also assume that $X_i \neq t_i$ for every $1 \leq i \leq n$. The result of applying θ to an expression E (e.g., a term, an atom, a goal clause, etc.), denoted $E\theta$, is the expression obtained from E by simultaneously replacing each occurrence of a variable X_i in E with t_i iff X_i/t_i belongs to θ. Substitutions can be composed as follows. Given two substitutions $\theta = \{X_1/t_1, \ldots, X_n/t_n\}$ and $\vartheta = \{Y_1/u_1, \ldots, Y_m/u_m\}$, their composition, denoted $\theta \circ \vartheta$, is the substitution obtained from the set $\{X_1/t_1\vartheta, \ldots, X_n/t_n\vartheta, Y_1/u_1, \ldots, Y_m/u_m\}$ by removing every $X_i/t_i\vartheta$ such that $X_i = t_i\vartheta$ and every Y_j/u_j such that $Y_j \in \{X_1, \ldots, X_n\}$. A substitution θ is *more general* than a substitution ϑ if there exists a substitution η such that $\vartheta = \theta \circ \eta$.

Example 3.5   Consider the atom $A = p(X, Y)$ and the substitution $\theta = \{X/b, Y/X\}$. Then, $A\theta = p(b, X)$. Consider now two substitutions $\theta = \{X/Y, Y/Z\}$ and $\vartheta = \{X/a, Y/b, Z/Y\}$. Then, $\theta \circ \vartheta = \{X/b, Z/Y\}$.

Given two atoms A_1 and A_2, a *unifier* of A_1 and A_2 is a substitution θ such that $A_1\theta = A_2\theta$. When a unifier of A_1 and A_2 exists, we say that A_1 and A_2 are *unifiable*. A unifier θ of A_1 and A_2 is called a *most general unifier* (mgu) of A_1 and A_2 if it is more general than any other unifier of A_1 and A_2. If there exists a unifier of A_1 and A_2, then there exists an mgu of A_1 and A_2. Indeed, the mgu is unique modulo renaming of variables. There exists an algorithm that yields an mgu for any two atoms if they are unifiable and report nonexistence of a unifier otherwise (for more details, see, e.g., Lloyd [1987] and Apt [1991]).

Example 3.6   The two atoms $A_1 = p(X, Z)$ and $A_2 = p(Y, a)$ are unifiable, as, for instance, a unifier is $\sigma = \{X/a, Y/a, Z/a\}$. A most general unifier of A_1 and A_2 is $\theta = \{Y/X, Z/a\}$. Notice that $\sigma = \theta \circ \{X/a\}$ and thus θ is more general than σ.

In order to find a proof for $B_1, \ldots, B_m$, SLD resolution starts with the goal clause $\leftarrow B_1, \ldots, B_m$; then, it iteratively derives a new goal clause from a previous goal clause (as described in the following) until the empty goal clause is reached—when the empty goal clause is reached the procedure is successful. Below we detail SLD resolution. Let gc be a non-empty goal clause of the form

$$\leftarrow B_1, \ldots, B_{i-1}, B_i, B_{i+1}, \ldots, B_m,$$

and r be a Datalog rule of the form

$$A_0 \leftarrow A_1, \ldots, A_n$$

such that gc and r have no variable in common (this can always be ensured by renaming variables of r) and B_i, A_0 have an mgu θ. Then, the *resolvent* of gc and r using θ is the goal clause

$$\leftarrow (B_1, \ldots, B_{i-1}, A_1, \ldots, A_n, B_{i+1}, \ldots, B_m)\theta$$

and B_i is called the *selected atom* of gc.

Let P be a Datalog program, D a database, and gc a goal clause. An *SLD derivation* from gc with P_D is a sequence $gc_0, gc_1, gc_2, \ldots$ of goal clauses and a sequence $\theta_1, \theta_2, \ldots$ of substitutions such that

- $gc_0 = gc$, and

- gc_i is the resolvent of gc_{i-1} and some rule in P_D using θ_i, for $i \geq 1$.

An SLD derivation can be finite or infinite. An *SLD refutation* of gc with P_D is an SLD derivation $gc, gc_1, \ldots, gc_k$ from gc with P_D s.t. $gc_k = \square$.

SLD resolution is a technique that provides proofs of atoms. An SLD refutation of a goal clause gc of the form $\leftarrow B_1, \ldots, B_m$ with P_D means that from the assumption that the goal clause gc holds in the presence of P_D, we get the empty clause $\square$, which stands for a contradiction. This can be viewed as a proof of the negation of gc from P_D, that is, the proof of $\exists \overline{X} B_1 \wedge \cdots \wedge B_m$, where $\overline{X}$ are all variables in gc (variables $\overline{X}$ are implicitly universally quantified at the beginning of gc). Moreover, an SLD refutation whose sequence of substitutions is $\theta_1, \ldots, \theta_k$ provides a proof of $(B_1 \wedge \cdots \wedge B_m)\theta_1 \circ \cdots \circ \theta_k$. Importantly, SLD resolution produces only correct proofs (soundness) and and all true facts (completeness). More formally, let P be a program, D a database, and gc a goal clause $\leftarrow B_1, \ldots, B_m$. If there exists an SLD refutation of gc with P_D whose substitutions are $\theta_1, \ldots, \theta_k$, then P_D semantically implies $(B_1 \wedge \cdots \wedge B_m)\theta_1 \circ \cdots \circ \theta_k$. If P_D semantically implies $\neg gc$, then there exists a refutation of gc with P_D.

As SLD resolution is sound and complete, it provides an adequate top-down technique for obtaining the ground atoms in the answer to a Datalog program. To prove that a ground atom is in the answer, one must search for a refutation of the corresponding goal clause, and there can be many of them. There are two sources of nondeterminism in searching for a refutation: *(i)* the choice of the selected atom and *(ii)* the choice of the rule whose head atom unifies with the chosen atom. Assuming a rule for choosing which atom to select at each step in a refutation (e.g., as in Prolog, always take the leftmost atom) we can systematically search for all possible unifying rules.

It turns out that the proof-theoretic semantics gives the same set of ground atoms as the model-theoretic and the fixpoint semantics. Thus, a ground atom A is in the least model of a program iff there is a proof tree for A from D and P.

Example 3.7 Let D be the database and P the Datalog program of Example 3.1. Suppose we want to find a proof a $tc(a, c)$. An SLD refutation of $\leftarrow tc(a, c)$ with P_D, where the selected atom is always the leftmost, is as follows. We start with the goal clause

$$\leftarrow tc(a, c).$$

The resolvent of the goal clause above and the second rule of P using $\theta = \{X/a, Y, c\}$ is the goal clause

$$\leftarrow edge(a, Z), tc(Z, c).$$

The resolvent of the goal clause above and the first fact of D using $\theta = \{Z/b\}$ is the goal clause

$$\leftarrow tc(b, c).$$

The resolvent of the goal clause above and the first rule of P using $\theta = \{X/b, Y/c\}$ is the goal clause

$$\leftarrow edge(b, c).$$

The resolvent of the goal clause above and the second fact of using the empty substitution is the empty goal clause $\square$ and thus $tc(a, c)$ is successfully proven.

3.3   PROGRAM EVALUATION

In this section, we report algorithms to evaluate a Datalog program P over a database D, that is, to compute the semantics of P_D.

3.3.1   EVALUATION OF NON-RECURSIVE PROGRAMS

We start by presenting an algorithm to evaluate non-recursive Datalog programs.

The algorithm to evaluate a non-recursive program P over a database D consists of deriving a relational algebra expression for each derived predicate symbol p of P; the evaluation of this expression over D yields the same answer relation for p as when P is evaluated over D. If a program P is not recursive, then its dependency graph $\mathcal{G}_P$ has no cycles and thus it is possible to determine a topological sorting of the graph, that is, an ordering $p_1, \ldots, p_n$ of the graph vertices such that if (p_i, p_j) is an edge of $\mathcal{G}_P$, then p_i comes before p_j in the ordering. The relational algebra expressions for the derived predicate symbols of P are computed following the order determined by a topological sorting of $\mathcal{G}_P$. The expression for a predicate symbol p is obtained by computing an expression for each rule having p in the head and then taking the union of the expressions obtained for all rules having p in the head.

Let r be a rule of the form

$$A_0 \leftarrow A_1, \ldots, A_n,$$

where A_0 is an atom of the form $p(t_1, \ldots, t_m)$, and, for ease of presentation, assume the t_i's are all variables. Moreover, assume to have a relation R_i for each atom A_i in the body of r—evaluating rules according to a topological sorting of $\mathcal{G}_P$ ensures that we always have a relation for each atom appearing in the body of r. If two atoms A_i and A_j have the same predicate symbol, then R_i and R_j are the same relation. We define *Eval-rule*$(r, R_1, \ldots, R_n)$ as the relational algebra expression obtained as follows.

1. Let E be the relational algebra expression $\sigma_F(R_1 \times \cdots \times R_n)$ where F is a conjunction of conditions obtained as follows: if position k in the body of r has a constant c, then F has the condition $\$k = c$; if positions k and l in the body of r both contain the same variable, then F has the condition $\$k = \$l$. As an example, if the body of r is $p_1(X, Y), p_2(Y, Z, Z), p_3(X, a)$, then F is $\$1 = \$6 \wedge \$2 = \$3 \wedge \$4 = \$5 \wedge \$7 = a$. Notice that F can be empty and in this case it is always satisfied by any tuple.

2. Finally, $Eval\text{-}rule(r, R_1, \ldots, R_n)$ is the relational algebra expression $\pi_V(E)$ where V has m (i.e., the arity of p) components defined as follows: if the i-th term of A_0 is a variable X, then the i-th component of V is one of the positions where X appears in the body of r. As an example, if $p(X, Z)$ is the head of r and the body of r is as above, then we get $\pi_{\$1\$4}(E)$.

Thus, $Eval\text{-}rule(r, R_1, \ldots, R_n)$ gives a relational algebra expression for rule r. The relational algebra expressions for the derived predicate symbols of a program P are obtained by considering predicate symbols according to a topological sorting of $\mathcal{G}_P$ and for each predicate symbol p_i we do the following.

1. For each rule r in P having p_i in the head, compute a relational algebra expression E using $Eval\text{-}rule$.

2. As we are following a topological sorting of $\mathcal{G}_P$, for each derived predicate symbol in the body of r, there is a relational algebra expression (defined using base relations only). Substitute each occurrence of a derived relation in E with the corresponding relational algebra expression.

3. Take the union of the expressions obtained at the second step.

Example 3.8   Consider again the graph database of Example 3.1 and the following non-recursive Datalog program:

$$
\begin{array}{rrcl}
r_1: & onehop(X, Y) & \leftarrow & edge(X, Y). \\
r_2: & twohops(X, Y) & \leftarrow & edge(X, Z), onehop(Z, Y). \\
r_3: & ans(X) & \leftarrow & onehop(a, X). \\
r_4: & ans(X) & \leftarrow & twohops(a, X).
\end{array}
$$

Intuitively, the first rule computes pairs (X, Y) such that Y can be reached from X by going through one edge, while the second rule computes pairs (X, Y) such that Y can be reached from X by going through two edges. The last two rules compute those vertices that can be reached from vertex a by going through one or two edges.

Clearly, $twohops$ depends on $onehop$, while ans depends on both $onehop$ and $twohops$. Thus, a topological sorting of the dependency graph is $onehop, twohops, ans$.

Denoting with *Edge* the edge relation, we consider the first predicate symbol according to the topological sorting above, namely *onehop*, and get

$$Eval\text{-}rule(r_1, Edge) = \pi_{\$1\$2}(Edge).$$

Since the definition of *onehop* consists only of r_1, then the relational algebra expression to compute the relation for *onehop* is:

$$Onehop = \pi_{\$1\$2}(Edge).$$

Obviously, the previous expression might be simplified into the equivalent one *Onehop = Edge*. Next, considering the second predicate symbol according to the topological sorting, namely *twohops*, we have

$$Eval\text{-}rule(r_2, Edge, Onehop) = \pi_{\$1\$4}(\sigma_{\$2=\$3}(Edge \times Onehop)).$$

Since the definition of *twohops* consists only of r_2, the relational algebra expression for *twohops* is:

$$Twohops = \pi_{\$1\$4}(\sigma_{\$2=\$3}(Edge \times \pi_{\$1\$2}(Edge))).$$

Finally, when we consider the last predicate symbol, namly *ans*, we get

$$Eval\text{-}rule(r_3, Onehop) = \pi_{\$2}(\sigma_{\$1=a}(Onehop))$$

$$Eval\text{-}rule(r_4, Twohops) = \pi_{\$2}(\sigma_{\$1=a}(Twohops))$$

and the relational algebra expression for *ans* is

$$Ans = \pi_{\$2}(\sigma_{\$1=a}(\pi_{\$1\$2}(Edge))) \cup \pi_{\$2}(\sigma_{\$1=a}(\pi_{\$1\$4}(\sigma_{\$2=\$3}(Edge \times \pi_{\$1\$2}(Edge))))).$$

3.3.2   EVALUATION OF RECURSIVE PROGRAMS

In the following, we report algorithms to evaluate possibly recursive Datalog programs. Specifically, we first present a "naïve" algorithm and then an improvement of it called "semi-naïve" algorithm (see also Abiteboul et al. [1995] and Ullman [1988]).

Algorithm Naïve

Consider a program P and a database D. Let $R_1, \ldots, R_k$ be the base relations and $P_1, \ldots, P_m$ the derived relations. For each derived predicate symbol p_i, we define $Eval(p_i, R_1, \ldots, R_k, P_1, \ldots, P_m)$ as the result of evaluating the union of the expressions given by *Eval-rule* over all rules with p_i in the head.

Given a possibly recursive Datalog program P and a database D, where the base predicate symbols are $r_1, \ldots, r_k$, the derived predicate symbols are $p_1, \ldots, p_m$, and the base relations are $R_1, \ldots, R_k$, the following algorithm performs the evaluation of P over D.

Algorithm 1 Naive-Evaluation

1: **for** $i := 1$ **to** m **do**
2:    $P_i := \emptyset$;
3: **repeat**
4:    **for** $i := 1$ **to** m **do**
5:       $P'_i := P_i$;
6:    **for** $i := 1$ **to** m **do**
7:       $P_i := Eval(p_i, R_1, \ldots, R_k, P'_1, \ldots, P'_m)$;
8: **until** $P_i = P'_i$ for all $1 \leq i \leq m$
9: **return** $P_1, \ldots, P_m$

The algorithm above iteratively computes *Eval* for every derived predicate symbol until none of the derived relations changes anymore. At each iteration, the updated derived relations obtained in the previous iteration are used in the computation of *Eval*.

One simple optimization that can be applied to the algorithm above is the following. Given a possibly recursive Datalog program P, we first determine the strongly connected components of the dependency graph $\mathcal{G}_P$. If each strongly connected component is contracted to a single vertex, the resulting graph is a directed acyclic graph $\mathcal{G}'_P$. Then, we apply Algorithm Naive-Evaluation to each connected component following the order given by a topological sorting of $\mathcal{G}'_P$. Applying Algorithm Naive-Evaluation to a connected component means applying the algorithm to the subprogram of P consisting of those rules which have a predicate symbol belonging to the connected component in the head, and considering the relations for predicate symbols in previous components as base relations.

Example 3.9   Consider the database and the Datalog program of Example 3.1, which are reported below for the reader's convenience.

$$edge(a, b).$$
$$edge(b, c).$$
$$edge(c, d).$$

$$r_1: \quad tc(X, Y) \leftarrow edge(X, Y).$$
$$r_2: \quad tc(X, Y) \leftarrow edge(X, Z), tc(Z, Y).$$

Clearly, *edge* is the only base predicate symbol and *tc* is the only derived predicate symbol. Let $Edge = \{(a, b), (b, c), (c, d)\}$ be the base relation corresponding to predicate symbol *edge*. Initially, $Tc = \emptyset$ (lines 1–2). Then, the repeat-until loop of lines 3–8 proceeds as follows. Iteration 1:

$$Tc' = Tc = \emptyset.$$
$$Tc = Eval(tc, Edge, Tc') = Edge \cup \pi_{\$1\$4}(\sigma_{\$2=\$3}(Edge \times Tc')) = \{(a, b), (b, c), (c, d)\}$$

Iteration 2:

$Tc' = Tc = \{(a, b), (b, c), (c, d)\}.$
$Tc = Eval(tc, Edge, Tc') = Edge \cup \pi_{\$1\$4}(\sigma_{\$2=\$3}(Edge \times Tc')) = \{(a, b), (b, c), (c, d)\} \cup$
$\{(a, c), (b, d)\}$

Iteration 3:

$Tc' = Tc = \{(a, b), (b, c), (c, d), (a, c), (b, d)\}.$
$Tc = Eval(tc, Edge, Tc') = Edge \cup \pi_{\$1\$4}(\sigma_{\$2=\$3}(Edge \times Tc')) = \{(a, b), (b, c), (c, d)\} \cup$
$\{(a, c), (b, d)\} \cup$
$\{(a, d)\}$

Iteration 4:

$Tc' = Tc = \{(a, b), (b, c), (c, d), (a, c), (b, d), (a, d)\}.$
$Tc = Eval(tc, Edge, Tc') = Edge \cup \pi_{\$1\$4}(\sigma_{\$2=\$3}(Edge \times Tc')) = \{(a, b), (b, c), (c, d)\} \cup$
$\{(a, c), (b, d)\} \cup$
$\{(a, d)\}$

As in the last iteration $Tc = Tc'$, the repeat-until loop terminates and the derived relation Tc is returned.

Suppose adding the following rule to the program considered above:

$$reachable\text{-}from\text{-}a(X) \leftarrow tc(a, X).$$

With this addition, the dependency graph has two strongly connected components, one consisting of tc and another one containing *reachable-from-a*. We can first apply Algorithm Naive-Evaluation to the subprogram containing the first two rules, as detailed above. Then, Algorithm Naive-Evaluation can be applied to the subprogram consisting only of the last rule using the relation Tc computed at the previous step as a base relation.

Algorithm Semi-naïve

One shortcoming of Algorithm Naive-Evaluation is that at each iteration, all tuples computed in the previous iteration are recomputed (e.g., see Example 3.9). We now present an algorithm that tries to overcome this inefficiency by incrementally computing the new relations at each iteration.

We start by introducing an incremental version of *Eval-rule* seen in Section 3.3.1. Consider a rule r of the form

$$A_0 \leftarrow A_1, \ldots, A_n,$$

and assume to have a relation R_i and an "incremental" relation ΔR_i for each atom A_i in the body of r. We define the incremental version of *Eval-rule* as follows:

$$Eval\text{-}rule\text{-}incr(r, R_1, \ldots, R_n, \Delta R_1, \ldots, \Delta R_n) =$$
$$\bigcup_{1 \leq i \leq n} Eval\text{-}rule(r, R_1, \ldots, R_{i-1}, \Delta R_i, R_{i+1}, \ldots, R_n).$$

Consider a program P and a database D. Let $R_1, \ldots, R_k$ be the base relations and $P_1, \ldots, P_m$ the derived relations. For each P_i, we also have an "incremental" relation ΔP_i. For each derived predicate symbol p_i, we define $Eval\text{-}incr(p_i, R_1, \ldots, R_k, P_1, \ldots, P_m, \Delta P_1, \ldots, \Delta P_m)$ as the result of evaluating the union of the expressions given by $Eval\text{-}rule\text{-}incr$ over all rules with p_i in the head. In the evaluation of $Eval\text{-}rule\text{-}incr$, the incremental relations for base predicate symbols are the empty set.

Algorithm Seminaive-Evaluation performs the evaluation of P over D and improves over Algorithm Naive-Evaluation by incrementally computing the derived relations.

Algorithm 2 Seminaive-Evaluation

1: **for** $i := 1$ **to** m **do**
2: $\quad \Delta P_i := Eval(p_i, R_1, \ldots, R_k, \emptyset, \ldots, \emptyset);$
3: $\quad P_i := \Delta P_i;$
4: **repeat**
5: $\quad$ **for** $i := 1$ **to** m **do**
6: $\quad\quad \Delta P_i' := \Delta P_i;$
7: $\quad$ **for** $i := 1$ **to** m **do**
8: $\quad\quad \Delta P_i := Eval\text{-}incr(p_i, R_1, \ldots, R_k, P_1, \ldots, P_m, \Delta P_1', \ldots, \Delta P_m');$
9: $\quad\quad \Delta P_i := \Delta P_i - P_i;$
10: $\quad$ **for** $i := 1$ **to** m **do**
11: $\quad\quad P_i := P_i \cup \Delta P_i;$
12: **until** $\Delta P_i = \emptyset$ for all $1 \leq i \leq m$
13: **return** $P_1, \ldots, P_m$

Example 3.10   Consider the database and the Datalog program of Example 3.9. Once again, $Edge = \{(a, b), (b, c), (c, d)\}$ is the base relation corresponding to predicate symbol $edge$. Moreover, $\Delta Edge = \emptyset$ as $edge$ is a base predicate symbol. Initially, relation ΔTc is computed as follows (line 2):

$$\Delta Tc := Eval(tc, Edge, \emptyset) = Edge \cup \pi_{\$1\$4}(\sigma_{\$2=\$3}(Edge \times \emptyset)) = \{(a, b), (b, c), (c, d)\}.$$

Then, $Tc = \Delta Tc = \{(a, b), (b, c), (c, d)\}$ (line 3). Next, the repeat-until loop of lines 4–12 proceeds as follows.

Iteration 1:

$$
\begin{aligned}
\Delta Tc' &= \Delta Tc = \{(a,b), (b,c), (c,d)\}. \\
\Delta Tc &= \textit{Eval-incr}(tc, Edge, Tc, \Delta Tc') \\
&= \textit{Eval-rule-incr}(r_1, Edge, \Delta Edge) \cup \textit{Eval-rule-incr}(r_2, Edge, Tc, \Delta Edge, \Delta Tc') \\
&= \textit{Eval-rule}(r_1, \Delta Edge) \cup \textit{Eval-rule}(r_2, \Delta Edge, Tc) \cup \textit{Eval-rule}(r_2, Edge, \Delta Tc') \\
&= \emptyset \cup \emptyset \cup \pi_{\$1\$4}(\sigma_{\$2=\$3}(Edge \times \Delta Tc')) \\
&= \{(a,c), (b,d)\} \\
\Delta Tc &= \Delta Tc - Tc = \{(a,c), (b,d)\} \\
Tc &= Tc \cup \Delta Tc = \{(a,b), (b,c), (c,d), (a,c), (b,d)\}
\end{aligned}
$$

Iteration 2:

$$
\begin{aligned}
\Delta Tc' &= \Delta Tc = \{(a,c), (b,d)\}. \\
\Delta Tc &= \textit{Eval-incr}(tc, Edge, Tc, \Delta Tc') \\
&= \textit{Eval-rule-incr}(r_1, Edge, \Delta Edge) \cup \textit{Eval-rule-incr}(r_2, Edge, Tc, \Delta Edge, \Delta Tc') \\
&= \textit{Eval-rule}(r_1, \Delta Edge) \cup \textit{Eval-rule}(r_2, \Delta Edge, Tc) \cup \textit{Eval-rule}(r_2, Edge, \Delta Tc') \\
&= \emptyset \cup \emptyset \cup \pi_{\$1\$4}(\sigma_{\$2=\$3}(Edge \times \Delta Tc')) \\
&= \{(a,d)\} \\
\Delta Tc &= \Delta Tc - Tc = \{(a,d)\} \\
Tc &= Tc \cup \Delta Tc = \{(a,b), (b,c), (c,d), (a,c), (b,d), (a,d)\}
\end{aligned}
$$

Iteration 3:

$$
\begin{aligned}
\Delta Tc' &= \Delta Tc = \{(a,d)\}. \\
\Delta Tc &= \textit{Eval-incr}(tc, Edge, Tc, \Delta Tc') \\
&= \textit{Eval-rule-incr}(r_1, Edge, \Delta Edge) \cup \textit{Eval-rule-incr}(r_2, Edge, Tc, \Delta Edge, \Delta Tc') \\
&= \textit{Eval-rule}(r_1, \Delta Edge) \cup \textit{Eval-rule}(r_2, \Delta Edge, Tc) \cup \textit{Eval-rule}(r_2, Edge, \Delta Tc') \\
&= \emptyset \cup \emptyset \cup \pi_{\$1\$4}(\sigma_{\$2=\$3}(Edge \times \Delta Tc')) \\
&= \emptyset \\
\Delta Tc &= \Delta Tc - Tc = \emptyset \\
Tc &= Tc \cup \Delta Tc = \{(a,b), (b,c), (c,d), (a,c), (b,d), (a,d)\}
\end{aligned}
$$

As in the last iteration $\Delta Tc = \emptyset$, the repeat-until loop terminates and the derived relation Tc is returned by Algorithm Seminaive-Evaluation.

3.4   EXPRESSIVITY AND COMPLEXITY

Recall that a query is a function that takes a database as input and gives another database as output. Furthermore, queries have to be generic, that is, invariant under renamings of the database domain. Queries can be expressed using query languages and the expressive power of a given query language is measured in terms of the set of queries that can be expressed using that language.

A *Datalog query* Q is a pair $\langle P, G \rangle$ where P is a Datalog program and G is an atom $g(t_1, \ldots, t_m)$, called *query goal*, s.t. g appears in the head of some rule in P. Let $t_{i_1}, \ldots, t_{i_k}$ be the terms of G that are variables, where $1 \leq i_1 < \cdots < i_k \leq m$. The *answer* to Q over a database D, denoted $Q(D)$, is the set of all tuples of constants $(c_1, \ldots, c_k)$ s.t. the atom obtained from G by replacing every t_{i_j} with c_j ($1 \leq j \leq k$) belongs to the least model of $P \cup D$. When $k = 0$ (i.e., the query goal is ground), the Datalog query is Boolean an returns *true* if G belongs to the least model of $P \cup D$, *false* otherwise.

Two Datalog queries Q and Q' are *equivalent*, denoted $Q \equiv Q'$, iff $Q(D) = Q'(D)$ for every database D.

Datalog allows us to express only *monotonic queries* (a monotonic query is such that if a database D_1 is a subset of a database D_2, then the result of the query over D_1 is a subset of the result of the query over D_2). Datalog can express only a proper subset of the queries computable in polynomial time. Indeed, Datalog cannot even express all monotonic queries computable in polynomial time [Afrati et al., 1995]. As already mentioned before, recursion allows Datalog to express queries which cannot be expressed in relational algebra and calculus, such as computing the transitive closure of a binary relation [Aho and Ullman, 1979]. Non-recursive Datalog has the same expressive power as the fragment of relational algebra using only projection, positive selection (i.e., selection conditions are restricted to be conjunctions of equalities), union, Cartesian product (in other words, non-recursive Datalog can express union of conjunctive queries). Datalog needs to be extended with negation in order to get (at least) the same expressive power as relational algebra and safe relational calculus. We will consider negation in Chapter 4.

There are three interesting complexity issues connected to Datalog and its extensions.

- The **data complexity** is the complexity of checking whether $D \cup P \models A$ for a *fixed* Datalog program P, and *variable* input database D and ground atoms A.

- The **program complexity** is the complexity of checking whether $D \cup P \models A$ for *variable* Datalog program P and ground atoms A, and *fixed* input database D.

- The **combined complexity** is the complexity of checking whether $D \cup P \models A$ for *variable* Datalog program P, input database D, and ground atoms A.

The data complexity of Datalog is P-complete. The program and combined complexity of Datalog are EXPTIME-complete. The data complexity of linear Datalog is NL-complete. The program and combined complexity of linear Datalog are PSPACE-complete. The data complexity of conjunctive queries expressed in Datalog is L, while their program and combined complexity are NP-complete. The following table reports these results.

Table 3.1: The complexity of Datalog

Query Language	Data Complexity	Program and Combined Complexity
Conjunctive queries	L	NP-complete
Linear Datalog	NL-complete	PSPACE-complete
Datalog	P-complete	EXPTIME-complete

BIBLIOGRAPHIC NOTES

For early applications of logic to databases we refer to Gallaire and Minker [1978], Gallaire et al. [1984] and Minker [1988]. An overview of logic programming and databases can be found in Ceri et al. [1990]; see also Minker et al. [2014].

Fixpoint semantics was explored in the context of logic programming in van Emden and Kowalski [1976] and Apt and van Emden [1982] and in the database context in Chandra and Harel [1982].

Resolution was originally proposed in the context of automatic theorem proving [Robinson, 1965], while SLD resolution was developed in [van Emden and Kowalski, 1976]. These form the basis of logic programming as introduced by Kowalski [1974] (see also Kowalski [1986]).

Safety conditions on datalog programs have been studied in Kifer et al. [1988], Krishnamurthy et al. [1988], Ramakrishnan et al. [1987], Sagiv and Vardi [1989] and Zaniolo [1986].

The seminaive evaluation of Datalog programs has been considered in several papers [Balbin and Ramamohanarao, 1987, Bancilhon and Ramakrishnan, 1986, Fong and Ullman, 1976] and [Paige and Schwartz, 1977].

For a more detailed treatment of Datalog we also refer to Abiteboul et al. [1995] and Ullman [1988].

A survey of various complexity and expressiveness results for different forms of logic programming can be found in Dantsin et al. [1997, 2001].

CHAPTER 4

Negation

Even if Datalog provides recursion and allows us to express queries that cannot be expressed in the relational algebra or calculus (e.g., computing the transitive closure of a graph), its expressive power remains limited. In fact, Datalog allows us to express only a proper subset of the queries computable in polynomial time, and only monotonic ones. Simple nonmonotonic queries, such as checking whether the active domain of an input database has an even number of elements or computing the difference of two relations, cannot be expressed. Indeed, Datalog cannot even express all monotonic queries computable in polynomial time [Afrati et al., 1995].

Datalog needs to be extended with negation in order to get (at least) the same expressive power as the relational algebra and the safe relational calculus. Negation is an important feature to formalize common sense reasoning in knowledge representation as it enables us to express non-monotonic queries, and thus perform nonmonotonic reasoning. The problem of finding a suitable semantics for Datalog programs with negation has been an important and difficult problem that has received considerable attention over the years, leading to different semantics.

In this chapter, we consider Datalog augmented with negation (in rule bodies)—the resulting language will be referred to as Datalog$^\neg$. We start by defining the general syntax of Datalog$^\neg$. Then, we focus on restricted subsets of Datalog$^\neg$ where only a limited use of negation is allowed, namely *semipositive*, *stratified*, and *locally stratified* Datalog$^\neg$ programs. After that, we consider the full Datalog$^\neg$ language and present the *stable model* and the *well-founded* semantics. Finally, we consider Datalog extended with a limited form of negation embedded in the *choice* construct.

At the end of the chapter, we also briefly discuss the extension of Datalog with disjunction.

4.1 SYNTAX

In this section, the syntax of Datalog$^\neg$ programs is introduced.

A *Datalog$^\neg$ rule r* is of the form:

$$A \leftarrow L_1, \ldots, L_n,$$

where $n \geq 0$, A is an atom, and the L_i's are literals (i.e., atoms or negated atoms). Function symbols are not allowed and thus terms appearing in a Datalog$^\neg$ rule are constants and variables. Once again, A is called the *head* of r and is denoted by $head(r)$; the conjunction $L_1, \ldots, L_n$ is called the *body* of r and is denoted by $body(r)$. *Comparison atoms* of the form $t_1 \; op \; t_2$ are allowed in the body, where *op* is a comparison predicate symbol (i.e., $op \in \{\geq, >, \leq, <, =, \neq\}$) and t_1 and t_2 are terms.

Every rule must be *safe*. The safety condition presented in Section 3.1 for Datalog is generalized as follows to accommodate negation and comparison atoms. For every Datalog¬ rule, every variable must be *limited* in the following sense:

- a variable X is limited if it appears in a positive literal of the body whose predicate symbol is not a comparison predicate symbol;

- a variable X is limited if it appears in a comparison atom of the form $X = c$ or $c = X$, where c is a constant; and

- a variable X is limited if it appears in a comparison atom of the form $X = Y$ or $Y = X$, where Y is a limited variable.

Notice that the first two conditions above are base cases to determine if a variable is limited, while the last condition can be iteratively applied to determine new variables as limited.

Example 4.1   Consider the following Datalog¬ rule

$$p(X) \leftarrow q(X), \neg s(Y), X = Y.$$

Variable X is limited because it appears in the positive body literal $q(X)$ and q is not a comparison predicate symbol. Then, we can conclude that Y is limited as well, because it appears in the comparison atom $X = Y$ and X has been determined as limited. Thus, the rule is safe.

A *Datalog¬ program* is a finite set of (safe) Datalog¬ rules. The dependency graph $\mathcal{G}_P$ of a Datalog¬ program P is defined in the same way as for Datalog programs (see Section 3.1). Once again, we use *ground(P)* to denote the set of all ground rules obtained from the rules of P by replacing all variables with constants.

4.2   SEMIPOSITIVE PROGRAMS

The most restricted use of negation that we consider is *semipositive Datalog¬*, which will be referred to as Datalog¬^{sp}. The following definition introduces Datalog¬^{sp} programs.

Definition 4.2   A Datalog¬ program P is *semipositive* if for every rule $r \in P$ and every negative literal L in the body of r, the predicate symbol of L is a base predicate symbol.

Essentially, Datalog¬^{sp} allows negation to be applied only to base atoms.

Example 4.3   Consider a directed graph stored in a database by means of facts of the form *vertex(v)*, meaning that v is a vertex of the graph, and facts of the form *edge(v_1, v_2)*, meaning that there is an edge from vertex v_1 to vertex v_2 in the graph (obviously, *vertex* and *edge* are base predicate symbols).

Below is a Datalog$^{\neg sp}$ program P to compute the pairs of vertices (v_1, v_2) such that the edge from v_1 to v_2 does not belong to the graph:

$$no\text{-}edge(X_1, X_2) \leftarrow vertex(X_1), vertex(X_2), \neg edge(X_1, X_2).$$

Datalog$^{\neg sp}$ allows us to compute the difference of two (base) relations, which cannot be expressed in Datalog. As an example, if p and q are base predicate symbols of arity 1, then the Datalog$^{\neg sp}$ rule $diff(X) \leftarrow p(X), \neg q(X)$ computes the set-theoretic difference of p and q. Notice that even in the presence of this limited form of negation the existence of a unique minimal model, which is the case for Datalog programs, is no longer guaranteed. For instance, if we consider the Datalog$^{\neg sp}$ program P consisting of the aforementioned rule and the database D consisting only of the fact $p(a)$, then P_D has two minimal models, namely $\{p(a), diff(a)\}$ and $\{p(a), q(a)\}$—intuitively, only the former is the intended one and, indeed, is the one assigned by the semantics presented below.

The semantics of a Datalog$^{\neg sp}$ program P and a database D is given by the semantics of the Datalog program P' and the database D' obtained as follows.

- Program P' is obtained from P by eliminating negation in the following way: each negative literal $\neg p(t_1, \ldots, t_n)$ in the body of a rule is replaced with a positive literal $p'(t_1, \ldots, t_n)$.

- Database D' is obtained by adding to D, for each base predicate symbol p, a new relation whose predicate symbol is p' and which is defined as the complement (w.r.t. the Herbrand universe of P_D) of the relation in D for p.

Basically, a ground negative literal $\neg A$ is interpreted as true if A does not belong to D, otherwise it is interpreted as false.

Example 4.4   Consider the Datalog$^{\neg sp}$ program P of Example 4.3 and suppose we are given a database D containing the following facts:

$$
\begin{array}{ll}
edge(a, b). & vertex(a). \\
edge(b, b). & vertex(b). \\
edge(b, c). & vertex(c). \\
edge(c, b). &
\end{array}
$$

The semantics of P and D is given by the Datalog program P' consisting of the following rule:

$$no\text{-}edge(X_1, X_2) \leftarrow vertex(X_1), vertex(X_2), edge'(X_1, X_2)$$

and the database D' obtained by adding the following facts to D

$$edge'(a, a),$$
$$edge'(a, c),$$
$$edge'(b, a),$$
$$edge'(c, a),$$
$$edge'(c, c).$$

Then, the *no-edge*-atoms that can be derived are

$$no\text{-}edge(a, a),$$
$$no\text{-}edge(a, c),$$
$$no\text{-}edge(b, a),$$
$$no\text{-}edge(c, a),$$
$$no\text{-}edge(c, c).$$

Datalog$^{\neg sp}$ is strictly more expressive than Datalog. For instance, the difference of two relations can be expressed in Datalog$^{\neg sp}$ but not in Datalog. Datalog$^{\neg sp}$ queries can be evaluated in polynomial time (data complexity).

4.3   STRATIFIED PROGRAMS

We now present a natural generalization of semipositive Datalog$^\neg$ called *stratified Datalog$^\neg$* [Apt et al., 1988, Chandra and Harel, 1985, Lifschitz, 1988, Van Gelder, 1989]. Stratified Datalog$^\neg$ programs restrict the manner in which recursion and negation may occur together.

First, we need to introduce some additional notions. Let P be a Datalog$^\neg$ program. A partition $S_1, \ldots, S_m$ of the set of predicate symbols in P, where the S_i's are called *strata*, and S_j is *lower* than S_k if $j < k$, is a *stratification* of P iff the following condition holds for every rule in P:

1. if p is the head predicate symbol and q is the predicate symbol of a positive body literal, then q belongs to a stratum lower than or equal to the stratum of p; and

2. if p is the head predicate symbol and q is the predicate symbol of a negative body literal, then q belongs to a stratum lower than the stratum of p.

Stratified Datalog programs are defined as follows.

Definition 4.5   A Datalog$^\neg$ program P is *stratified* if it has a stratification.

We will refer to stratified Datalog$^\neg$ also as Datalog$^{\neg s}$. It is worth noting that there can be different stratifications for a Datalog$^{\neg s}$ program.

Example 4.6   Consider again a directed graph stored in a database by means of facts of the form $vertex(v)$ and $edge(v_1, v_2)$. The following Datalog$^\neg$ program P computes the pairs of vertices

(v_1, v_2) for which there is no path from v_1 to v_2 in the graph.

$$
\begin{aligned}
r_1 : & \quad tc(X, Y) & \leftarrow & \quad edge(X, Y). \\
r_2 : & \quad tc(X, Y) & \leftarrow & \quad edge(X, Z), tc(Z, Y). \\
r_3 : & \quad non\text{-}reachable(X_1, X_2) & \leftarrow & \quad vertex(X_1), vertex(X_2), \neg tc(X_1, X_2).
\end{aligned}
$$

As negation is applied to the derived atom $tc(X_1, X_2)$ in the third rule, P is not semipositive.

However, P is stratified. In fact, a possible stratification is given by $S_1 = \{vertex, edge, tc\}$ and $S_2 = \{non\text{-}reachable\}$. Notice that there exist other stratifications. For instance, another stratification is given by $S_1 = \{vertex, edge\}$, $S_2 = \{tc\}$, and $S_3 = \{non\text{-}reachable\}$. Because of rule r_3, in any stratification, the stratum of tc must be lower than the stratum of $non\text{-}reachable$.

An equivalent definition of Datalog$^{\neg s}$ programs can be given by imposing some restrictions on the structure of the dependency graph associated with a Datalog$^\neg$ program. Specifically, a Datalog$^\neg$ program P is stratified iff every rule r in P satisfies the following condition: if p is the head predicate symbol, then for every derived predicate symbol q appearing in a negative literal of the body of r, there is no path in $\mathcal{G}_P$ from p to q. Thus, the condition above prevents recursion through negation.

Clearly, non-recursive Datalog$^\neg$ programs are always stratified. Moreover, Datalog$^{\neg sp}$ programs are stratified as well.

We now define the semantics of Datalog$^{\neg s}$ programs in terms of the *iterated fixed point model*. Consider a Datalog$^{\neg s}$ program P and a database D. First of all, we generalize the immediate consequence operator $\mathcal{T}_{P_D}$ (cf. Section 3.2.2) to deal with negative literals in rule bodies. Given a set I of ground atoms, then

$$
\begin{aligned}
\mathcal{T}_{P_D}(I) = \{A_0 \mid & \ A_0 \leftarrow A_1, \ldots, A_k, \neg A_{k+1}, \ldots, \neg A_n \text{ is a ground rule in } ground(P_D), \text{ and} \\
& A_i \in I \text{ for every } 1 \leq i \leq k, \text{ and} \\
& A_i \notin I \text{ for every } k + 1 \leq i \leq n\}.
\end{aligned}
$$

A stratification $S_1, \ldots, S_m$ of P induces a partition of P into m sets $P_1, \ldots, P_m$ such that P_i consists of the rules of P defining the predicate symbols in S_i. Let

$$
\begin{aligned}
M_1 &= \mathcal{T}^{\omega}_{P_1 \cup D}(\emptyset), \\
M_2 &= M_1 \cup \mathcal{T}^{\omega}_{P_2}(M_1), \\
&\vdots \\
M_m &= M_{m-1} \cup \mathcal{T}^{\omega}_{P_m}(M_{m-1}).
\end{aligned}
$$

Then, M_m is an *iterated fixed point model* of P. Even if there might be different stratifications for a Datalog$^{\neg s}$ program, they all yield the same iterated fixed point model, which is thus unique for any Datalog$^{\neg s}$ program.

Example 4.7   Consider the Datalog$^{\neg s}$ program P of Example 4.6 and the stratification consisting of $S_1 = \{vertex, edge, tc\}$ and $S_2 = \{non\text{-}reachable\}$. The partition of P determined by such a stratification is $P_1 = \{r_1, r_2\}$ and $P_2 = \{r_3\}$. Suppose we are given a database D containing the following facts:

$$
\begin{array}{ll}
edge(a,b). & vertex(a). \\
edge(b,b). & vertex(b). \\
edge(b,c). & vertex(c). \\
edge(c,b). &
\end{array}
$$

Then,

$$
\begin{aligned}
M_1 &= \mathcal{T}^{\omega}_{P_1 \cup D}(\emptyset) = D \cup \{tc(a,b), tc(a,c), tc(b,b), tc(b,c), tc(c,b), tc(c,c)\}, \\
M_2 &= M_1 \cup \mathcal{T}^{\omega}_{P_2}(M_1) = \\
&= M_1 \cup \{non\text{-}reachable(a,a), non\text{-}reachable(b,a), non\text{-}reachable(c,a)\}.
\end{aligned}
$$

The iterated fixed point model of P_D is M_2.

While in Datalog$^{\neg sp}$ negation is restricted only to base atoms, in Datalog$^{\neg s}$ negation can be applied also to derived atoms (in a restricted way, though). The existence of stratifications allows us to choose one of them and evaluate the induced subprograms following the order dictated by the stratification. When evaluating a subprogram P_i, predicate symbols defined by rules in subprograms that have been already evaluated (i.e., those subprograms P_j with $j < i$) can be seen as base predicate symbols—thus, in this sense, P_i can be seen as a semipositive program.

The computation of the iterated fixed point model can be carried out by computing each M_i by means of the algorithms presented in Chapter 3, with the only difference being how the relations corresponding to negative body literals are defined. In this regard, consider a predicate symbol q and let Q be the corresponding relation computed after the stratum of q has been processed. When *Evalrule* (cf. Section 3.3) is called for a rule having a negative body literal of the form $\neg q(t_1, \ldots, t_k)$, the relation for such a negative literal is defined as $(Dom)^k - Q$, where Dom is the set of constants appearing in P_D.

From the discussion above, it is easy to see that the computation of the iterated fixed point model can be carried out in polynomial time in the data complexity; indeed, the data complexity of Datalog$^{\neg s}$ is P-complete [Apt et al., 1988].

Datalog$^{\neg s}$ is strictly more expressive than Datalog$^{\neg sp}$ [Abiteboul et al., 1995]. Datalog$^{\neg s}$ without recursion has the same expressive power as the relational algebra and the safe relational calculus [Abiteboul et al., 1995]. Thus, Datalog$^{\neg s}$ (with recursion allowed) is strictly more expressive than the relational algebra and the safe relational calculus (e.g., it can express the transitive closure of a graph, which cannot be expressed using the other two languages).

4.4   LOCALLY STRATIFIED PROGRAMS

Locally stratified programs, originally introduced by Przymusinski [1988], generalize stratified programs. The basic idea is illustrated in the following example.

Example 4.8   Consider the following Datalog$^\neg$ program:

$$p(a) \leftarrow \neg p(c).$$
$$p(b) \leftarrow \neg p(c).$$

It is easy to check that the program is not stratified, since predicate symbol p depends on itself "through negation." If the program had been written as below, using three different (0-ary) predicate symbols p_a, p_b, p_c rather than a single one, it would be stratified:

$$p_a \leftarrow \neg p_c.$$
$$p_b \leftarrow \neg p_c.$$

This example suggests that we might use a more fine-grained version of the Datalog$^{\neg s}$ condition, looking for a stratification of ground atoms rather than a stratification of predicate symbols—this is the basic idea of locally stratified programs, which are formally defined as follows.

Definition 4.9   Let P be a Datalog$^\neg$ program. A partition $B_1, \ldots, B_m$ of the Herbrand base B_P, where the B_i's are called *local strata* and B_j is lower than B_k if $j < k$, is a *local stratification* of P iff the following condition holds for every ground rule in $ground(P)$:

1. if H is the head atom and A is a positive body literal, then A belongs to a local stratum lower than or equal to the local stratum of H; and

2. if H is the head atom and $\neg A$ is a negative body literal, then A belongs to a local stratum lower than the local stratum of H.

We say that P is *locally stratified* if admits a local stratification.

The class of locally stratified Datalog$^\neg$ programs will be also referred to as Datalog$^{\neg ls}$. There is a simple analogy between stratification of Datalog$^{\neg s}$ programs and local stratification of Datalog$^{\neg ls}$ programs: the latter treats ground atoms and ground rules in the same way as the former treats predicate symbols and arbitrary rules.

Example 4.10   Consider again the Datalog$^\neg$ program of Example 4.8, whose Herbrand base is $\{p(a), p(b), p(c)\}$. The program is locally stratified as $B_1 = \{p(c)\}$ and $B_2 = \{p(a), p(b)\}$ form a local stratification.

Similar to Datalog$^{\neg s}$ programs, for a locally stratified program there can be different local stratifications. For instance, $B_1 = \{p(c)\}$, $B_2 = \{p(a)\}$, and $B_3 = \{p(b)\}$ is another local stratification of the Datalog$^\neg$ program of Example 4.8.

Datalog$^{\neg ls}$ programs can be equivalently defined using a "ground version" of the dependency graph. More precisely, given a Datalog$^\neg$ program P, the *ground dependency graph* of P is a directed graph whose nodes are the ground atoms in the Herbrand base B_P of P. There is an edge from a ground atom A to a ground atom H iff there is a rule in *ground*(P) whose head is H and one of the body literals is either A or $\neg A$. A Datalog$^\neg$ program is locally stratified iff every ground rule r in *ground*(P) satisfies the following condition: if H is the head atom, then for every negative literal $\neg A$ in the body of r, there is no path in the ground dependency graph from H to A.

We now define the semantics of Datalog$^{\neg ls}$ programs. Consider a Datalog$^\neg$ program P and a database D such that P_D is locally stratified. The semantics of P and D is given by the *perfect model* defined as follows. Let $B_1, \ldots, B_m$ be a local stratification of P_D and $P_1, \ldots, P_m$ be the partition of *ground*(P_D) such that P_i consists of the rules of *ground*(P) whose head atom is in B_i. Similar to stratified programs, we define

$$
\begin{aligned}
M_1 &= \mathcal{T}^\omega_{P_1 \cup D}(\emptyset), \\
M_2 &= M_1 \cup \mathcal{T}^\omega_{P_2}(M_1), \\
&\;\;\vdots \\
M_m &= M_{m-1} \cup \mathcal{T}^\omega_{P_m}(M_{m-1}).
\end{aligned}
$$

Then, M_m is the *perfect model* of P. Even if P_D can have different local stratifications, they all yield the same perfect model, which is thus unique for any Datalog$^{\neg ls}$ program.

Notice that in the definition of a perfect model above, the more general definition of the immediate consequence operator is used (cf. Section 4.3), that is, the one which deals with negative literals in rule bodies.

Example 4.11   Consider the Datalog$^{\neg ls}$ program of Example 4.8 and the local stratification consisting of the local strata $B_1 = \{p(c)\}$, $B_2 = \{p(a)\}$, and $B_3 = \{p(b)\}$.
Then,

$$
\begin{aligned}
P_1 &= \emptyset, \\
P_2 &= \{p(a) \leftarrow \neg p(c).\}, \text{ and} \\
P_3 &= \{p(b) \leftarrow \neg p(c).\}
\end{aligned}
$$

and

$$
\begin{aligned}
M_1 &= \emptyset, \\
M_2 &= \{p(a)\}, \text{ and} \\
M_3 &= \{p(a), p(b)\}.
\end{aligned}
$$

Thus, the perfect model is M_3.

In a sense, compared with stratified Datalog$^\neg$ programs, locally stratified Datalog$^\neg$ programs allow us to handle situations where recursion through negation is apparent, but not real, as in the previous example, where a natural semantics can be given to the program.

We notice that the notion of a perfect model has been proposed by Przymusinski [1988, 1989] for a class of Datalog$^\neg$ programs more general than Datalog$^{\neg ls}$ programs.

Every Datalog$^{\neg s}$ program is locally stratified and its iterated fixed point model coincides with its perfect model. Note that a Datalog$^\neg$ program is stratified if all ground atoms with the same predicate symbol can be assigned the same local stratum B_i.

The data complexity of locally stratified Datalog$^\neg$ programs is still polynomial time.

4.5   UNSTRATIFIED NEGATION

In the previous sections we considered subclasses of Datalog$^\neg$ by imposing restrictions on the use of negation, with the more general subclass being Datalog$^{\neg ls}$. There are Datalog$^\neg$ programs that are not locally stratified and for which we cannot rely on the semantics previously discussed.

In this section, we remove any limitation on the use of negation and thus consider the full Datalog$^\neg$ language. We present two different semantics for Datalog$^\neg$ programs, namely the *stable model semantics* and the *well-founded semantics*, which both generalize the semantics discussed so far.[1]

4.5.1   STABLE MODEL SEMANTICS

The *stable model* semantics has been proposed by Gelfond and Lifschitz [1988]. It is more general than the perfect model semantics of Datalog$^{\neg ls}$ programs and is applicable to Datalog$^\neg$ programs that are not locally stratified.

Consider a Datalog$^\neg$ program P and a database D. As usual, the Herbrand universe H_{P_D} of P_D is the set of constants appearing in P_D, the Herbrand base B_{P_D} of P_D is the set of ground atoms which can be built using predicate symbols appearing in P_D and constants in H_{P_D}, and an interpretation of P_D is any subset of B_{P_D}.

Given an interpretation I of P_D, let $P_D{}^I$ denote the ground Datalog program derived from $ground(P_D)$ by deleting

- every rule that contains a negative literal $\neg A$ in its body with $A \in I$, and

- all negative literals in the bodies of the remaining rules.

An interpretation I of P_D is a *stable model* of P_D if and only if I is the least model of $P_D{}^I$—notice that $P_D{}^I$ has a (unique) least model as it is a Datalog program, cf. Section 3.2.1.

Example 4.12   [Gelfond and Lifschitz, 1988] Consider the following Datalog$^\neg$ program P

$$q(X) \leftarrow p(X, Y), \neg q(Y)$$

---

[1]Other interesting semantics for Datalog$^\neg$ programs have been proposed, see the bibliographic notes of this chapter.

and a database D containing only the fact $p(1, 2)$. Here p is a base predicate symbol and q is a derived one. Clearly, P_D is as follows:

$$p(1, 2).$$
$$q(1) \leftarrow p(1, 2), \neg q(2).$$
$$q(1) \leftarrow p(1, 1), \neg q(1).$$
$$q(2) \leftarrow p(2, 2), \neg q(2).$$
$$q(2) \leftarrow p(2, 1), \neg q(1).$$

Notice that P_D is not locally stratified.

Consider the interpretation $I_1 = \{q(2)\}$. Then, $P_D{}^{I_1}$ is the following Datalog program

$$p(1, 2).$$
$$q(1) \leftarrow p(1, 1).$$
$$q(2) \leftarrow p(2, 1).$$

whose least model is $\{p(1, 2)\}$, which is different from I_1. Hence, I_1 is not a stable model.

Consider now the interpretation $I_2 = \{p(1, 2), q(1)\}$. Then, $P_D{}^{I_2}$ is the following Datalog program

$$p(1, 2).$$
$$q(1) \leftarrow p(1, 2).$$
$$q(2) \leftarrow p(2, 2).$$

whose least model is I_2. Hence, I_2 is a stable model. Indeed, I_2 is the only stable model of P.

The underlying idea of the stable model semantics is the following. If an interpretation I is the set of ground atoms that are considered to be true, then any rule having a negative literal $\neg A$ in its body with $A \in I$ is useless and any negative literal $\neg A$ with $A \notin I$ is trivial. Then, $ground(P_D)$ can be simplified into $P_D{}^I$. If I happens to be precisely the set of atoms that logically follow from the simplified program $P_D{}^I$, then I is a stable model. Thus, in a sense, a stable model is able to "reproduce" itself.

A Datalog$\neg$ program can have zero, one, or many stable models. As an example, the Datalog$\neg$ program consisting only of the rule $p \leftarrow \neg p$ has no stable models. The Datalog$\neg$ program consisting of the two rules $p \leftarrow \neg q$ and $q \leftarrow \neg q$ has two stable models, namely $\{p\}$ and $\{q\}$.

Stable models are minimal models. Furthermore, the stable model semantics generalizes all the semantics considered in the previous sections. Hence, locally stratified Datalog$\neg$ programs have a unique stable model which is equal to the perfect model. Obviously, since the perfect model semantics restricted to stratified Datalog$\neg$ programs coincides with the iterated fixed point semantics, we can also conclude that a stratified Datalog$\neg$ program has a unique stable model which is identical to its iterated fixed point model.

Notice that when we consider Datalog programs, $P_D{}^I$ coincides with $ground(P_D)$ for every interpretation I and thus the only interpretation that is a stable model is the the least model of P_D.

The data complexity of Datalog⁻ under the stable model semantics is co-NP-complete and the program complexity is co-NEXPTIME-complete [Dantsin et al., 2001, Kolaitis and Papadim-itriou, 1991, Marek and Truszczynski, 1991, Schlipf, 1995]. Marek and Truszczynski [1991] showed that even for a propositional (i.e., all predicate symbols have arity 0 and thus there are no variables) Datalog⁻ program, checking whether it has a stable model is NP-complete.

Datalog⁻ under the stable model semantics is able to express exactly all queries whose evaluation complexity is in co-NP [Schlipf, 1995].[2]

4.5.2 WELL-FOUNDED SEMANTICS

The well-founded semantics has been proposed by Van Gelder et al. [1988, 1991].

In the semantics considered so far, a stable model provides a truth value for every atom in the Herbrand base of a given program, provided that a semantics can be assigned to the considered program (e.g., the Datalog⁻ program $p \leftarrow \neg p$ has no stable models). The well-founded semantics is based on the idea that a program may not necessarily provide such information for all ground atoms, and thus the truth value of some ground atoms can be unknown. Such a relaxation allows the well-founded semantics to assign a natural semantics to all Datalog⁻ programs (including, for instance, the program consisting of the rule $p \leftarrow \neg p$, for which no stable model exists). The price to pay is that total information is no longer guaranteed, that is, there might be ground atoms whose truth value is unknown.

In a sense, the well-founded semantics tries to give a reasonable meaning to as much of the program as possible in the unfavorable cases, when only a partial model exists (i.e., the truth values of some ground atoms is unknown), as an extension of the semantics for the favorable cases, which have a total model (i.e., the truth value of every ground atom is known—it is either true or false).

Another aspect of the well-founded semantics is that it treats negative and positive literals in a more uniform way in the following sense. One can no longer assume that $\neg A$ is true simply because A is not inferred. Instead, both negative and positive literals must be inferred.

Roughly speaking, another way of looking at the well-founded semantics is that it assigns value "unknown" to an atom if it is defined by unstratified negation.

Before formally defining the well-founded semantics, we introduce some needed notation and terminology. A positive literal A and the negative literal $\neg A$, where A is an atom, are said to be *complements* of each other. We say that a set of literals is *consistent* if it does not contain both a literal and its complement. Given a set of literals U, we use $\neg U$ to denote the set of literals built by taking the complement of each literal in U.

Let P be a Datalog⁻ program and D a database. A *partial interpretation* I of P_D is a consistent set of ground literals whose atoms are taken from the Herbrand base B_{P_D}. A *total interpretation* is a partial interpretation that contains every atom of B_{P_D} or its negation.

---

[2]The evaluation complexity of a query is the complexity of checking whether a given atom belongs to the query result, or, in the case of Boolean queries, whether the query evaluates to true.

A ground literal L is *true w.r.t.* I if L is in I and *false* if its complement is in I.

A conjunction of ground literals is *true w.r.t.* I if all its literals are *true* w.r.t. I, and is *false w.r.t.* I if any of its literals is *false* w.r.t. I.

We say that a ground rule r is

- *satisfied* w.r.t. I if the head is true w.r.t. I or some body literal is false w.r.t. I,

- *falsified* w.r.t. I if the head is false w.r.t. I and all body literals are true w.r.t. I, and

- *weakly falsified* w.r.t. I if the head is false w.r.t. I but no body literal is false w.r.t. I.

A *total model* of P_D is a total interpretation of P_D such that every ground rule in $ground(P_D)$ is satisfied.

A *partial model* of P_D is a partial interpretation of P_D that can be extended to a total model of P_D. Thus, for a partial model, there might be some ground rules that are not satisfied, but all rules can be satisfied by adding some ground literals to the partial model (the resulting set of literals must be consistent). Clearly, this is impossible if the partial model falsifies a ground rule in $ground(P_D)$. If the partial interpretation only weakly falsifies a ground rule, then the addition of some literal may be necessary to satisfy the rule.

Intuitively, a partial interpretation I says that the truth value of each atom $A \in I$ is true, the truth value of each atom A s.t. $\neg A \in I$ is false, and the truth value of other atoms is unknown. Thus, a partial interpretation may contain incomplete information. The natural ordering on partial interpretations is $\subseteq$. Given two partial interpretations I and I', if $I \subseteq I'$ then I' contains all the information in I, both positive and negative, and possibly more.

We now present the important notion of an *unfounded set*.

Definition 4.13   Let P be a Datalog$^{\neg}$ program and D a database. A subset U of the Herbrand base B_{P_D} is an *unfounded set* w.r.t. a partial interpretation I of P_D if each atom $A \in U$ satisfies the following condition: for every ground rule in $ground(P_D)$ whose head is A, at least one of the following conditions hold:

1. some (positive or negative) body literal is false w.r.t. I and

2. some positive body literal belongs to U.

Intuitively, we can look at I as what we already know about the intended model of P_D (possibly partial). Rules satisfying the first condition above cannot be used to infer anything as their bodies are false w.r.t. I. The second condition above is the *unfoundedness* condition: of all the rules that still might be usable to derive something in the set U, each requires an atom in U to be true. In other words, there is no one atom in U that can be *first* to be established as true by the rules of P_D (starting from knowing I). Consequently, if we choose to infer that some or all atoms in U are false, there is no way we could later have to infer one to be true.

The well-founded semantics uses the two aforementioned conditions to draw negative conclusions. Essentially, it simultaneously infers all atoms in U to be false.

Example 4.14   [Van Gelder et al., 1991] Consider the following (ground) Datalog$^\neg$ program:

$$p(a) \leftarrow p(c), \neg p(b).$$
$$p(b) \leftarrow \neg p(a).$$
$$p(e) \leftarrow \neg p(d).$$
$$p(c).$$
$$p(d) \leftarrow q(a), \neg q(b).$$
$$p(d) \leftarrow q(b), \neg q(c).$$
$$q(a) \leftarrow p(d).$$
$$q(b) \leftarrow q(a).$$

The set $U = \{p(d), q(a), q(b), q(c)\}$ is an unfounded set with respect to the partial interpretation $\emptyset$. In particular, there is no rule with $q(c)$ in the head so the condition in Definition 4.13 is trivially satisfied for $q(c)$. For each of $p(d)$, $q(a)$, and $q(b)$, the second condition of Definition 4.13 applies as there is no way to establish $p(d)$ as true without first establishing $q(a)$ or $q(b)$ as true, there is no way to establish $q(a)$ as true without first establishing $p(d)$ as true, and likewise for $q(b)$. Clearly, $q(c)$ can never be proven, but we can also see that among $p(d)$, $q(a)$, and $q(b)$, none can be the first one to be proven.

In contrast, it can be easily verified that $\{p(a), p(b)\}$ is not an unfounded set with respect to the partial interpretation $\emptyset$.

It is easy to see that the union of arbitrary unfounded sets is an unfounded set. Given a Datalog$^\neg$ program P and a database D, the *greatest unfounded set* with respect to a partial interpretation I, denoted $U_{P_D}(I)$, is the union of all sets that are unfounded with respect to I.

We now introduce three operators that will be used to define the well-founded semantics.

Definition 4.15   Let P be a Datalog$^\neg$ program, D a database, and I a partial interpretation of P_D. We define the operators $T_{P_D}, U_{P_D}, W_{P_D}$, which take a set of literals and return a set of literals, as follows:

- a ground atom A belongs to $T_{P_D}(I)$ iff there is some ground rule in *ground*(P_D) whose head is A and such that every body literal is true w.r.t. I;

- $U_{P_D}(I)$ is the greatest unfounded set with respect to I; and

- $W_{P_D}(I) = T_{P_D}(I) \cup \neg U_{P_D}(I)$.

Intuitively, given a partial interpretation I (which can be seen as what we already know about the intended model of P_D), $T_{P_D}(I)$ infers ground atoms that are established as true,

$U_{P_D}(I)$ infers ground atoms that can be established as false, and W_{P_D} simply combines the result of the two operators. It is easy to see that the three operators are monotone.

Notice that when the $T_{P_D}(I)$ operator is applied and we want to determine whether we can infer the head atom of a ground rule r, to decide whether a negative literal $\neg A$ in the body of r is true w.r.t. I, the presence of $\neg A$ in I is required. This is different from other semantics that look for the absence of A from I—see, e.g., the more general version (able to deal with negative body literals) of the immediate consequence operator $\mathcal{T}_{P_D}$ reported in Section 4.3.

Definition 4.16   Consider a Datalog$^\neg$ program P and a database D. We define the sets I_γ and I^∞, whose elements are ground literals built from the atoms in the Herbrand base of P_D, as follows:

1. $I_0 = \emptyset$;

2. $I_{\gamma+1} = W_{P_D}(I_\gamma)$, for $\gamma \geq 0$; and

3. $I^\infty = \bigcup_\gamma I_\gamma$.

We are now ready to define the well-founded semantics.

Definition 4.17   Consider a Datalog$^\neg$ program P and a database D. The *well-founded semantics* of P_D is given by the least fixed point of W_{P_D} (or the limit I^∞).

Indeed, the least fixed point of W_{P_D} is a partial model, and is called *well-founded model*. The well-founded model is unique and always exists, in contrast to the stable model semantics for which there exist Datalog$^\neg$ programs that have no stable models.

Every positive literal in the well-founded model denotes that its atom is true, every negative literal denotes that its atom is false, and missing atoms have no truth value assigned by the semantics.

The well-founded semantics coincides with the perfect model semantics on locally stratified Datalog$^\neg$ programs (thus, it also coincides with the stable model semantics on such programs). Thus, for locally stratified Datalog$^\neg$ programs the well-founded model is total. Furthermore, there are Datalog$^\neg$ programs that are not locally stratified but have a total well-founded model. For instance, considering the Datalog$^\neg$ program P and the database D of Example 4.12, we have that P_D is not locally stratified but it has a total well-founded model, which is the unique stable model of P_D (see Example 4.12).

While stratification is a syntactic property of a Datalog$^\neg$ program, for an unstratified Datalog$^\neg$ program, whether it has a total well-founded model depends in general on the database.

For arbitrary Datalog$^\neg$ programs (thus, beyond locally stratified ones) the relation between the stable model and the well-founded semantics has been investigated in [Van Gelder et al., 1991]. If a Datalog$^\neg$ program has a total well-founded model, then that model is the unique stable model of the program. However, the converse does not hold, that is, there are programs that do not have a total well-founded model but do have a unique stable model, as shown in the following example.

Example 4.18   [Van Gelder et al., 1991] Consider the following Datalog¬ program P:

$$a \leftarrow \neg b.$$
$$b \leftarrow \neg a.$$
$$p \leftarrow \neg p.$$

There exist two minimal models for P, namely $\{a, p\}$ and $\{b, p\}$. It can be easily verified that P has no stable model while its well-founded model is $\emptyset$, which is not total.

Consider now the Datalog¬ program P' obtained by adding the following rule to P

$$p \leftarrow \neg b.$$

Then, P' has a unique stable model, namely $\{a, p\}$ while its well-founded model is still the empty set. In a sense, the addition of the aforementioned rule to P "stabilizes" one of the two minimal models of P.

Below is another example reporting a Datalog¬ program that has a unique stable model but does not have a total well-founded model.

Example 4.19   [Van Gelder et al., 1991] Consider the following Datalog¬ program P:

$$a \leftarrow \neg b.$$
$$b \leftarrow \neg a.$$
$$c \leftarrow a, b.$$
$$a \leftarrow \neg c.$$

The well-founded model of P is the empty set, while its unique stable model is $\{a\}$.

The well-founded model of a Datalog¬ program P is a subset of every stable model of P [Van Gelder et al., 1991].[3]

The data complexity of the well-founded semantics is P-complete, while the program complexity is EXPTIME-complete [Dantsin et al., 2001, Van Gelder et al., 1991].

4.6   CHOICE

In this section, we extend Datalog with the *choice* construct [Giannotti et al., 1991, 2001, Saccà and Zaniolo, 1990].[4] The choice construct allows us to get an increase in expressive power and to

---

[3]In Section 4.5.1 we represented stable models as subsets of the Herbrand base B_{P_D}, and thus they are sets of atoms; here it is assumed that a stable model M can be seen as the set of literals $M \cup \neg(B_{P_D} \setminus M)$.

[4]A choice construct called *static choice* was considered by Krishnamurthy and Naqvi [1988] and Naqvi and Tsur [1989]. A different choice construct called *dynamic choice* was considered in Giannotti et al. [1991, 2001], Saccà and Zaniolo [1990]. In this section, we consider the dynamic choice and call it simply choice.

obtain simple declarative formulations of classical combinatorial problems, such as those which can be solved by means of greedy algorithms [Greco and Zaniolo, 2001]. The declarative semantics of the choice construct is given in terms of Datalog¬ rules, so augmenting Datalog with the choice means introducing a restricted form a negation (embedded in the choice construct).

We also discuss the *choice-least* and *choice-most* constructs [Greco and Zaniolo, 2001], which specialize the choice construct so as to force greedy selections among alternative choices— these turn out to be particularly useful to express classical greedy algorithms.

4.6.1 SYNTAX

We start by introducing the basic idea of the choice construct with an example.

Example 4.20   Consider a database schema {*student*(*Name*, *Major*, *Year*), *professor*(*Name*, *Major*)} and a university database over such a schema containing the following facts:

$$student(john, ee, senior).$$
$$professor(ohm, ee).$$
$$professor(bell, ee).$$

Also, suppose that the major of a student must match his/her advisor's major area of specialization. Then, eligible advisors can be computed with the following rule:

$$elig\_adv(S, A) \leftarrow student(S, M, Y), professor(A, M)$$

which yields *elig_adv*(*john*, *ohm*) and *elig_adv*(*john*, *bell*).

Now, suppose we want to enforce that a student can have only one advisor. This can be obtained by adding the atom *choice*((*S*), (*A*)) in the body of the rule above, which forces the selection of a unique advisor, out of the eligible advisors, for a student. The resulting rule is:

$$actual\_adv(S, A) \leftarrow student(S, M, Y), professor(A, M), choice((S), (A)).$$

Intuitively, the rule above forces each student *S* to be associated with a unique professor *A*.

The goal *choice*((*S*), (*A*)) can also be viewed as enforcing the *functional dependency* $S \rightarrow A$ on the set of atoms derived by means of the rule; thus, in *actual_adv*, the second column (professor name) is functionally dependent on the first one (student name).

The result of executing the rule is *nondeterministic*: it can give either *actual_adv*(*john*, *ohm*) or *actual_adv*(*john*, *bell*).

Choice rules and programs are defined as follows.

Definition 4.21   A *choice rule* is of the form:

$$A \leftarrow B(\overline{Z}), choice((\overline{X}_1), (\overline{Y}_1)), \ldots, choice((\overline{X}_k), (\overline{Y}_k)),$$

where $k > 0$, A is an atom whose variables appear in $\overline{Z}$,[5] $B(\overline{Z})$ is a conjunction of atoms, $\overline{Z}$ is a list of the variables occurring in $B(\overline{Z})$, $\overline{X}_i$, and $\overline{Y}_i$ are lists of variables such that $\overline{X}_i \cap \overline{Y}_i = \emptyset$ and $\overline{X}_i, \overline{Y}_i \subseteq \overline{Z}$, for all $1 \leq i \leq k$.

A *choice program* is a finite set of Datalog rules and choice rules.

In a choice rule of the form reported in the preceding definition, each of the $choice((\overline{X}_i), (\overline{Y}_i))$'s is called *choice atom*.

In this section, we are interested in choice programs having at least one choice rule—in fact, when this is not the case, we are dealing with simple Datalog programs. Thus, in the rest of this section, a choice program is understood to have at least one choice rule.

4.6.2   STABLE-MODEL DECLARATIVE SEMANTICS

The semantics of a choice program P is defined in terms of the stable model semantics of a Datalog$^\neg$ program derived from P, called *first-order equivalent* of P. In the following definition, we use $\circ$ to denote the operator that concatenates (ordered) lists of variables.

Definition 4.22   Given a choice program P, the *first-order equivalent* of P, denoted $foe(P)$, is the Datalog$^\neg$ program obtained from P by replacing every choice rule r of the form

$$A \leftarrow B(\overline{Z}), choice((\overline{X}_1), (\overline{Y}_1)), \ldots, choice((\overline{X}_k), (\overline{Y}_k))$$

with the following set of rules:

$$
\begin{aligned}
A &\leftarrow B(\overline{Z}), chosen_r(\overline{X}, \overline{Y}). \\
chosen_r(\overline{X}, \overline{Y}) &\leftarrow B(\overline{Z}), \neg diff\_choice_r(\overline{X}, \overline{Y}). \\
diff\_choice_r(\overline{X}, \overline{Y}_1, \ldots, \overline{Y}_k) &\leftarrow chosen_r(\overline{X}, \overline{Y}'_1, \ldots, \overline{Y}'_k), \overline{Y}_i \neq \overline{Y}'_i. \qquad \forall i \in [1, k],
\end{aligned}
$$

where $\overline{X} = \overline{X}_1 \circ \cdots \circ \overline{X}_k, \overline{Y} = \overline{Y}_1 \circ \cdots \circ \overline{Y}_k$, and $\overline{Y}'_i$ is the list of variables obtained by "priming" every variable in $\overline{Y}_i$. Moreover, the intended meaning of $\overline{Y}_i \neq \overline{Y}'_i$ is that it is true if $Y \neq Y'$ is true for some variable $Y \in \overline{Y}_i$ and its primed counterpart Y'.[6]

Definition 4.23   The semantics of a choice program P and a database D is given by the stable models of $foe(P) \cup D$, which are called *choice models* of P_D.

Example 4.24   Consider the choice program P consisting only of the following choice rule r (taken from Example 4.20):

$$actual\_adv(S, A) \leftarrow student(S, M, Y), professor(A, M), choice((S), (A)).$$

---

[5]This is a safety condition.

[6]Notice that the last kind of rules does not satisfy the safety condition as variables $\overline{Y}_i$ are not limited (cf. Section 4.1). However, such rules might be made safe by adding a suitable atom $d(\overline{Y}_i)$ in the rule body which dictates what are the values that variables $\overline{Y}_i$ can take.

The first-order equivalent of P is reported below (it can be read as a statement that a professor will be assigned to a student with the same major whenever a different professor has not been assigned to the same student):

$$
\begin{aligned}
actual\_adv(S, A) &\leftarrow student(S, M, Y), professor(A, M), chosen_r(S, A). \\
chosen_r(S, A) &\leftarrow student(S, M, Y), professor(A, M), \neg diff\_choice_r(S, A). \\
diff\_choice_r(S, A) &\leftarrow chosen_r(S, A'), \ A \neq A'.
\end{aligned}
$$

Consider now the following database D (taken again from Example 4.20)

$$
\begin{aligned}
&student(john, ee, senior). \\
&professor(ohm, ee). \\
&professor(bell, ee).
\end{aligned}
$$

Then, P_D has two choice models whose $actual\_adv$-atoms are $\{actual\_adv(john, ohm)\}$ and $\{actual\_adv(john, bell)\}$, respectively.

The body of a choice rule may contain a choice atom of the form $choice((), \overline{X}))$, that is, the first argument is the empty list. The intuitive meaning is that a unique value for $\overline{X}$ is nondeterministically chosen. This kind of choice atom is illustrated in the following example.

Example 4.25   Consider again the university database schema of Example 4.20 and suppose we are given the following database D:

$$
\begin{aligned}
&student(john, ee, senior). \\
&student(alice, ee, senior). \\
&professor(ohm, ee). \\
&professor(bell, ee).
\end{aligned}
$$

Let P be the choice program consisting of the following choice rule r

$$
adv(S, A) \leftarrow student(S, M_1, Y), professor(A, M_2), choice((), (A)).
$$

This choice rule assigns to all students the same (nondeterministically chosen) advisor A and thus the adv relation will contain a single professor. Then, P_D has two choice models whose adv-atoms are $\{adv(john, ohm), adv(alice, ohm)\}$ and $\{adv(john, bell), adv(alice, bell)\}$, respectively.

Notice also that that the first-order equivalent of P is the following Datalog$^\neg$ program

$$
\begin{aligned}
adv(S, A) &\leftarrow student(S, M_1, Y), professor(A, M_2), chosen_r(A). \\
chosen_r(S, A) &\leftarrow student(S, M_1, Y), professor(A, M_2), \neg diff\_choice_r(A). \\
diff\_choice_r(A) &\leftarrow chosen_r(A'), \ A \neq A'.
\end{aligned}
$$

In general, program $foe(P)$ has the following properties [Giannotti et al., 2001]:

- *foe*(*P*) has one or more stable models and

- the *chosen$_r$* atoms in each stable model of *foe*(*P*) obey the functional dependencies defined by the choice atoms.

It is worth noting that the functional dependency enforced by a choice atom in the body of a choice rule *r* is "local" to *r*, that is, what is derived through the application of *r* must satisfy the functional dependency; however, there might be some other rules in the considered program that allow us to derive atoms that violate the functional dependency. This aspect is illustrated in the following example.

Example 4.26 Consider again the choice program *P* and the database *D* of Example 4.24. Recall that *P* contains only one choice rule assigning a single advisor to each student. Thus, P_D has two choice models whose *actual_adv*-atoms are {*actual_adv*(*john, ohm*)} and {*actual_adv*(*john, bell*)}, respectively.
Consider the choice program *P'* obtained by adding to *P* the following Datalog rule:

$$actual\_adv(S, A) \leftarrow student(S, M, Y), professor(A, M).$$

Now P'_D has only one choice model whose *actual_adv*-atoms are {*actual_adv*(*john, ohm*), *actual_adv*(*john, bell*)}. The addition of the rule above allows us to derive more atoms that lead to the violation of the functional dependency enforced by the choice rule.

Below we report different examples showing how some classical combinatorial problems can be easily expressed using the choice construct.

Example 4.27 Consider a bipartite undirected graph $G = \langle (V_1, V_2), E \rangle$, that is, an undirected graph where vertices are partitioned into two subsets V_1 and V_2, and each edge in *E* connects a vertex in V_1 with a vertex in V_2.
Consider the problem of finding a *matching*, i.e., a subset *E'* of *E*, such that for every vertex $v \in V_1 \cup V_2$ at most one edge of *E'* is incident on *v*. Suppose that we have a fact *edge*(*x, y*) for each edge joining vertex $x \in V_1$ with vertex $y \in V_2$. The problem can be expressed with the following choice rule:

$$matching(X, Y) \leftarrow edge(X, Y), choice((Y), (X)), choice((X), (Y)).$$

Intuitively, the choice rule says that any edge might be included in the matching provide that the matching relation satisfies the conditions imposed by the choice atoms, that is, if an edge (*X, Y*) is included in the matching then *X* is joined only with *Y* in the matching, and, likewise, *Y* is joined only with *X* in the matching.

Example 4.28 Consider an undirected graph stored in a database as follows: for each edge connecting vertex *x* with vertex *y* there are two facts *edge*(*x, y*) and *edge*(*y, x*) in the database. A spanning tree starting from the root vertex a can be computed by means of the following choice program:[7]

$$st(root, a).$$
$$st(X, Y) \leftarrow st(Z, X), edge(X, Y), Y \neq a, Y \neq X, choice((Y), (X)).$$

To illustrate the presence of multiple choice models for this choice program, consider a simple graph consisting of the following edges:

$$edge(a, b).\quad edge(b, a).$$
$$edge(b, c).\quad edge(c, b).$$
$$edge(a, c).\quad edge(c, a).$$

Initially, the recursive rule could derive $st(a, b)$ and $st(a, c)$. No further edges can be added after those, since the addition of $st(c, b)$ or $st(b, c)$ would violate the functional dependency enforced by $choice((Y), (X))$. Notice that $st(root, a)$ is always derived by the first rule and thus there are no "chosen" atoms with the second argument equal to the source vertex a. Therefore, to avoid the addition of $st(b, a)$ or $st(c, a)$, the atom $Y \neq a$ was added to the recursive rule.

The choice program has three different choice models, for which we list only the st-atoms below:

- $\{st(a, b), st(a, c)\}$

- $\{st(a, b), st(b, c)\}$

- $\{st(a, c), st(c, b)\}$.

4.6.3   FIXPOINT SEMANTICS

In this section, we present a fixpoint semantics for choice programs. This semantics will be specialized in Section 4.6.4 to define the *greedy choice*.

Given a choice program P, we use P_C to denote the set of rules in $foe(P)$ that define a predicate $chosen_r$ (for some r in P), and use P_S to denote the remaining rules of $foe(P)$, i.e., $P_S = foe(P) - P_C$. We can associate P_C (resp. P_S) with an immediate consequence operator $\mathcal{T}_{P_C}$ (resp. $\mathcal{T}_{P_S}$). Clearly, for any interpretation I of $foe(P)$, the following holds:

$$\mathcal{T}_{foe(P)}(I) = \mathcal{T}_{P_C}(I) \cup \mathcal{T}_{P_S}(I).$$

---

[7]For illustrative purposes, here we are slightly abusing the syntax of choice programs (cf. Definition 4.21) by allowing inequalities in the body of a rule. However, the semantics of such more general choice programs can be defined in the same way as in Definition 4.22 as it is given in terms of the stable models of Datalog$^{\neg}$ programs.

We now introduce a general operator for computing the nondeterministic fixpoints of a choice program P. We will denote by FD_P the functional dependencies defined by the choice atoms in P.

Definition 4.29 Given a choice program P, its *nondeterministic immediate consequence operator* Ψ_P is a mapping from an interpretation of $foe(P)$ to a set of interpretations of $foe(P)$ defined as follows:

$$\Psi_P(I) = \{\mathcal{T}_{P_S}^\omega(I \cup \Delta C) \cup \Delta C \mid \Delta C \in \Gamma_P(I)\},$$

where

$$\Gamma_P(I) = \begin{cases} \{\emptyset\} & \text{if } \mathcal{T}_{P_C}(I) = \emptyset \\ \{\Delta C \mid \emptyset \subset \Delta C \subseteq \mathcal{T}_{P_C}(I) \setminus I \text{ and } I \cup \Delta C \models FD_P\}, & \text{otherwise.} \end{cases}$$

$I \cup \Delta C \models FD_P$ denotes that $I \cup \Delta C$ satisfies the dependencies in FD_P.

Basically, the Ψ_P operator is the composition of two operators. Given an interpretation I, the first operator computes all the admissible subsets $\Delta C \subseteq \mathcal{T}_{P_C}(I) \setminus I$; that is, those where $I \cup \Delta C$ obeys the functional dependencies FD_P. The second operator derives the logical consequence for each admissible subset using the fixpoint of $\mathcal{T}_{P_S}$.

The definition of $\Gamma_P(I)$ is such that ΔC is not empty iff $\mathcal{T}_{P_C}(I) \setminus I$ is not empty. Thus, if there are possible new choices, then at least one has to be taken. The Ψ_P operator formalizes a single step of a bottom-up evaluation of a choice program.

Observe that, given the presence of the condition $I \cup \Delta C \models FD_P$, we can eliminate the atoms $diff\_choice_r(\overline{X}, \overline{Y})$ from the rules defining predicate symbols $chosen_r$. In fact, if $\mathcal{T}_{P_C'}$ denotes the immediate consequence operator for the set of rules obtained from P_C by deleting the atoms $diff\_choice_r(\overline{X}, \overline{Y})$, then $\mathcal{T}_{P_C'}$ can replace $\mathcal{T}_{P_C}$ in the definition of $\Gamma_P(I)$ (cf. Definition 4.29 above), without affecting the final result.

Definition 4.30 Given a choice program P, an *inflationary choice fixpoint computation* for P is a sequence $\langle I_n \rangle_{n \geq 0}$ of interpretations such that:

1. $I_0 = \emptyset$,

2. $I_{n+1} \in \Psi_P(I_n)$, for $n \geq 0$.

Inasmuch as every sequence $\langle I_n \rangle_{n \geq 0}$ is monotonic, it has a unique limit for $n \to \infty$; this limit will be called an *inflationary choice fixpoint* for the choice program P.

Given a choice program P and a Herbrand interpretation M of $foe(P)$, then M is a choice model of P iff M is an inflationary choice fixpoint for P [Giannotti et al., 1991]. Thus, the inflationary choice fixpoint computation is *sound* (every inflationary choice fixpoint is a choice model) and *complete* (for each choice model there is some inflationary choice fixpoint computation producing it).

The data complexity (i.e., the computational complexity evaluated with respect to the size of the database) of computing a choice model for a choice program P is polynomial time [Giannotti et al., 1991]. Therefore, the computation of one of the stable models of $foe(P)$ can be performed in polynomial time using the inflationary choice fixpoint computation. This contrasts with the general intractability of finding stable models of Datalog$^\neg$ programs: in fact, as already mentioned in Section 4.5.1, checking if a Datalog$^\neg$ program has a stable model is NP-complete [Marek and Truszczynski, 1991].

The choice construct allows us to capture a special subclass of Datalog$^\neg$ programs that have a stable model semantics but are amenable to efficient implementation and are appealing to intuition. Evaluating these programs only requires memorization of the $chosen_r$ predicates; from these, the $diff\_choice_r$ predicates can be generated on-the-fly, thus eliminating the need to store $diff\_choice_r$ explicitly. Moreover, the model of memorizing tables to enforce functional dependencies provides a simple enough metaphor for a programmer to make effective usage of this construct without having to become cognizant on the subtleties of non-monotonic semantics.

We also mention that, although we are considering Datalog programs with choice, the framework can be trivially extended to consider stratified negation. The computation of a choice model for a Datalog$^{\neg s}$ program with choice can be carried out by partitioning the program into an ordered number of suitable subprograms and computing the choice fixpoints of every subprogram in their order.

4.6.4   GREEDY CHOICE

In this section, we focus on a specialization of the choice construct called *greedy choice* [Greco and Zaniolo, 1998, 2001, Greco et al., 1992]. The interest in such a specialization follows from the observation that it is frequently desirable to select a value that is the *least* or the *most* among a set of candidate values, and still satisfy the functional dependencies defined by the choice atoms.

A *choice-least* (resp. *choice-most*) *atom* is of the form *choice-least*$((\overline{X}), (C))$ (resp. *choice-most*$((\overline{X}), (C)))$, where $\overline{X}$ is a list of variables and C is a single variable ranging over an ordered domain.

A *choice-least rule* (resp. *choice-most rule*) is a Datalog rule that contains one choice-least (resp. one choice-most) atom, and zero or more choice atoms (besides standard atoms, of course).

A *choice-least* (resp. *choice-most*) *program* is a finite set of choice-least (resp. choice-most) rules, choice rules, and Datalog rules. In the rest of this section, we assume that a choice-least (resp. choice-most) program has at least one choice-least (resp. *choice-most*) rule as when this is not the case we are dealing with choice programs or Datalog programs, which have been already discussed before.

A *choice-least*$((\overline{X}), (C))$ (resp. *choice-most*$((\overline{X}), (C)))$ atom in a rule indicates that the functional dependency defined by the atom *choice*$((\overline{X}), (C))$ is to be satisfied, and the C value assigned to a certain value of $\overline{X}$ has to be the minimum (resp. maximum) one among the candidate values. For instance, a rule of the form

$$p(X, Y, C) \leftarrow q(X, Y, C), choice((X), (Y)), choice\text{-}least((X), (C))$$

imposes the functional dependency $X \rightarrow Y, C$ on the possible instances of p. In addition, for each value of X, the minimum among the candidate values of C must be chosen. For instance, assuming that q is defined by the facts $q(a, b, 1)$ and $q(a, c, 2)$, from the rule above we might derive either $p(a, b, 1)$ or $p(a, c, 2)$. However, the choice-least atom introduces the additional requirement that the minimum value on the third attribute has to be chosen, so that only $p(a, b, 1)$ is derived. This means that, by using the choice-least and choice-most constructs, we introduce some preference criteria on the stable models of the program.

Choice-least and choice-most programs have dual properties; thus, in the following we will consider choice-least programs with the understanding that the corresponding properties for choice-most programs are implicitly defined by this duality.

The correct evaluation of choice-least programs can be defined by specializing the nondeterministic immediate consequence operator (Definition 4.29) by ensuring that *(i)* ΔC is a set containing only one element, and *(ii)* a least-cost tuple among those that are candidates is chosen.

In order to define such an operator, we first define a "lazy" version of the nondeterministic immediate consequence operator, called *lazy immediate consequence operator*, where ΔC is specialized into a singleton set δ. The specialized version of Ψ_P so derived will be denoted Ψ_P^{lazy}. As proven in Giannotti et al. [1991], the inflationary choice fixpoint computation restricted so as to use Ψ_P^{lazy} still provides a sound and nondeterministically complete computation for the choice models of P. After that, we define an immediate consequence operator called *least-cost immediate consequence operator*, which ensures that a least-cost tuple among the candidate ones is chosen.

Given a choice-least program P, the *first-order equivalent* of P, denoted $foe(P)$, is defined as for standard choice programs (cf. Definition 4.22), by treating choice-least atoms as choice atoms. As for choice programs, P_C denotes the set of rules in $foe(P)$ that define a predicate $chosen_r$ (for some r in P), and P_S denotes the remaining rules of $foe(P)$, i.e., $P_S = foe(P) - P_C$. We start by defining Ψ_P^{lazy}.

Definition 4.31 Let P be a choice-least program and I an interpretation of $foe(P)$. The *lazy immediate consequence operator* Ψ_P^{lazy} for P is defined as follows:

$$\begin{aligned}
\Theta_I &= \{\delta \mid \delta \in \mathcal{T}_{P_C}(I) \setminus I \text{ and } I \cup \{\delta\} \models FD_P\} \\
\Gamma_P^{lazy}(I) &= \{I \cup \{\delta\} \mid \delta \in \Theta_I\} \cup \{I \mid \Theta_I = \emptyset\} \\
\Psi_P^{lazy}(I) &= \{\mathcal{T}_{P_S}^\omega(J) \mid J \in \Gamma_P^{lazy}(I)\}.
\end{aligned}$$

Given an interpretation I, a set $\Delta C \in \Gamma_P(I)$, and two atoms $t_1, t_2 \in \Delta C$, we write $t_1 < t_2$ if both atoms are inferred only by choice-least rules, and the cost of t_1 is less than the cost of t_2 according to some choice-least atom. For instance, consider the choice-least rule

$$p(X, Y, C) \leftarrow q(X, Y, C), choice\text{-}least((X), (C)),$$

where the "cost" of p-atoms with respect to the choice-least atom *choice-least*$((X), (C))$ is their third argument. Suppose t_1 and t_2 are the atoms $p(a, b, 1)$ and $p(a, b, 2)$, respectively. Then, the cost of t_1 is less than the cost of t_2.

Furthermore, we denote with *least*(ΔC) the set of atoms of ΔC with least cost, i.e., *least*$(\Delta C) = \{t \mid t \in \Delta C \text{ and } \nexists u \in \Delta C \text{ s.t. } u < t\}$. The implementation of the least-cost immediate consequence operator is simply obtained by replacing $\delta \in \Theta_I$ with $\delta \in \text{least}(\Theta_I)$ in the definition of the lazy immediate consequence operator.

Definition 4.32   Let P be a choice-least program and I an interpretation of *foe*(P). The *least-cost immediate consequence operator* Ψ_P^{least} for P is defined as follows:

$$
\begin{aligned}
\Theta_I &= \{\delta \mid \delta \in \mathcal{T}_{P_C}(I) \setminus I \text{ and } I \cup \{\delta\} \models FD_P\} \\
\Gamma_P^{least}(I) &= \{I \cup \{\delta\} \mid \delta \in \text{least}(\Theta_I)\} \cup \{I \mid \Theta_I = \emptyset\} \\
\Psi_P^{least}(I) &= \{\mathcal{T}_{P_S}^{\omega}(J) \mid J \in \Gamma_P^{least}(I)\}.
\end{aligned}
$$

Likewise, the dual definition of the *most-cost immediate consequence operator* can be easily derived.

Definition 4.33   Given a choice-least program P, an *inflationary least choice fixpoint computation* for P is a sequence $\langle I_n \rangle_{n \geq 0}$ of interpretations such that:

- $I_0 = \emptyset$ and

- $I_{n+1} \in \Psi_P^{least}(I_n)$,   for $n \geq 0$.

Thus, all atoms that do not violate the functional dependencies defined by choice atoms (including those imposed by choice-least atoms) are considered, and one is chosen that has the least value for the cost argument. For a choice-least program P,

1. every inflationary least choice fixpoint for P is a choice model for the choice program obtained from P by treating choice-least atoms as choice atoms; and

2. every inflationary least choice fixpoint of P can be computed in polynomial time.

As for the first property, observe that every computation of the inflationary least choice fixpoint is also a computation of the lazy choice fixpoint.

The second property follows from the fact that the complexity of the inflationary lazy choice fixpoint is polynomial time, and the cost of selecting an atom with least cost is also polynomial.

The model so constructed will be called *greedy choice models*.

In a system that adopts a semantics based on the least choice fixpoint, a programmer will specify a *choice-least*$((X), (Y))$ atom to ensure that only particular choice models rather than arbitrary ones are produced through the greedy selection of the least values of Y at each step.

The specialization of choice atoms into choice-least or choice-most atoms yields a convenient and efficient formulation of many greedy algorithms, such as Dijkstra's shortest path (for which arithmetic operators are needed as well) and Prim's minimum-spanning tree algorithms [Greco and Zaniolo, 1998].

Example 4.34   Consider a weighted directed graph stored by means of facts of the form $edge(x, y, c)$, meaning that there is an edge in the graph from vertex x to vertex y with cost c. An algorithm for finding a minimum spanning tree starting from a source vertex a can be formulated as follows, yielding the well-known Prim's algorithm.

$$st(root, a, 0).$$
$$st(X, Y, C) \leftarrow st(Z, X, W), edge(X, Y, C), \ Y \neq a,$$
$$choice((Y), (X)), choice\text{-}least((Y), (C)).$$

Greedy algorithms often provide efficient approximate solutions to NP-complete problems; the following algorithm yields heuristically effective approximations of optimal solutions for the traveling salesperson problem [Papadimitriou and Steiglitz, 1982].

Example 4.35   Given a complete undirected graph, the first rule of the following program simply selects an arbitrary vertex X from which to start the search. Then, the second rule greedily chooses at each step an edge (X, Y, C) of least cost C having X as endpoint.

$$spath(root, X, 0) \leftarrow vertex(X), choice((), X).$$
$$spath(X, Y, C) \leftarrow spath(W, X, K), edge(X, Y, C), spath(root, Z, 0), Y \neq Z,$$
$$choice((X), (Y)), choice((Y), (X)), choice\text{-}least((Y), (C)).$$

The examples above show that the choice constructs provide a logic-based approach for the design of greedy algorithms. In a nutshell, the design approach is as follows: *(i)* formulate the all-answer solution to the problem at hand (e.g., find all the costs of all paths from a source vertex to the other vertices), *(ii)* use choice-induced functional dependency constraints so that the original logic program generates non-deterministic single answers (e.g., find a cost from the source vertex to each other vertex), and *(iii)* specialize the choice atoms into choice-least or choice-most atoms to force a greedy heuristics upon the generation of single answers (thus computing the least-cost paths). This approach yields conceptual simplicity and simple programs.

4.7   DISJUNCTION

In this section, we briefly discuss the extension of Datalog and Datalog$^\neg$ with disjunction (in rule heads). The resulting languages will be referred to as *Datalog*$^\vee$ and *Datalog*$^{\vee,\neg}$, respectively.

Disjunction is an important feature for knowledge representation, database querying, and for representing incomplete information.

We start by defining the syntax of Datalog$^\vee$. A *Datalog$^\vee$ rule r* is of the form:

$$H_1 \vee \cdots \vee H_m \leftarrow A_1, \ldots, A_n,$$

where $m \geq 1, n \geq 0$, and both the H_i's and the A_i's are atoms (function symbols are not allowed). The disjunction $H_1 \vee \cdots \vee H_m$ is called the *head* of r while the conjunction $A_1, \ldots, A_n$ is called the *body* of r. A *Datalog$^\vee$ program* is a finite set of Datalog$^\vee$ rules.

The safety condition of Datalog programs (cf. Section 3.1) is generalized by requiring that every variable appearing in the head must appear in at least one atom of the body, for every Datalog$^\vee$ rule.

The semantics of a Datalog$^\vee$ program is given by its minimal Herbrand models as defined below. Consider a Datalog$^\vee$ program P and a database D. As usual, the Herbrand universe H_{P_D} of P_D (recall that P_D denotes $P \cup D$) is the set of constants appearing in P_D, and the Herbrand base B_{P_D} of P_D is the set of ground atoms which can be built using predicate symbols appearing in P_D and constants in H_{P_D}. An interpretation of P_D is any subset of B_{P_D}. Once again, we use *ground*(P_D) to denote the set of all ground rules obtained from the rules of P_D by replacing all variables with constants.

The truth value of a ground atom A w.r.t. an interpretation I is *true* if $A \in I$, *false* otherwise. A ground rule r is *satisfied* by I if there is a ground atom in the head of r which is *true* w.r.t. I or there is a ground atom in the body of r which is *false* w.r.t. I. An interpretation of P_D is a *model* of P_D if it satisfies every ground rule in *ground*(P_D). A model M of P_D is minimal if no proper subset of M is a model of P_D.

The model-theoretic semantics of a Datalog$^\vee$ program P_D is given by its minimal models. Obviously, this semantics is a generalization of the model-theoretic semantics for Datalog programs presented in Section 3.2.1. Notice that while every Datalog program has a unique minimal model (the least model), a Datalog$^\vee$ program might have more than one minimal model.

Example 4.36   Consider the Datalog$^\vee$ program P consisting of the following Datalog$^\vee$ rule, saying that a person X is either male or female

$$male(X) \vee female(X) \leftarrow person(X).$$

Consider also the database D consisting only of the fact *person*(a). Then, P_D has two minimal models, namely {*person*(a), *male*(a)} and {*person*(a), *female*(a)}.

The language obtained by extending Datalog$^\neg$ with disjunction is denoted as *Datalog$^{\vee,\neg}$*. More specifically, a *Datalog$^{\vee,\neg}$ rule* is of the form

$$H_1 \vee \cdots \vee H_m \leftarrow L_1, \ldots, L_n,$$

where $m \geq 1$, $n \geq 0$, the H_i's are atoms, and the L_i's are literals (i.e., atoms or negated atoms); function symbols are not allowed. The safety condition is the same as for Datalog$^\neg$ (cf. Section 4.1).

A *Datalog$^{\vee,\neg}$ program* is a finite set of Datalog$^{\vee,\neg}$ rules.

The stable model semantics for Datalog$^\neg$ programs is easily generalized to Datalog$^{\vee,\neg}$ programs as follows [Gelfond and Lifschitz, 1991, Przymusinski, 1991].

Consider a Datalog$^{\vee,\neg}$ program P and a database D. The Herbrand universe H_{P_D}, the Herbrand base B_{P_D}, and interpretations of P_D are defined in the usual way as well as $ground(P_D)$. Given an interpretation I of P_D, let $P_D{}^I$ denote the ground Datalog$^\vee$ program derived from $ground(P_D)$ by deleting

- every rule that contains a negative literal $\neg A$ in its body with $A \in I$, and

- all negative literals in the bodies of the remaining rules.

An interpretation I of P_D is a *disjunctive stable model* of P_D if and only if I is a minimal model of $P_D{}^I$. Clearly, this is a generalization of the stable model semantics for Datalog$^\neg$ programs (cf. Section 4.5.1).

Notice that if P is a Datalog$^\vee$ program, then $P_D{}^I = ground(P_D)$ for any interpretation I of P_D and thus the disjunctive stable models of P_D are exactly the minimal models of P_D. Thus, the disjunctive stable model semantics also generalizes the minimal model semantics discussed above for Datalog$^\vee$ programs.

The expressive power and the complexity of Datalog$^{\vee,\neg}$ and several sublanguages of it, under different semantics, are thoroughly studied in Dantsin et al. [2001], Eiter et al. [1997a]. Here we just mention that Datalog$^{\vee,\neg}$ is more expressive than Datalog$^\neg$ (unless the polynomial hierarchy collapses).

BIBLIOGRAPHIC NOTES

Other interesting semantics (which have not been reported in this chapter) have been proposed for Datalog$^\neg$ programs, such as the inflationary and noninflationary semantics, partial stable models, maximal partial stable models, regular models, perfect models, two- and three-valued completion semantics, and fixpoint models [Abiteboul and Vianu, 1991, Abiteboul et al., 1995, Bidoit and Hull, 1986, Dudakov, 1999, Eiter et al., 1997b, Furfaro et al., 2007, Kolaitis and Papadimitriou, 1991, Przymusinski, 1988, Saccà, 1995, Saccà and Zaniolo, 1991, 1997, Schlipf, 1995, You and Yuan, 1995].

A extension of the class of locally stratified Datalog$^\neg$ programs, called *weakly stratified programs*, has been proposed by Przymusinska and Przymusinski [1988].

The expressivity and the complexity of various subclasses of Datalog$^\neg$ under different semantics have been studied in Abiteboul et al. [1995], Buccafurri et al. [1997], Cadoli and Palopoli [1998], Cholak and Blair [1994], Dantsin et al. [2001], Eiter et al. [1998], Greco and Saccà [1996,

1997a,b, 1999], Greco et al. [2001], Kolaitis [1991], Kolaitis and Vardi [1995], Palopoli [1992], Saccà [1997].

The expressive power of the choice construct has been studied in Giannotti and Pedreschi [1998], Giannotti et al. [2001], Greco et al. [1995], where it is shown that it is more powerful than other nondeterministic constructs, including the *witness operator* Abiteboul and Vianu [1991], and the original version of choice (called static choice) proposed in Krishnamurthy and Naqvi [1988]. For instance, it has been shown in Giannotti et al. [1991] that the task of ordering a domain or checking whether a relation contains an even number of elements cannot be performed by Datalog programs with static choice or the witness operator [Abiteboul and Vianu, 1991]. Because of the ability of choice programs to order the elements of a set, Datalog$^{\neg s}$ with choice allows us to express all problems in P.

An extension of Datalog with the choice construct and weak constraints has been studied in Greco [1996, 1998a].

For a more complete treatment of disjunctive logic programming, we refer the reader to Eiter et al. [1997a], Lobo et al. [1992], Minker [1994], Minker and Seipel [2002].

We conclude by mentioning various systems for Datalog and different extensions of it, including negation and disjunction: *Clasp* [Gebser et al., 2012], *DeALS* [Mazuran et al., 2013, Shkapsky et al., 2015], *DLV* [Leone et al.], *LogicBlox* [Aref et al., 2015], *NP Datalog* [Greco et al., 2006, 2010], and *Smodels* [Simons et al., 2002].

CHAPTER 5

Function Symbols

Function symbols are widely acknowledged as an important feature, as they often make modeling easier, and the resulting encodings more readable and concise. They also increase the expressive power and allow us to overcome the inability of dealing with infinite domains.

The main problem with the introduction of function symbols in Datalog is that the least model of a program can be infinite—equivalently, the bottom-up program evaluation might not terminate. Unfortunately, it is undecidable whether the evaluation terminates. In order to cope with this issue, recent research has focused on identifying classes of programs allowing only a restricted use of function symbols while ensuring finiteness and computability of the least model. These approaches provide conditions, called *termination criteria*, specifying sufficient conditions for the (bottom-up) program evaluation to terminate.

This chapter presents termination criteria recently proposed in the literature. It also presents an orthogonal technique, based on program adornment, that can be used in conjunction with current termination criteria to make them more effective.

5.1 SYNTAX AND SEMANTICS

In this chapter, we consider the extension of Datalog with uninterpreted function symbols (i.e., they are not evaluated)—the resulting language will be referred to as Datalog^f.

In addition to infinite sets of constants, variables, and predicate symbols, we assume to have an infinite set of function symbols. Each function symbol is associated with a fixed arity, which is a positive integer. Besides constants and variables (which are called *simple* terms), terms now include also expressions of the form $f(t_1, \ldots, t_m)$, where f is a function symbol of arity m and the t_i's are terms—terms of this form are called *complex*.

As for the syntax, a *Datalog^f rule* simply is a Datalog rule (see Section 3.1) where complex terms can occur. In this chapter, we sometimes call Datalog^f rules simply rules. A *Datalog^f program* is a finite set of Datalog^f rules.

The three semantics for Datalog programs discussed in Chapter 3 can be straightforwardly generalized to the case where function symbols are allowed.

Compared with the model-theoretic semantics of Datalog programs (cf. Section 3.2.1), the main difference is that the Herbrand universe H_P of a Datalog^f program P contains the set of ground terms which can be built using constants and function symbols appearing in P (while for Datalog programs the Herbrand universe contains only constants). The Herbrand base B_P of P remains defined as the set of ground atoms which can be built using predicate symbols appearing in P and ground terms of H_P. The ground instances of atoms, Datalog^f rules, and Datalog^f programs are still obtained by replacing variables with ground terms of H_P. However, notice that since H_P can contain complex terms, the Herbrand base and the ground instantiations can contain complex terms as well. Thus, in a nutshell, the main difference between Datalog and Datalog^f is that ground terms are not only constants, but also include complex terms built from function symbols and constants. The other definitions of Section 3.2.1 remain unmodified and the same notation and terminology therein will be used in the following.

It is important to note that the Herbrand universe is infinite if P contains at least one function symbol and one constant. As a consequence, the Herbrand base is infinite, and interpretations and models can be infinite too. A Datalog^f program has a unique least model, which can be infinite.

The immediate consequence operator can be defined for Datalog^f programs in the same way as for Datalog programs (cf. Section 3.2.2), with the only difference that the ground instantiations of Datalog^f rules and programs are obtained by replacing variables with constants and ground complex terms built from function symbols and constants. As for Datalog^f programs, the least model coincides with the least fixpoint of the immediate consequence operator.

Example 5.1   Consider the following Datalog^f program which counts the number of elements in a list:

$$r_0 : \quad count([a, b, c], 0).$$
$$r_1 : \quad count(L, s(I)) \leftarrow count([X|L], I).$$

The bottom-up evaluation of the program terminates yielding the set of atoms $count([a, b, c], 0)$, $count([b, c], s(0))$, $count([c], s(s(0)))$, and $count([], s(s(s(0))))$. The length L of list $[a, b, c]$ can be retrieved from the atom $count([], L)$ by counting the number of s in L, which 3 in this case.[1]

To make function symbols more explicit, the program above can be rewritten into the following Datalog^f program:

$$r_0 : \quad count(lc(a, lc(b, lc(c, nil))), 0).$$
$$r_1 : \quad count(L, s(I)) \leftarrow count(lc(X, L), I).$$

Here lc is a binary function symbol denoting the list constructor operator, and nil denotes the empty list.

5.2   TERMINATION CRITERIA

The main problem with the introduction of function symbols in Datalog is that the least model can be infinite and thus cannot be fully and explicitly computed. To deal with this issue, subclasses of Datalog^f imposing a restricted use of function symbols, but guaranteeing the computability of

---

[1]Notice that the program has been written so as to count the number of elements in a list when evaluated in a bottom-up fashion, and therefore differs from the classical formulation relying on a top-down evaluation strategy. However, programs relying on a top-down evaluation strategy can be rewritten into programs whose bottom-up evaluation gives the same result.

the least model have been proposed—this section surveys several of such subclasses proposed in the literature. We start by introducing some additional notation and terminology used throughout the chapter.

The binary relation *subterm* over terms is recursively defined as follows: every term is a subterm of itself; if t is a complex term of the form $f(t_1, \ldots, t_m)$, then every t_i is a subterm of t, for $1 \le i \le m$; if t_1 is a subterm of t_2 and t_2 is a subterm of t_3, then t_1 is a subterm of t_3.

Given a predicate symbol p of arity n, the i-th *argument* of p is an expression of the form $p[i]$, for $1 \le i \le n$. If p is a base (resp. derived) predicate symbol, then $p[i]$ is said to be a *base* (resp. *derived*) argument. The set of all predicate symbols appearing in a Datalog^f program P is denoted by $pred(P)$. The set of all arguments of P is denoted by $arg(P)$, that is, $arg(P) = \{p[i] \mid p \text{ belongs to } pred(P), \text{ and has arity } n \text{ and } 1 \le i \le n\}$.

The following subsections present current termination criteria.

5.2.1 λ-RESTRICTED PROGRAMS

In this section, we present the class of λ-restricted programs [Gebser et al., 2007].

Given a Datalog^f program P, we use $V(r)$ to denote the set of variables appearing in a rule $r \in P$ and $B(X, r)$ to denote the set of predicate symbols of the atoms in the body of r which contain variable X. Moreover, recall that $def(p, P)$ denotes the definition of a predicate symbol p in P, that is, the set of rules of P having p in the head atom.

Definition 5.2 λ-restricted program.   A Datalog^f program P is λ-*restricted* if there exists a mapping $\lambda : pred(P) \to \mathbb{N}$ such that, for every predicate symbol $p \in pred(P)$, the following holds:

$$\max\{\max\{\min\{\lambda(p') \mid p' \in B(X, r)\} \mid X \in V(r)\} \mid r \in def(p, P)\} < \lambda(p).$$

Intuitively, the condition stated in the definition above means that, for each predicate symbol p, all the variables in rules defining p are "bounded" by predicate symbols p' in the body such that $\lambda(p') < \lambda(p)$. If this is the case, the feasible ground instances of rules in $def(p, P)$ are completely determined by predicate symbols from lower levels than the one of p.

Example 5.3   The following Datalog^f program is λ-restricted:

$$\begin{aligned} p(f(X)) &\leftarrow q(X). \\ q(X) &\leftarrow p(X), r(X). \end{aligned}$$

In fact, it can be easily verified that the mapping λ defined as $\lambda(r) = 1$, $\lambda(q) = 2$, $\lambda(p) = 3$ satisfies the condition of Definition 5.2.

One limitation of λ-restriction is that some Datalog programs (thus, without function symbols) are not recognized as λ-restricted—however, the least model of a Datalog program is always finite and the bottom-up evaluation always terminates. An example is the following Datalog program:

$$p(X) \leftarrow q(X).$$
$$q(X) \leftarrow p(X).$$

To satisfy the condition of Definition 5.2, any mapping λ from predicate symbols to natural numbers should be s.t. $\lambda(p) > \lambda(q)$ (because of the first rule) and $\lambda(q) > \lambda(p)$ (because of the second rule); since such a mapping does not exist, the program above is not λ-restricted. Thus, by relying on the λ-restriction criterion, no conclusion can be drawn on the termination of the program above.

5.2.2   FINITE DOMAIN PROGRAMS

Finite domain programs have been introduced by Calimeri et al. [2008]. The definition relies on the notion of *argument graph*, defined below, which represents the propagation of values among arguments of a Datalog^f program.

Definition 5.4   Argument graph.   The *argument graph* of a Datalog^f program P, denoted $G(P)$, is a directed graph whose set of nodes is $arg(P)$, and there is an edge $(q[j], p[i])$ iff there is a rule $r \in P$ such that

- an atom $p(t_1, \ldots, t_n)$ appears in $head(r)$,

- an atom $q(u_1, \ldots, u_m)$ appears in $body(r)$, and

- terms t_i and u_j have a common variable.

Example 5.5   Consider the following Datalog^f program, where *base* is a base predicate symbol.

$$q(X, Y) \quad \leftarrow \quad p(X), base(Y).$$
$$p(f(X, Y)) \quad \leftarrow \quad q(X, Y).$$

The argument graph is depicted in Figure 5.1.

Given a Datalog^f program P, an argument $p[i]$ is said to be *recursive* if it appears in a cycle of $G(P)$; two arguments $p[i]$ and $q[j]$ are *mutually recursive* if there exists a cycle in $G(P)$ involving both $p[i]$ and $q[j]$. For instance, considering the Datalog^f program of Example 5.5, arguments $base[1]$ and $q[2]$ are not recursive while $p[1]$ and $q[1]$ are recursive. Moreover, $p[1]$ and $q[1]$ are mutually recursive.

Definition 5.6   Finite domain program.   Given a Datalog^f program P, the set of *finite domain arguments* of P is the maximal set $FD(P)$ of arguments of P such that, for each argument $q[k] \in FD(P)$, every rule r whose predicate symbol in the head is q satisfies the following condition. Let t be the term corresponding to argument $q[k]$ in the head of r. Then, either

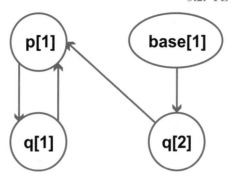

Figure 5.1: Argument graph.

1. t is variable-free,

2. t is a subterm of a term corresponding to a finite domain argument of a body predicate symbol, or

3. every variable appearing in t also appears in a term corresponding to a finite domain argument of a body predicate symbol which is not mutually recursive with $q[k]$.

If all arguments of P are finite domain (i.e., $FD(P) = arg(P)$), then P is a *finite domain* program.

Example 5.7 Consider the following simple Datalog^f program

$$q(X) \leftarrow q(f(X)).$$

Obviously, $q[1]$ is mutually recursive with itself. It can be easily verified that the program above is finite domain (by applying the second condition of Definition 5.6).

Checking whether a Datalog^f program P is finite domain or not can be done by first assuming that all arguments are in $FD(P)$ and then iteratively eliminating arguments appearing in the head of a rule such that none of the three conditions of Definition 5.6 holds. Thus, checking whether a Datalog^f program is finite domain is decidable.

Notice that all Datalog programs (i.e., no function symbols are allowed) are finite domain: by assuming that all arguments of a Datalog program are finite domain, it is easy to see that, for all of them, the first or second condition of Definition 5.6 is always satisfied.

Moreover, the class of finite domain programs is not comparable with the class of λ-restricted programs.

Example 5.8 Consider the two Datalog^f programs of Example 5.3. As discussed before, the first one is λ-restricted while the second one is not. On the other hand, the second program is finite domain (in fact, it is a Datalog program) while the first one is not. To see why the first program is not finite domain, it suffices to notice that if we assume that all arguments are finite domain, then $p[1]$ and the first rule do not satisfy any of the conditions of Definition 5.6.

5.2.3   ARGUMENT-RESTRICTED PROGRAMS

The class of argument-restricted programs has been introduced by Lierler and Lifschitz [2009]. Before presenting its definition, some additional notation is introduced. For any atom A of the form $p(t_1, \ldots, t_n)$, we use A^0 to denote predicate symbol p and A^i to denote term t_i, for $1 \leq i \leq n$. The *depth* $d(X, t)$ of a variable X in a term t that contains X is recursively defined as follows:

$$d(X, X) = 0,$$
$$d(X, f(t_1, \ldots, t_m)) = 1 + \max_{i \; : \; t_i \text{ contains } X} d(X, t_i).$$

Definition 5.9   Argument-restricted program.   An *argument ranking* for a Datalog^f program P is a function ϕ from $arg(P)$ to integers such that the following condition is satisfied for every rule r of P. Let A be the atom in the head of r. For every variable X occurring in a term A^i, $body(r)$ contains an atom B such that X occurs in a term B^j satisfying the condition

$$\phi(A^0[i]) - \phi(B^0[j]) \geq d(X, A^i) - d(X, B^j).$$

A Datalog^f program is *argument-restricted* if it has an argument ranking.

Example 5.10   The two programs of Example 5.3 are both argument-restricted. For the first one, an argument ranking is $\phi(p[1]) = 1$, $\phi(q[1]) = \phi(r[1]) = 0$. For the second program, an argument ranking is $\phi(p[1]) = \phi(q[1]) = 0$.

Argument-restricted programs strictly include λ-restricted and finite domain programs [Lierler and Lifschitz, 2009]. An algorithm for checking whether a Datalog^f program is argument-restricted can be found in Lierler and Lifschitz [2009].

5.2.4   SAFE PROGRAMS

The class of *safe programs* [Greco et al., 2012b] is an extension of the class of finite domain programs. Its definition is based on the notions of *activation graph* and *safe argument*.

Let P be a Datalog^f program and r_1, r_2 be (not necessarily distinct) rules of P. We say that r_1 *activates* r_2 iff there exist two ground rules $r_1' \in ground(r_1)$, $r_2' \in ground(r_2)$ and an interpretation I such that *(i)* $I \not\models r_1'$, *(ii)* $I \models r_2'$, and *(iii)* $I \cup head(r_1') \not\models r_2'$. This intuitively means that if I does not satisfy r'_1, I satisfies r'_2, and $head(r'_1)$ is added to I to satisfy r'_1, this causes r'_2 not to be satisfied anymore (and then to be "activated").

Definition 5.11 Activation graph.   The *activation graph* of a Datalog^f program P, denoted $\Omega(P)$, is a directed graph whose nodes are the rules of P, and there is an edge (r_i, r_j) in the graph iff r_i activates r_j.

Example 5.12   Consider the following Datalog^f program:

$$
\begin{aligned}
r_0 : & \quad p(X) & \leftarrow & \quad base(X). \\
r_1 : & \quad q(f(X)) & \leftarrow & \quad p(X). \\
r_2 : & \quad p(g(X)) & \leftarrow & \quad q(X),
\end{aligned}
$$

where *base* is a base predicate symbol. It is easy to see that r_0 activates r_1, but not vice versa; r_1 activates r_2 and vice versa. The activation graph is shown in Figure 5.2.

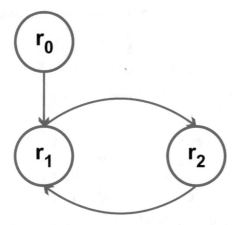

Figure 5.2: Activation graph.

Definition 5.13 Safe program.   Given a Datalog^f program P, the set of *safe arguments safe(P)* is computed by first setting $safe(P) = FD(P)$ (cf. Definition 5.6) and next iteratively adding each argument $q[k]$ of P such that for every rule $r \in P$ where q appears in the head,

• r does not appear in a cycle of $\Omega(P)$, or

• if $q(t_1, \ldots, t_n)$ is the head atom, then for every variable X appearing in t_k, there is an atom $p(u_1, \ldots, u_m)$ in $body(r)$ and a term u_i $(1 \leq i \leq m)$ s.t. X appears in u_i and $p[i]$ is safe.

A Datalog^f program P is said to be *safe* if all its arguments are safe.

Example 5.14   The following Datalog^f program, where *base* is a base predicate symbol, is safe as its activation graph does not have cycles (notice that rule r_2 does not activate itself):

$$
\begin{array}{rrcl}
r_1: & p(X, X) & \leftarrow & base(X). \\
r_2: & p(f(X), g(X)) & \leftarrow & p(X, X).
\end{array}
$$

Although the class of safe programs strictly includes λ-restricted programs, the classes of safe and argument-restricted programs are not comparable, as shown in the following example.

Example 5.15   The Datalog^f program of Example 5.14 is safe, but not argument-restricted. On the other hand, the following Datalog^f program, where *base* is a base predicate symbol, is argument-restricted, but not safe:

$$
\begin{array}{rrcl}
r_1: & q(X, f(X)) & \leftarrow & p(X). \\
r_2: & r(X, Y) & \leftarrow & q(X, Y). \\
r_3: & p(X) & \leftarrow & r(Y, X), base(X). \\
r_4: & t(X, X) & \leftarrow & q(Y, X). \\
r_5: & q(X, X) & \leftarrow & t(X, Y). \\
r_6: & t(X, g(X, Y_1, Y_2)) & \leftarrow & t(Y_1, X), q(Y_2, X).
\end{array}
$$

It can be readily verified that the function ϕ defined as follows is an argument ranking, and thus, the program above is argument-restricted:

$$
\begin{array}{ll}
\phi(p[1]) = 0, & \phi(base[1]) = 0, \\
\phi(q[1]) = 1, & \phi(q[2]) = 1, \\
\phi(r[1]) = 1, & \phi(r[2]) = 1, \\
\phi(t[1]) = 1, & \phi(t[2]) = 2.
\end{array}
$$

The set of finite domain arguments is $\{base[1], p[1]\}$, which is also the set of safe arguments. Thus, the program above is not safe.

5.2.5 Γ-ACYCLIC PROGRAMS

Γ-acyclic programs have been introduced by Greco et al. [2012b]. The definition of Γ-acyclic programs relies on the notion of propagation graph defined below.

Definition 5.16   Propagation graph.   The *(labeled) propagation graph* $\Delta(P)$ of a Datalog^f program P is a labeled directed graph defined as follows. The set of nodes is the set of non-safe arguments (see Definition 5.13) of P, also-called *affected arguments* and denoted as *aff*(P). The set of (labeled) edges is defined in the following way: for each pair of nodes $p[i], q[j] \in$ *aff*(P) and for every rule $r \in P$ such that

- there is an atom $p(t_1, \ldots, t_n)$ in the head of r,

- there is an atom $q(u_1, \ldots, u_m)$ in the body of r, and

- the same variable X occurs in both t_i and u_j,

there is a labeled edge $(q[j], p[i], \alpha) \in E$, where α is defined as follows:

- $\alpha = \epsilon$ if $t_i = u_j$,

- $\alpha = f$ if $u_j = X$ and $t_i = f(\ldots, X, \ldots)$, and

- $\alpha = \overline{f}$ if $u_j = f(\ldots, X, \ldots)$ and $t_i = X$.

In the previous definition, ϵ is used to denote the empty string. Furthermore, without loss of generality, we assumed that if the same variable occurs in two terms appearing in the head and in the body of a rule, then one term is a subterm of the other and the nesting level of the complex terms is at most one.

The definition of Γ-acyclic programs relies also on the grammar introduced in the following definition.

Definition 5.17 Grammar Γ_P. Let P be a Datalog^f program and F_P the set of function symbols occurring in P. The *grammar* Γ_P is a 4-tuple (N, T, R, S), where $N = \{S, S_1, S_2\}$ is the set of nonterminal symbols, S is the start symbol, $T = \{f \mid f \in F_P\} \cup \{\overline{f} \mid f \in F_P\}$ is the set of terminal symbols, and R is the set consisting of the following production rules:

- $S \rightarrow S_1 f S_2$, $\forall f \in F_P$;

- $S_1 \rightarrow f S_1 \overline{f} S_1 \mid \epsilon$, $\forall f \in F_P$;

- $S_2 \rightarrow (S_1 \mid f) S_2 \mid \epsilon$, $\forall f \in F_P$.

The language $\mathcal{L}(\Gamma_P)$ is the set of strings generated by Γ_P.

A path π in a propagation graph $\Delta(P)$ is a sequence $(a_1, b_1, \alpha_1), \ldots, (a_k, b_k, \alpha_k)$ of labeled edges of $\Delta(P)$, where $k \geq 1$ and $b_i = a_{i+1}$ for all $1 \leq i < k$. If $a_1 = b_k$, then π is also called a cycle. For any path π as above, we denote with $\lambda(\pi)$ the string $\alpha_1 \ldots \alpha_k$. Given a grammar $\Gamma_P = (N, T, R, S)$ and a propagation graph $\Delta(P)$, we say that path π in $\Delta(P)$ spells a string $w \in \mathcal{L}(\Gamma_P)$ if $\lambda(\pi) = w$. We are now ready to define Γ-acyclic programs.

Definition 5.18 Γ-acyclic program. A Datalog^f program P is Γ-*acyclic* if there is no cycle in $\Delta(P)$ spelling a string of $\mathcal{L}(\Gamma_P)$.

It straightforwardly follows from the definition above that the class of safe programs is a subset of the class of Γ-acyclic programs. In fact, for every safe program, the propagation graph is empty (because the set of affected arguments is empty, cf. Definition 5.16), and thus, the condition of Γ-acyclicity of Definition 5.18 is trivially satisfied. The class of Γ-acyclic programs strictly contains that of safe programs, while it is not comparable with that of argument-restricted programs, as shown in the following example.

Example 5.19   As already discussed, the Datalog^f program of Example 5.14 is safe, but not argument-restricted. Since the program is safe, then it is also Γ-acyclic.

The following Datalog^f program is Γ-acyclic but not safe (it is not argument-restricted either):

$$
\begin{array}{rrcl}
r_1: & r(f(X)) & \leftarrow & s(X). \\
r_2: & q(f(X)) & \leftarrow & r(X). \\
r_3: & p(X) & \leftarrow & q(X). \\
r_4: & n(X) & \leftarrow & p(g(X)). \\
r_5: & s(X) & \leftarrow & n(X).
\end{array}
$$

Notice that all arguments are affected. The propagation graph has a single cycle going through all arguments of the program, and the corresponding string is $ff\overline{g}$. Since the string does not belong to the language $\mathcal{L}(\Gamma_P)$, the program is Γ-acyclic.

As already shown, the Datalog^f program of Example 5.15 is argument-restricted. It can be easily verified that the corresponding propagation graph has a cycle spelling a string of $\mathcal{L}(\Gamma_P)$ (e.g., there is a cycle going through $t[1]$ and $t[2]$ whose associated string is g). Thus, the program is not Γ-acyclic.

5.2.6   BOUNDED PROGRAMS

A termination criterion more general than the ones presented thus far has been proposed by Greco et al. [2013a], who introduced the class of *bounded programs*, which strictly includes the classes of programs presented in the previous sections.

The criterion relies on two powerful tools: *(i)* the *labeled argument graph*, a directed graph whose edges are labeled with useful information on how terms are propagated from the body to the head of rules, and *(ii)* the activation graph presented before (Definition 5.11). The labeled argument graph is used in synergy with the activation graph for a better understanding of how terms are propagated.

Another relevant aspect that distinguishes the criterion presented in this section from the the termination criteria previously discussed is that the latter analyze one group of arguments (depending on each other) at a time, without looking at how groups of arguments are related. On the contrary, the criterion of bounded programs can be used to perform an analysis of how groups of arguments affect each other.

For instance, none of the termination criteria discussed in the previous sections is able to realize that the bottom-up evaluation of the program of Example 5.1 terminates. Intuitively, this is because they analyze how the first argument of *count* affects itself and how the second argument of *count* affects itself, but miss noticing that the growth of the latter is bounded by the reduction of the former. One of the novelties of the criterion presented in this section is the capability of doing this kind of reasoning—indeed, it is able to realize that the bottom-up evaluation of the program above terminates.

We start by introducing some notation and terminology used in the following. We define a *partial argument ranking* for a Datalog^f program P as a partial function ϕ from $arg(P)$ to non-negative integers, such that the following condition is satisfied for every rule r of P. Let A be the atom occurring in the head of r. For every variable X occurring in a term A^i, if $\phi(A^0[i])$ is defined, then $body(r)$ contains an atom B such that X occurs in a term B^j, $\phi(B^0[j])$ is defined, and the following condition is satisfied:

$$\phi(A^0[i]) - \phi(B^0[j]) \geq d(X, A^i) - d(X, B^j).$$

The set of *restricted arguments* of P is $AR(P) = \{p[i] \mid p[i] \in arg(P) \wedge$ there exists a partial argument ranking ϕ s.t. $\phi(p[i])$ is defined$\}$.

An argument $p[i]$ in $arg(P)$ is said to be *limited* iff for any finite database D, the set $\{t_i \mid p(t_1, \ldots, t_i, \ldots, t_n) \in M\}$ is finite, where M is the least model of P_D.

For ease of presentation, we assume that if the same variable occurs in two terms appearing in the head and in the body of a rule, then one term is a subterm of the other, and complex terms are of the form $f(t_1, \ldots, t_m)$ with the t_i's being simple terms. There is no loss of generality in such assumptions as every Datalog^f program can be rewritten into an equivalent one satisfying such conditions (e.g., a rule of the form $p(f(h(X))) \leftarrow q(g(X))$ can be rewritten into the three rules $p(f(X)) \leftarrow p'(X)$, $p'(h(X)) \leftarrow p''(X)$, and $p''(X) \leftarrow q(g(X))$).

Below we introduce the first tool used to define bounded programs. It is a new graph derived from the argument graph by labeling edges with additional information.

Definition 5.20 Labeled argument graph.   The *labeled argument graph* of a Datalog^f program P, denoted $G_L(P)$, is a directed graph whose set of nodes is $arg(P)$, and the set of labeled edges is defined as follows. For each pair of nodes $p[i], q[j] \in arg(P)$, and for every rule $r \in P$ such that

1. there is an atom $p(t_1, \ldots, t_n)$ in $head(r)$,

2. there is an atom $q(u_1, \ldots, u_m)$ in $body(r)$, and

3. terms t_i and u_j have a common variable X;

there exists an edge $(q[j], p[i], \langle \alpha, r, k \rangle)$, where k is a natural number denoting the position of $q(u_1, \ldots, u_m)$ in $body(r)$,[2] and

- $\alpha = \epsilon$ if $u_j = t_i$;

---

[2]We assume that atoms in the body are ordered with the first one being associated with 1, the second one with 2, etc. The order is used only for the purpose of identifying body atoms.

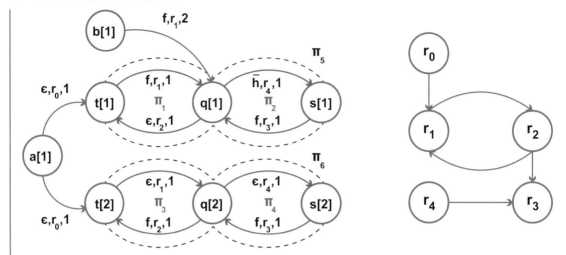

Figure 5.3: Labeled argument and activation graphs.

- $\alpha = f$ if $u_j = X$ and $t_i = f(\ldots, X, \ldots)$; and

- $\alpha = \overline{f}$ if $u_j = f(\ldots, X, \ldots)$ and $t_i = X$.

Example 5.21   Consider the following Datalog^f program

$$
\begin{array}{rrcl}
r_0: & t(X, X) & \leftarrow & a(X). \\
r_1: & q(f(X), Y) & \leftarrow & t(X, Y), b(X). \\
r_2: & t(X, f(Y)) & \leftarrow & q(X, Y). \\
r_3: & q(f(X), f(Y)) & \leftarrow & s(X, Y). \\
r_4: & s(X, Y) & \leftarrow & q(h(X), Y),
\end{array}
$$

where a and b are base predicate symbols. The labeled argument and activation graphs of the program above are depicted in Figure 5.3. For instance, the edge $(t[1], q[1], \langle f, r_1, 1 \rangle)$ says that the first atom in the body of r_1 is an atom whose predicate symbol is t, its first term is a variable, say X, and the atom in the head of r_1 is an atom whose predicate symbol is q and whose first term is of the form $f(\ldots, X, \ldots)$. We will show how this kind of information can be profitably used to analyze Datalog^f programs (e.g., to keep track of how complex terms are generated from argument to argument).

A *path* ρ from a_1 to b_m in a labeled argument graph $G_L(P)$ is a non-empty sequence $(a_1, b_1, \langle \alpha_1, r_1, k_1 \rangle), \ldots, (a_m, b_m, \langle \alpha_m, r_m, k_m \rangle)$ of labeled edges of $G_L(P)$ s.t. $b_i = a_{i+1}$ for all $1 \leq i < m$. If the first and last nodes coincide (i.e., $a_1 = b_m$), then ρ is called a *cyclic path*. We define $\lambda_1(\rho) = \alpha_1 \ldots \alpha_m$ as the sequence of ϵ and function symbols labeling the edges of ρ, $\lambda_2(\rho) = $

$r_1, \ldots, r_m$ as the sequence of rules labeling the edges of ρ, and $\lambda_3(\rho) = \langle r_1, k_1 \rangle \ldots \langle r_m, k_m \rangle$ as the sequence of pairs $\langle$rule, body atom identifier$\rangle$ labeling the edges of ρ. In the case where the indication of the start edge is not relevant, we will call a cyclic path a *cycle*. Given a cycle π consisting of n labeled edges $e_1, \ldots, e_n$, we can derive n different cyclic paths starting from each of the e_i's—we use $\tau(\pi)$ to denote the set of such cyclic paths. As an example, if π is a cycle consisting of labeled edges e_1, e_2, e_3, then $\tau(\pi) = \{(e_1, e_2, e_3), (e_2, e_3, e_1), (e_3, e_2, e_1)\}$. Given two cycles π_1 and π_2, we write $\pi_1 \approx \pi_2$ iff there exist $\rho_1 \in \tau(\pi_1)$ and $\rho_2 \in \tau(\pi_2)$ such that $\lambda_3(\rho_1) = \lambda_3(\rho_2)$. A cycle is *basic* if it does not contain two occurrences of the same edge.

We say that a node $p[i]$ of $G_L(P)$ *depends on* a node $q[j]$ of $G_L(P)$ iff there is a path from $q[j]$ to $p[i]$ in $G_L(P)$. Moreover, we say that $p[i]$ *depends on* a cycle π iff it depends on a node $q[j]$ appearing in π. Clearly, nodes belonging to a cycle π depend on π. We say that $\lambda_2(\rho) = r_1, \ldots, r_m$ denotes a cyclic path in the activation graph $\Omega(P)$ iff $(r_1, r_2), \ldots, (r_{m-1}, r_m), (r_m, r_1)$ are edges of the activation graph $\Omega(P)$.

Definition 5.22   Active cycle.   Given a Datalog^f program P, we say that a cycle π in $G_L(P)$ is *active* iff $\exists \rho \in \tau(\pi)$ such that $\lambda_2(\rho)$ denotes a cyclic path in the activation graph $\Omega(P)$.

Thus, checking if a cycle in the labeled argument graph is active requires looking at the activation graph. Here the basic idea is to check, based on the information reported in the activation graph, if the propagation of terms along a cycle of the labeled argument graph can really take place. We illustrate this with the following example.

Example 5.23   Consider the labeled argument graph and the activation graph of Example 5.21 (cf. Figure 5.3). Cycles π_1 and π_3 in Figure 5.3 are active as $(r_1, r_2), (r_2, r_1)$ is a cyclic path in the activation graph. On the contrary, it is easy to check that cycles π_2 and π_4 in Figure 5.3 are not active.

In the previous example, the labeled edges of the non-active cycle π_4 say that a complex term with function symbol f might be generated from $s[2]$ to $q[2]$ (using rule r_3), be propagated from $q[2]$ to $s[2]$ (using rule r_4), and so on and so forth, possibly causing the generation of complex terms of unbounded size. However, in order for this to happen, rules r_3 and r_4 should activate each other, which is not the case from an analysis of the activation graph. Thus, we can conclude that the generation of unbounded terms cannot really happen.

On the other hand, active cycles might lead to the generation of terms of unbounded size. To establish whether this can really be the case, a deeper analysis of the cycles in the labeled argument graph is performed. Specifically, grammars are used to analyze edge labels to get a better understanding of what terms can be propagated among arguments. We use two distinct languages which allows us to distinguish between "growing" paths, which could give rise to terms of infinite size, and "balanced" paths, where propagated terms do not grow (see Definition 5.25).

In addition to the grammar Γ_P of Definition 5.17, we define the grammar Γ_P' below.

Definition 5.24   Grammar Γ_P'.   Let P be a Datalog^f program and F_P the set of function symbols occurring in P. The *grammar* Γ_P' is a 4-tuple (N, T, R, S) where $N = \{S\}$ is the set of nonterminal symbols, S is the start symbol, $T = \{f \mid f \in F_P\} \cup \{\overline{f} \mid f \in F_P\}$ is the set of terminal symbols, R contains the production rule:

- $S \rightarrow f\, S\, \overline{f}\, S \mid \epsilon, \qquad \forall f \in F_P.$

The language $\mathcal{L}(\Gamma_P')$ is the set of strings generated by Γ_P'.

Notice that $\mathcal{L}(\Gamma_P) \cap \mathcal{L}(\Gamma_P') = \emptyset$. Recall that grammar Γ_P has been introduced in Greco et al. [2012b] to analyze cycles of the propagation graph. Here we consider a more detailed analysis of the relationships among arguments by considering also Γ_P'. Intuitively, strings in $\mathcal{L}(\Gamma_P)$ describe growing sequences of functions symbols used to compose and decompose complex terms, so that, starting from a given term we obtain a larger term. On the other hand, strings in $\mathcal{L}(\Gamma_P')$ describe "balanced" sequences of functions symbols used to compose and decompose complex terms, so that starting from a given term we obtain the same term.

Definition 5.25   Classification of cycles.   *Given a Datalog^f program P and a cycle π in $G_L(P)$, we say that π is*

- growing *if there is $\rho \in \tau(\pi)$ s.t. $\lambda_1(\rho) \in \mathcal{L}(\Gamma_P)$,*

- balanced *if there is $\rho \in \tau(\pi)$ s.t. $\lambda_1(\rho) \in \mathcal{L}(\Gamma_P')$, and*

- failing *otherwise.*

Consider the labeled argument graph in Figure 5.3. Cycles π_1, π_3, and π_4 are growing, whereas cycle π_2 is failing. Observe that, in general, a failing cycle is not active, but the inverse is not true. In fact, cycle π_4 from Figure 5.3 is not active even if it is not failing.

The tools introduced so far are used to define the *binding* operator Ψ_P (Definition 5.26 below). The idea is to compute the fixpoint of Ψ_P starting from a set of limited arguments, so as to get a set of limited arguments, which can be used as an underestimation of the limited arguments of the program. If the fixpoint computation gives us all arguments of P, then P is *bounded*.

Definition 5.26 Ψ_P operator.   Let P be a Datalog^f program and $A \subseteq arg(P)$. We define $\Psi_P(A)$ as the set of arguments $q[k]$ of P such that, for each cycle π in $G_L(P)$ on which $q[k]$ depends, at least one of the following conditions holds:

1. π is not active or is not growing;

2. π contains an edge $(s[j], p[i], \langle f, r, l \rangle)$ and, letting $p(t_1, \ldots, t_n)$ be the atom in the head of r, for every variable X in t_i, there is an atom $b(u_1, \ldots, u_m)$ in $body(r)$ s.t. X appears in a term u_h and $b[h] \in A$; and

3. there is a cycle π' in $G_L(P)$ s.t. $\pi' \approx \pi$, π' is not balanced, and π' passes only through arguments in A.

The following example illustrates the Ψ_P operator.

Example 5.27   Consider the Datalog^f program of Example 5.21, whose labeled argument and activation graphs are reported in Figure 5.3. Notice that cycles π_1 and π_3 are growing and active, π_2 is failing and non-active, π_4 is growing and non-active. The cycle π_5 composed by π_1 and π_2 (denoted by a dashed line) is failing and non-active, and the cycle π_6 composed by π_3 and π_4 (denoted by a dashed line) is growing and non-active. Furthermore, base arguments $a[1]$ and $b[1]$ do not depend on any cycle; $t[1], q[1], s[1]$ depend on π_1, π_2, and π_5; $t[2], q[2], s[2]$ depend on π_3, π_4, and π_6. By iteratively applying operator Ψ_P starting from $\emptyset$ we have:

- $A_1 = \Psi_P(\emptyset) = \{a[1], b[1]\}$;

- $A_2 = \Psi_P(A_1) = A_1 \cup \{t[1], q[1], s[1]\}$ as Condition 2 of Definition 5.26 applies to π_1, and Condition 1 applies to π_2 and π_5; and

- $A_3 = \Psi_P(A_2) = A_2 \cup \{t[2], q[2], s[2]\}$ as Condition 1 applies to π_4 and π_6, and Condition 3 applies to π_3 (in fact, $\pi_1 \approx \pi_3$, π_1 is not balanced and goes only through nodes in A_3).

Therefore, we derive that all arguments are limited.

We are now ready to define the class of *bounded programs*. Given a Datalog^f program P, we start with the set of restricted arguments $AR(P)$, which gives a good and efficiently computable approximation of the set of limited arguments; then, we iteratively apply operator Ψ_P trying to infer more limited arguments. If, eventually, all arguments in $arg(P)$ are determined as limited, then P is bounded.

More formally, given a Datalog^f program P, the i-th iteration of Ψ_P ($i \geq 1$) w.r.t. a set $A \subseteq arg(P)$ is defined as follows: $\Psi_P^1(A) = \Psi_P(A)$ and $\Psi_P^i(A) = \Psi_P(\Psi_P^{i-1}(A))$ for $i > 1$. It can be easily verified that Ψ_P always has a fixpoint, denoted by $\Psi_P^\infty(A)$.

Definition 5.28   Bounded programs.   The set of *bounded* arguments of a Datalog^f program P is $\Psi_P^\infty(AR(P))$. We say that P is *bounded* iff all its arguments are bounded.

Bounded programs strictly include argument-restricted and Γ-acyclic programs [Greco et al., 2013a].

5.3   PROGRAM ADORNMENT

The termination criteria discussed in the previous section are not able to identify as terminating even simple Datalog^f programs whose bottom-up evaluation always terminates. For instance, consider the following example.

Example 5.29   Consider the following Datalog^f program

$$
\begin{aligned}
p(X, X) &\leftarrow base(X).\\
q(X, Y) &\leftarrow p(X, Y).\\
p(f(X), g(X)) &\leftarrow q(X, X),
\end{aligned}
$$

where *base* is a base predicate symbol. The bottom-up evaluation of the program terminates whatever set of facts for *base* is added to it. Nevertheless, none of the termination criteria introduced so far is able to realize that the bottom-up evaluation terminates.

In this section, we present an orthogonal technique that, used in conjunction with current termination criteria, allows us to detect more Datalog^f programs whose evaluation terminates. The technique has been introduced in Greco et al. [2013b]. It takes a Datalog^f program P and transforms it into an "adorned" Datalog^f program P^μ with the aim of applying termination criteria to P^μ rather than P. The transformation is sound in that if P^μ satisfies a certain termination criterion, then the bottom-up evaluation of P terminates.

Applying termination criteria to adorned programs rather than the original ones makes termination criteria (strictly) more effective, that is, (strictly) more programs whose evaluation terminates are recognized. Roughly speaking, each adorned rule is obtained from a rule in the original program by adding adornments, which keep track of the structure of the terms that can be propagated during the bottom-up evaluation. Here the basic idea is to generate only rules that have a chance to trigger, and disregard those rules that have no chance to trigger (because what can actually be derived during the program evaluation does not comply with the structure of the body). As adorning predicate symbols possibly breaks "cyclic" dependencies among arguments and/or rules, this often allows us to recognize more Datalog^f programs as terminating than if termination criteria are applied to the original Datalog^f programs. An example is provided below.

Example 5.30   Consider again the Datalog^f program of Example 5.29. The technique presented in this section transforms it into the following adorned Datalog^f program:

$$
\begin{aligned}
p^{\epsilon\epsilon}(X, X) &\leftarrow base^{\epsilon}(X).\\
q^{\epsilon\epsilon}(X, Y) &\leftarrow p^{\epsilon\epsilon}(X, Y).\\
p^{f_1 g_1}(f(X), g(X)) &\leftarrow q^{\epsilon\epsilon}(X, X).\\
q^{f_1 g_1}(X, Y) &\leftarrow p^{f_1 g_1}(X, Y).
\end{aligned}
$$

The adorned program above is "equivalent" to the original one of Example 5.29 in that the least model of the original program can be obtained from the least model of the transformed program by dropping adornments.

As opposed to the original program, the transformed program above is not recursive, and thus, it is easily recognized as terminating by all current termination criteria. This allows us to say that the bottom-up evaluation of the original program is terminating because of the aforementioned equivalence.

For the sake of simplicity and without loss of generality, we assume that databases do not contain complex terms (hence, we can assume that base atoms in rule bodies do not contain complex terms). For instance, the set of facts $\{base(a), base(f(b))\}$ can be replaced with the set of facts $\{base(a), base(b)\}$ and the rules $\{base_d(a) \leftarrow base(a), base_d(f(b)) \leftarrow base(b)\}$, where $base_d$ is a derived predicate symbol. Additionally, atoms appearing in rule bodies and having $base$ as predicate symbol are replaced with the same atoms where $base_d$ replaces $base$. Since databases are not relevant for the proposed technique, they are not shown in examples. In fact, as discussed in the following, the technique allows us to conclude that the evaluation of a Datalog^f program terminates for any database that is added to the program.

We start by introducing notation and terminology used hereafter. We will use the notation $p(\bar{t})$ to refer to an atom $p(t_1, \ldots, t_n)$ (here $\bar{t}$ is understood to be a sequence of n terms). Given a Datalog^f program P, we define the *adornment alphabet* $\Lambda = \{\epsilon\} \cup \{f_i \mid f$ is a function symbol in P and $i \in \mathbb{N}\}$; elements of Λ are called *adornment symbols*. An *adornment* α for a predicate symbol p of arity n is a string of length n over the alphabet Λ; the expression p^α is an *adorned predicate symbol*, and $p^\alpha(t_1, \ldots, t_n)$ is an *adorned atom*, where the t_i's are terms. An *adorned conjunction* is a conjunction of adorned atoms. An *adorned rule* is a rule containing only adorned atoms. Given an adornment symbol f_i in $\Lambda - \{\epsilon\}$, an *adornment definition* for f_i is an expression of the form $f_i = f(\alpha_1, \ldots, \alpha_m)$, where m is the arity of function symbol f and the α_i's are adornment symbols. As an example, if the transformation technique derives an adorned predicate symbol $p^{f_1 g_1}$ with adornment definitions $f_1 = f(\epsilon)$ and $g_1 = g(f_1)$, this means that the bottom-up evaluation of the considered Datalog^f program might yield atoms of the form $p(f(c_1), g(f(c_2)))$ with c_1 and c_2 being constants.[3] Intuitively, adornment definitions are used to keep track of what kind of complex terms can be propagated.

Roughly speaking, the transformation technique works as follows. It maintains a set of adorned predicate symbols, a set of adornment definitions, and a set of adorned rules. Whenever we find a rule whose body can be adorned in a "coherent" way (we will make clear what this means in Definition 5.33), we derive an adorned predicate symbol from the rule head (using the body adornments), and generate an adorned rule. In this step, new adornment definitions might

---

[3]Here predicate symbol p is assumed of arity 2, and function symbols f and g are assumed of arity 1.

be generated as well. New adorned predicate symbols are used to generate further adorned rules. Below is an example that illustrates the basic idea.

Example 5.31   Consider the following Datalog^f program, where *base* is a base predicate symbol:

$$
\begin{aligned}
r_0: & \quad p(X, f(X)) && \leftarrow && base(X). \\
r_1: & \quad p(X, f(X)) && \leftarrow && p(Y, X), base(Y). \\
r_2: & \quad\quad p(X, Y) && \leftarrow && p(f(X), f(Y)).
\end{aligned}
$$

First, base predicate symbols are adorned with strings of ϵ's; thus, we get the adorned predicate symbol $base^\epsilon$. This is used to adorn the body of r_0 so as to get

$$
\rho_0: \quad p^{\epsilon f_1}(X, f(X)) \leftarrow base^\epsilon(X)
$$

from which we derive the new adorned predicate symbol $p^{\epsilon f_1}$, and the adornment definition $f_1 = f(\epsilon)$. Next, $p^{\epsilon f_1}$ and $base^\epsilon$ are used to adorn the body of r_1 so as to get

$$
\rho_1: \quad p^{f_1 f_2}(X, f(X)) \leftarrow p^{\epsilon f_1}(Y, X), base^\epsilon(Y)
$$

from which we derive the new adorned predicate symbol $p^{f_1 f_2}$, and the adornment definition $f_2 = f(f_1)$. Intuitively, the body of ρ_1 is coherently adorned because Y is always associated with the same adornment symbol ϵ. Using the new adorned predicate symbol $p^{f_1 f_2}$, we can adorn rule r_2 and get

$$
\rho_2: \quad p^{\epsilon f_1}(X, Y) \leftarrow p^{f_1 f_2}(f(X), f(Y)).
$$

At this point, we are not able to generate new adorned rules (using the adorned predicate symbols generated so far) with coherently adorned bodies and the transformation terminates. For instance, we may attempt to adorn the body of r_1 as $p^{f_1 f_2}(Y, X), base^\epsilon(Y)$, but this is not coherently adorned because the same variable Y is associated with both f_1 and ϵ. As a further example, we may attempt to adorn the body of r_2 as $p^{\epsilon f_1}(f(X), f(Y))$, but again this is not coherently adorned because $f(X)$ does not comply with the term structure described by ϵ, which indicates that the first term of the atom should be a simple term.

The order according to which rules are adorned is irrelevant.

In the previous example, to determine termination of the bottom-up evaluation of the original program, we can apply current termination criteria to the transformed program $P^\mu = \{\rho_0, \rho_1, \rho_2\}$ rather than the original one. In fact, the adornment technique ensures that if P^μ is recognized as terminating, so is the original program. Notice that both the original program and the transformed one are recursive, but while some termination criteria (e.g., the argument-restricted, Γ-acyclicity, and bounded criteria) detect P^μ as terminating, none of the current termination criteria is able to realize that the original program's evaluation terminates.

For instance, consider argument-restriction (cf. Section 5.2.3). The original program of Example 5.31 above is not argument-restricted, as there is no argument ranking for it. In fact, every argument ranking must satisfy $\phi(p[2]) - \phi(p[2]) \geq 1$ (because of rule r_1), but this condition is clearly unsatisfiable. On the other hand, the transformed program $P^\mu = \{\rho_0, \rho_1, \rho_2\}$ is argument-restricted, as an argument ranking for it can be found. For instance, the function ϕ defined as follows is an argument ranking: $\phi(base^\epsilon[1]) = 0$, $\phi(p^{\epsilon f_1}[1]) = 0$, $\phi(p^{\epsilon f_1}[2]) = 1$, $\phi(p^{f_1 f_2}[1]) = 1$, $\phi(p^{f_1 f_2}[2]) = 2$.

Furthermore, the transformation technique allows current termination criteria to detect strictly more programs as terminating under bottom-up evaluation. As an example, the original program in the example above is not argument-restricted, so we could not say anything about the termination of its bottom-up evaluation on the basis of such a criterion. However, P^μ is argument-restricted and this allows us to conclude that the bottom-up evaluation of the original program terminates *for any database* added to it.

In the following, we formally present the transformation technique. First, we define how to determine the adornment symbols associated with the variables in an adorned conjunction, and how to check if the conjunction is coherently adorned. Then, we define how to determine the adornment of a rule head when its body is coherently adorned. Finally, we present the complete technique.

Checking adornment coherency.   The aim of adornment coherency is to check if the adorned conjunction in the body of an adorned rule satisfies two conditions that are necessary for the rule to "trigger." First, for each adorned atom $p^{\alpha_1 \cdots \alpha_n}(t_1, \ldots, t_n)$ in the conjunction, we check if t_i complies with the term structure corresponding to α_i. As an example, in the adorned atom $p^{f_1}(g(X))$ with adornment definition $f_1 = f(\epsilon)$, $g(X)$ does not comply with the term structure $f(c)$ corresponding to f_1, where c is an arbitrary constant. Second, we determine the adornment symbol associated with each variable occurrence in the conjunction and check if, for every variable, all its occurrences are associated with adornment symbols describing compatible term structures. As an example, if $p^{f_1 g_1}(X, X)$ is an atom in the conjunction with adornment definitions $f_1 = f(\epsilon)$ and $g_1 = g(\epsilon)$, then two different term structures are associated with two occurrences of the same variable X and the conjunction is not coherently adorned.

Function *TermAdn* below determines the adornment symbols associated with the variables in a term t_i in an adorned atom $p^{\alpha_1 \cdots \alpha_n}(t_1, \ldots, t_n)$ on the basis of α_i and a set of adornment definitions S. Function *BodyAdn* simply collects the adornment symbols for all variables in an adorned conjunction (using *TermAdn*), and is used to check if the conjunction is coherently adorned.

Definition 5.32   Let $body^\sigma$ be an adorned conjunction and S a set of adornment definitions. We define

$$BodyAdn(body^\sigma, S) = \bigcup_{\substack{p^{\alpha_1 \cdots \alpha_n}(t_1, \ldots, t_n) \,\in\, body^\sigma \,\wedge \\ 1 \leq i \leq n}} TermAdn(t_i, \alpha_i, S);$$

where *TermAdn* is recursively defined as follows:

1. $TermAdn(t_i, \epsilon, S) = \emptyset$, if t_i is a constant;

2. $TermAdn(t_i, \alpha_i, S) = \{t_i / \alpha_i\}$, if t_i is a variable;

3. $TermAdn(f(u_1, \ldots, u_m), f_i, S) = \bigcup\limits_{j=1}^{m} TermAdn(u_j, \alpha_j, S)$, if $f_i = f(\alpha_1, \ldots, \alpha_m)$ is in S;

and

4. $TermAdn(t_i, \alpha_i, S) = \{fail\}$, otherwise.

Notice that there is a non-deterministic choice to be made in item 3 above, when there are multiple adornment definitions for the same f_i in S. Depending on the choice, $BodyAdn(body^\sigma, S)$ can return different sets; we define $SBodyAdn(body^\sigma, S)$ as the set of all possible outcomes. Notice that if $body^\sigma$ is the empty conjunction, then $SBodyAdn(body^\sigma, S)$ contains only the empty set.

Definition 5.33 Consider an adorned conjunction $body^\sigma$ and a set of adornment definitions S, and let $W \in SBodyAdn(body^\sigma, S)$. We say that $body^\sigma$ is *coherently adorned* w.r.t. W iff $fail \notin W$ and for every two distinct X/α and X/β in W it is the case that $\alpha = f_i$ and $\beta = f_j$, where f is a function symbol and $i, j \in \mathbb{N}$.

Notice that the empty conjunction is coherently adorned. Given a set $W \in SBodyAdn(body^\sigma, S)$, we define $\mathcal{S}(W)$ as the set of all subsets T of W containing exactly one expression of the form X/α for every variable X in $body^\sigma$. The following example illustrates the previous definitions.

Example 5.34 Consider the set of adornment definitions $S = \{f_2 = f(f_1), f_1 = f(\epsilon), g_1 = g(\epsilon)\}$. For the adorned conjunction $p^{f_2 g_1}(f(f(X)), g(X))$, we have that $BodyAdn(p^{f_2 g_1}(f(f(X)), g(X)), S)$ can return only the set W obtained as follows:

$$
\begin{aligned}
W &= TermAdn(f(f(X)), f_2, S) \cup TermAdn(g(X), g_1, S) \\
&= TermAdn(f(X), f_1, S) \cup TermAdn(X, \epsilon, S) \\
&= TermAdn(X, \epsilon, S) \cup \{X/\epsilon\} \\
&= \{X/\epsilon\} \cup \{X/\epsilon\} = \{X/\epsilon\},
\end{aligned}
$$

and $p^{f_2 g_1}(f(f(X)), g(X))$ is coherently adorned w.r.t. W.

Considering $q^{f_2}(f(g(X)))$, we have that $BodyAdn(q^{f_2}(f(g(X))), S)$ can return only $W = TermAdn(f(g(X)), f_2, S) = TermAdn(g(X), f_1, S) = \{fail\}$, and $q^{f_2}(f(g(X)))$ is not coherently adorned w.r.t. W.

Considering $p^{f_2 g_1}(f(X), g(X))$, we have that $BodyAdn(p^{f_2 g_1}(f(X), g(X)), S)$ can return only the set W obtained as follows:

$$
\begin{aligned}
W &= TermAdn(f(X), f_2, S) \cup TermAdn(g(X), g_1, S) \\
&= TermAdn(X, f_1, S) \cup TermAdn(X, \epsilon, S) \\
&= \{X/f_1\} \cup \{X/\epsilon\} = \{X/f_1, X/\epsilon\},
\end{aligned}
$$

and $p^{f_2 g_1}(f(X), g(X))$ is not coherently adorned w.r.t. W.

Head adornment.   When the conjunction in the body of a rule can be coherently adorned, adornments are propagated from the body to the head. The adornment of the head predicate symbol is determined on the basis of *(i)* the structure of the terms in the head, and *(ii)* the adornment symbols associated with the variables in the body. As an example, consider the rule $p(X, f(X, g(X))) \leftarrow b(X)$ and the adorned body conjunction $b^\epsilon(X)$. The adornment symbol associated with variable X is ϵ, which intuitively means that the bottom-up evaluation of the considered Datalog^f program might yield atoms of the form $b(c)$, with c being a constant. As a consequence, the rule above might yield atoms of the form $p(c, f(c, g(c)))$. To keep track of this, the head predicate symbol is adorned as $p^{\epsilon f_1}$, and the adornment definitions $f_1 = f(\epsilon, g_1)$ and $g_1 = g(\epsilon)$ are derived.

We start by introducing a special (asymmetric) "union operator," denoted by $\sqcup$, which takes as input a set of adornment definitions S and a set containing a single adornment definition $f_h = f(\alpha_1, \ldots, \alpha_m)$, and gives as output a set S' of adornment definitions with $S \subseteq S'$. Operator $\sqcup$ is defined as follows:

- $S \sqcup \{f_h = f(\alpha_1, \ldots, \alpha_m)\} = S$, if there exists $f_k = f(\alpha_1, \ldots, \alpha_m)$ in S; and

- $S \sqcup \{f_h = f(\alpha_1, \ldots, \alpha_m)\} = S \cup \{f_h = f(\alpha_1, \ldots, \alpha_m)\}$, if there is no $f_k = f(\alpha_1, \ldots, \alpha_m)$ in S.

We are now ready to define how rule heads are adorned.

Definition 5.35   Consider a Datalog^f rule $p(t_1, \ldots, t_n) \leftarrow body$, a set of adornment definitions S_0, and an adorned conjunction $body^\sigma$ obtained by adding adornments to all atoms in $body$. Let W be an element of $SBodyAdn(body^\sigma, S_0)$ s.t. $body^\sigma$ is coherently adorned w.r.t. W, and $T \in \mathcal{S}(W)$. The adornment of the head atom $p(t_1, \ldots, t_n)$ w.r.t. T and S_0 is

$$SetHeadAdn(p(t_1, \ldots, t_n), T, S_0) = \langle p^{\alpha_1 \cdots \alpha_n}(t_1, \ldots, t_n), S_n \rangle,$$

where

$$\langle \alpha_1, S_1 \rangle = Adn(t_1, T, S_0)$$
$$\langle \alpha_2, S_2 \rangle = Adn(t_2, T, S_1)$$
$$\vdots$$
$$\langle \alpha_n, S_n \rangle = Adn(t_n, T, S_{n-1})$$

and function *Adn* is defined as follows:

- $Adn(t, T, S) = \langle \epsilon, S \rangle$, if t is a constant;

- $Adn(t, T, S) = \langle \alpha_i, S \rangle$, if t is a variable X and X/α_i is in T;[4]

- $Adn(f(u_1, \ldots, u_m), T, S) = \langle f_j, S' \rangle$, where

---

[4]Notice that X always appears in $body^\sigma$ because of the safety condition (cf. Section 3.1).

- $\langle \beta_1, S_1 \rangle = Adn(u_1, T, S)$;
- $\langle \beta_2, S_2 \rangle = Adn(u_2, T, S_1)$;

$$\vdots$$

- $\langle \beta_m, S_m \rangle = Adn(u_m, T, S_{m-1})$;
- $S' = S_m \sqcup \{f_i = f(\beta_1, \ldots, \beta_m)\}$, with $i = \max\{k \mid f_k = f(\gamma_1, \ldots, \gamma_m) \in S_m\} + 1$;
- j is s.t. $f_j = f(\beta_1, \ldots, \beta_m)$ is in S'.

Example 5.36   Consider the Datalog^f rule

$$p(f(a, nil), f(X, f(Y, nil))) \leftarrow base(X, Y)$$

and the adorned body $base^{\epsilon\epsilon}(X, Y)$. Then, $SBodyAdn(base^{\epsilon\epsilon}(X, Y), \emptyset)$ has one element, $W = \{X/\epsilon, Y/\epsilon\}$, and $T = \{X/\epsilon, Y/\epsilon\}$ is the only element in $\mathcal{S}(W)$. Then,

$$SetHeadAdn(p(f(a, nil), f(X, f(Y, nil))), T, \emptyset)$$

gives $\langle p^{f_1 f_2}(f(a, nil), f(X, f(Y, nil))), S_2 \rangle$, where $S_2 = \{f_1 = f(\epsilon, \epsilon), f_2 = f(\epsilon, f_1)\}$. In fact, by Definition 5.35,

- $Adn(f(a, nil), T, \emptyset)$ gives $\langle f_1, S_1 \rangle$, where $S_1 = \{f_1 = f(\epsilon, \epsilon)\}$, since

  - $Adn(a, T, \emptyset)$ gives $\langle \epsilon, \emptyset \rangle$, and
  - $Adn(nil, T, \emptyset)$ gives $\langle \epsilon, \emptyset \rangle$.

- Then, $Adn(f(X, f(Y, nil)), T, S_1)$ gives $\langle f_2, S_2 \rangle$ as

  - $Adn(X, T, S_1)$ gives $\langle \epsilon, S_1 \rangle$, and
  - $Adn(f(Y, nil), T, S_1)$ gives $\langle f_1, S_1 \rangle$ as
    * $Adn(Y, T, S_1)$ gives $\langle \epsilon, S_1 \rangle$, and
    * $Adn(nil, T, S_1)$ gives $\langle \epsilon, S_1 \rangle$.

Transformation function.   Before presenting the complete transformation technique, we introduce some further notations and terminology. An *adornment substitution* θ is a set of pairs the form f_i/f_j (i.e., the same function symbol is used, but with different subscripts) with $i > j$ that does not contain two pairs of the form f_i/f_j and f_j/f_k. Thus, a symbol f_i cannot be replaced by a symbol g_h, and a symbol f_j used to replace a symbol f_i cannot be substituted in θ by a symbol f_k—where f_i, f_j, f_k, g_h are in $\Lambda - \{\epsilon\}$. For instance, $\{f_2/f_1, g_3/g_1\}$ is an adornment substitution, but $\{f_1/g_1\}$ and $\{f_3/f_2, f_2/f_1\}$ are not. The result of applying θ to an adorned rule r, denoted $r\theta$, is the adorned rule obtained from r by substituting each f_i appearing in r with

---

Algorithm 3 Adorn

Input: Datalog^f program P.
Output: Adorned Datalog^f program P^μ.

1: $S = \emptyset$; $P^\mu = \emptyset$;
2: $AP = \{p^{\alpha_1 \cdots \alpha_n} \mid p$ is a base predicate symbol appearing in P of arity n and every $\alpha_i = \epsilon\}$;
3: **repeat**
4:     $AP' = AP$;
5:     **for each** rule $p(\bar{t}) \leftarrow body$ in P **do**
6:         **for each** $body^\sigma$ in $\mathcal{A}(body, AP)$ **do**
7:             **for each** W in $SBodyAdn(body^\sigma, S)$ **do**
8:                 **if** $body^\sigma$ is coherently adorned w.r.t. W **then**
9:                     **for each** T in $\mathcal{S}(W)$ **do**
10:                        $\langle p^\alpha(\bar{t}), S' \rangle = SetHeadAdn(p(\bar{t}), T, S)$;
11:                        $AP = AP \cup \{p^\alpha\}$; $S = S'$;
12:                        $ar = p^\alpha(\bar{t}) \leftarrow body^\sigma$;
13:                        $P^\mu = P^\mu \cup \{ar\}$;
14:                        **if** $\exists r \in P^\mu \wedge \exists substitution\ \theta \neq \emptyset\ s.t.\ ar\theta = r$ **then**
15:                            $P^\mu = P^\mu \theta$; $AP = AP\theta$; $S = S\theta$;
16: **until** $AP' = AP$
17: **return** P^μ;

---

f_j, where f_i/f_j belongs to θ. The result of applying θ to a set of adorned rules P^μ (resp. adorned predicate symbols AP, adornment definitions S), denoted $P^\mu\theta$ (resp. $AP\theta$, $S\theta$), is analogously defined.

The set of the *adorned versions* of an atom $p(\bar{t})$ w.r.t. a set of adorned predicate symbols AP is $\mathcal{A}(p(\bar{t}), AP) = \{p^\alpha(\bar{t}) \mid p^\alpha \in AP\}$. The set of the *adorned versions* of a conjunction of atoms $body = A_1, \ldots, A_k$ w.r.t. AP is $\mathcal{A}(body, AP) = \{AA_1, \ldots, AA_k \mid AA_i \in \mathcal{A}(A_i, AP)\ \text{for } 1 \leq i \leq k\}$. If $body$ is the empty conjunction, then $\mathcal{A}(body, AP)$ contains only the empty conjunction.

Function *Adorn* (Algorithm 3) performs the transformation of a Datalog^f program. It maintains a set of adornment definitions S, a set of adorned rules P^μ (eventually, this will be the output), and a set AP of adorned predicate symbols. Initially, S and P^μ are empty (line 1), and AP contains all base predicate symbols in P adorned with strings of ϵ's (line 2). Then, for each coherently adorned body $body^\sigma$ of a rule $p(\bar{t}) \leftarrow body$ in the original program, we determine the adorned head $p^\alpha(\bar{t})$ and the set of adornment definitions S' using function *SetHeadAdn* (line 10). The set AP is extended with p^α, S' is assigned to S (line 11), and a new adorned rule ar of the form $p^\alpha(\bar{t}) \leftarrow body^\sigma$ is added to P^μ (line 13). If there exists an adornment substitution θ that applied to ar gives a rule r in P^μ, then θ is applied to P^μ, AP, and S (line 15). This ensures termination of *Adorn*.

The following example shows the role of adornment substitutions.

Example 5.37   Consider the Datalog^f program below where *base* is a base predicate symbol:

$$p(X) \leftarrow base(X).$$
$$p(f(X)) \leftarrow p(X).$$

Starting from $S = \emptyset$, $P^\mu = \emptyset$, and $AP = \{base^\epsilon\}$, the transformation algorithm adds the following adorned rules to P^μ

$$\rho_0: \quad p^\epsilon(X) \leftarrow base^\epsilon(X).$$
$$\rho_1: \quad p^{f_1}(f(X)) \leftarrow p^\epsilon(X).$$
$$\rho_2: \quad p^{f_2}(f(X)) \leftarrow p^{f_1}(X).$$
$$\rho_3: \quad p^{f_3}(f(X)) \leftarrow p^{f_2}(X).$$

Furthermore, the adornment definitions $f_1 = f(\epsilon)$, $f_2 = f(f_1)$, $f_3 = f(f_2)$ are added to S, and the adorned predicate symbols p^ϵ, p^{f_1}, p^{f_2}, p^{f_3} are added to AP. At this point, the following adorned rule is derived and added to P^μ:

$$\rho_4: \quad p^{f_4}(f(X)) \leftarrow p^{f_3}(X).$$

The adornment definition $f_4 = f(f_3)$ is added to S and p^{f_4} is added to AP. However, since there is an adornment substitution $\theta = \{f_4/f_2, f_3/f_1\}$ such that $\rho_4\theta = \rho_2$, then θ is applied to P^μ, AP, and S. Thus, P^μ becomes $\{\rho_0, \rho_1, \rho_2, \rho_3\theta\}$, where $\rho_3\theta$ is

$$p^{f_1}(f(X)) \leftarrow p^{f_2}(X).$$

$AP = \{p^\epsilon, p^{f_1}, p^{f_2}\}$ and $S = \{f_1 = f(\epsilon), f_2 = f(f_1), f_1 = f(f_2)\}$. At this point, no new adorned rule can be generated and the algorithm terminates.

In the previous example, notice that both the original and the transformed programs are not recognized as terminating by current termination criteria. Indeed, for any database containing at least one fact *base(c)*, the least model is not finite and the bottom-up evaluation of both programs never terminates. Nevertheless, function *Adorn* terminates.

We conclude this section by mentioning different important properties of the transformation technique (more details can be found in Greco et al. [2013b]).

First of all, function *Adorn* always terminates.

An important property of the transformation technique is that the original Datalog^f program it takes as input and the transformed Datalog^f program it gives as output are "equivalent" in the following sense: the least model of the original program can be obtained from the least model of transformed program by dropping adornments.

Another crucial property of the transformation technique is its soundness: if the transformed program *Adorn(P)* satisfies one of the termination criteria presented in the previous section, then the bottom-up evaluation of the original Datalog^f program P terminates—indeed, we can state that the evaluation of $P \cup D$ terminates for any finite database D (recall that we assume that databases do not contain complex terms). Thus, the least model of $P \cup D$ is finite, and can be computed.

Finally, applying termination criteria to adorned programs as discussed in this section allows us to detect strictly more programs as terminating.

5.4 DEALING WITH DISJUNCTION AND NEGATION

The termination criteria presented in this chapter have been originally proposed for Datalog programs allowing function symbols, negation in the body, and disjunction in the head of rules. In this chapter, we have restricted attention to Datalog^f programs (where there is no negation in rule bodies and no disjunction in rule heads).

Nevertheless, a program P with disjunction in the head and negation in the body (e.g., see Example 5.38) can be analyzed by checking termination of a Datalog^f program $st(P)$ derived from P as follows: every rule $A_1 \vee \cdots \vee A_m \leftarrow body$ in P is replaced with m Datalog^f rules of the form $A_i \leftarrow body^+$ $(1 \leq i \leq m)$ where $body^+$ is obtained from $body$ by deleting all negative literals.

It is easy to see that if M is the least model of $st(P)$, then $SM \subseteq M$ for every stable model SM of P (because deleting literals from rule bodies and introducing multiple rules for head disjunctions allows us to infer more ground atoms). Hence, if $st(P)$ satisfies a termination criterion, then P has a finite number of stable models, and each of them has finite size and can be computed—e.g., by computing the stable models of the (finite) ground program $P' \subseteq ground(P)$ consisting only of those rules whose terms all appear in M.

Indeed, the analysis performed by current termination criteria over a program P (possibly with negation and disjunction) is equivalent to the analysis of $st(P)$, because the analysis ignores negation and looks at a rule $A_1 \vee \cdots \vee A_m \leftarrow body$ in the same way as m rules of the form $A_i \leftarrow body$, $1 \leq i \leq m$.

Example 5.38 Consider the following program P where disjunction and negation occur:

$$
\begin{aligned}
p(X) \vee q(f(X)) &\leftarrow s(X), \neg base(X). \\
s(X) &\leftarrow q(g(X)), \neg p(X).
\end{aligned}
$$

Then, $st(P)$ is as follows:

$$
\begin{aligned}
p(X) &\leftarrow s(X). \\
q(f(X)) &\leftarrow s(X). \\
s(X) &\leftarrow q(g(X)).
\end{aligned}
$$

If $st(P)$ satisfies a certain termination criterion, then P has a finite set of stable models and each of them has finite size and can be computed.

BIBLIOGRAPHIC NOTES

A significant body of work has been done on termination of logic programs under top-down evaluation [Baselice et al., 2009, Bonatti, 2004, Bruynooghe et al., 2007, Codish et al., 2005, De Schreye and Decorte, 1994, Marchiori, 1996, Nguyen et al., 2007, Nishida and Vidal, 2010, Ohlebusch, 2001, Schneider-Kamp et al., 2009a,b, 2010, Serebrenik and De Schreye, 2005, Voets and De Schreye, 2011].

The problem of checking termination of the bottom-up evaluation of Datalog^f programs is also akin to work done in the area of term rewriting [Arts and Giesl, 2000, Endrullis et al., 2008, Ferreira and Zantema, 1996, Sternagel and Middeldorp, 2008, Zantema, 1994, 1995].

In this chapter, we have considered the problem of checking if the bottom-up evaluation of a Datalog^f program terminates, and thus, as noticed and discussed in Alviano et al. [2010], Calimeri et al. [2008, 2010], all the works above cannot straightforwardly be applied to the setting considered in this chapter.

As for the context considered in this chapter, recent years have witnessed an increasing interest in the problem of identifying Datalog programs with function symbols for which a finite set of finite stable models exists and can be computed.

The class of *finitely-ground programs*, guaranteeing the aforementioned desirable property, has been proposed in Calimeri et al. [2008]. Since membership in the class is not decidable, recent research has concentrated on the identification of decidable sufficient conditions for a program to be finitely-ground. Efforts in this direction are *ω-restricted programs* [Syrjänen, 2001], *λ-restricted programs* [Gebser et al., 2007], and *finite domain programs* [Calimeri et al., 2008]. More general classes are *argument-restricted programs* [Lierler and Lifschitz, 2009], *safe* and *Γ-acyclic programs* [Calautti et al., 2015a, Greco et al., 2012b], *mapping-restricted programs* [Calautti et al., 2013], *bounded programs* [Greco et al., 2013a], *rule- and cycle-bounded programs* [Calautti et al., 2014, 2015c, 2016], and *size-restricted programs* [Calautti et al., 2015b]. We point out that the aforementioned techniques have been proposed for Datalog programs allowing function symbols, negation in the body, and disjunction in the head of rules. In this chapter, we restricted attention to Datalog^f programs (where there is no negation in rule bodies and no disjunction in rule heads). However, the analysis performed by current techniques over a program P, possibly with negation and disjunction, is indeed equivalent to the analysis of the Datalog^f program $st(P)$ (cf. Section 5.4).

Termination properties of query evaluation for programs under tabling were studied in Riguzzi and Swift [2014], Verbaeten et al. [2001].

The topic of this chapter is also related to research done in the database community on termination of the chase procedure, where existential rules are considered [Deutsch et al., 2008, Fagin et al., 2005, Grau et al., 2013, Greco and Spezzano, 2010, Greco et al., 2011, Krötzsch and Rudolph, 2011, Marnette, 2009b, Meier et al., 2009]. A survey on this topic can be found in Greco et al. [2012a].

Indeed, sufficient conditions ensuring termination of the bottom-up evaluation of logic programs can be directly applied to existential rules. Specifically, one can analyze the logic program obtained from the skolemization of existential rules, where existentially quantified variables are replaced with complex terms [Marnette, 2009a]. In fact, the evaluation of such a program behaves as the "semi-oblivious" chase [Marnette, 2009a], whose termination guarantees the termination of the standard chase [Meier, 2010, Onet, 2013]. Thus, if the program obtained from the skolemization of a set of existential rules satisfies a termination criterion, then its bottom-up evaluation terminates, which means that the semi-oblivious chase for the original set of existential rules terminates, which in turn implies that the standard chase for the original set of existential rules terminates.

On the other hand, termination criteria developed for the chase cannot directly applied to Datalog programs with function symbols. The rules obtained via skolemization of existential rules are of a very restricted form: function symbols appear only in rule heads, each function symbol occurs at most once, there is no nesting of function symbols. In contrast, we have considered a much more general setting allowing an arbitrary use of function symbols: they can appear in both the head and the body of rules, may be nested, and the same function symbol can appear multiple times.

CHAPTER 6

Aggregates

In this chapter, we extend Datalog to include aggregation constructs, such as *count*, *sum*, and *summation*, and show how they help express optimization problems.

Aggregates are an important feature of query languages and allow us to summarize a large amount of data into a single value—for instance, they can be used to count the number of products supplied by a certain supplier, or compute the total amount of a certain purchase.

We first discuss two classical aggregates, namely *count* and *sum*. Then, we present the *summation* aggregate proposed by Greco [1999a]. Finally, we consider the combination of the *summation* aggregate and the *choice-least* and *choice-most* constructs (cf. Section 4.6), and illustrate how they can be used to easily express classical optimization problems.

For all the aforementioned aggregate constructs, we provide a declarative semantics based on rewriting programs with aggregates into programs with choice and choice-least/most constructs.

6.1 SYNTAX

In this section, we discuss some common syntactical aspects of the languages considered in this chapter. In the following sections, we will individually consider different languages, each obtained by extending Datalog with a specific aggregate.

An *aggregate* is a function that takes a multiset of values as input and returns a single value as output. Indeed, besides allowing aggregates, in this chapter the syntax of Datalog is extended to allow arithmetic and comparison operators too.

We will make use of arithmetic on a finite subset N of the cardinal numbers. More specifically, given a program P, we assume the existence of a finite subset $N = \{0, \ldots, n_P\}$ of cardinal numbers, where n_P is the maximum number a programmer wants to manipulate in program P.

In contrast to other constants, which are uninterpreted, constants in N are interpreted, as well as the arithmetic operators defined on N. The operators we consider are the usual arithmetic operators of sum, difference, product, and so on, which are interpreted in the standard way. Observe that the assumption of a finite subset of the cardinal numbers guarantees that the Herbrand universe is finite and the the bottom-up evaluation of a program always terminates.

In the following, we assume that for each predicate symbol at most one argument, called *cost argument*, can take values from the ordered domain N whereas all the remaining arguments take values from the Herbrand universe. Variables appearing in cost arguments will be called *cost variables*. For the sake of simplicity, we also assume that the cost argument in a predicate, if any, is always the last one.

Comparison atoms of the form $t_1 \; op \; t_2$ are allowed in the body of rules, where *op* is a comparison predicate symbol (i.e., $op \in \{\geq, >, \leq, <, =, \neq\}$) and t_1 and t_2 are terms. Besides constants and variables, t_1 and t_2 can be complex arithmetic expressions involving arithmetic operators, constants from N, and variables. Such terms are interpreted in the standard way and then compared according to *op*. For instance, given the comparison atom $X = 2 \times Y$, its true ground instances are those where X is replaced with a value which is twice the value Y is replaced with.

Aggregates are expressed by means of *aggregate atoms* of the form $sum((\overline{X}), V, S)$, $count((\overline{X}), C)$, $summation((\overline{X}), V, S)$, where $\overline{X}$ is a list of variables, and V, S, and C are variables. The intuitive meaning as well as a formal semantics of such aggregate atoms will be discussed in the following sections. Aggregate atoms can appear only in the body of rules.

Thus, the body of a rule can contain standard atoms (i.e., atoms whose predicate symbol is neither a comparison predicate symbol nor an aggregate one), comparison atoms, and aggregate atoms.

Every rule must be *safe*. To accommodate the three different types of atoms that can occur in a rule, the safety condition is defined as follows. For every rule, every variable must be *limited* in the following sense:

- a variable X is limited if it appears in a standard atom in the body; and

- a variable X is limited if it appears in a comparison atom of the form $X = t$ or $t = X$, where t is a term whose variables are all limited (notice that t can be a complex arithmetic expression)—in the case that t is a constant, the condition is trivially satisfied.

In the rest of the chapter we first present the *sum* and *count* aggregates. Then, we consider the *summation* aggregate. After that, we discuss the combination of *summation* and *choice-least* and *choice-most*. We point out that the classical *min* and *max* aggregates can indeed be expressed by the *choice-least* and *choice-most* constructs, respectively.

Given a list of terms $\overline{X}$, we will use $var(\overline{X})$ to denote the list of variables occurring in $\overline{X}$.

6.2   SUM AND COUNT

The aggregates *sum* and *count* were first introduced in Mumick et al. [1990] and further investigated in several subsequent papers.

In the following, we define syntax and semantics of such aggregates. In particular, we present the semantics given by Greco [1999a], which is defined in terms of choice-most programs.

Sum aggregate.   The sum aggregate is expressed by means of atoms of the form $sum((\overline{X}), V, S)$, where $\overline{X}$ is a list of variables, and V and S are variables. The intuitive meaning is that, given a multiset T of tuples of the form $(\overline{x}, v)$, where $\overline{x}$ is a list of constants from the Herbrand universe called the $\overline{X}$-value of the tuple and v is a value from N called the V-value of the tuple, for each maximal subset T' of T of tuples having the same $\overline{X}$-value, all the V-values must be added, yielding S. Thus, the aggregate atom yields as many values for S as the number of distinct values of $\overline{X}$. An example is provided below.

Example 6.1   Consider the rule

$$p(X, S) \leftarrow q(X, Y, V), \; sum((X), V, S)$$

along with the following facts:

$$q(a, c, 2).$$
$$q(a, d, 4).$$
$$q(b, c, 3).$$

The evaluation of the rule above yields $p(a, 6)$ by summing up the V-values of the first two facts, and $p(b, 3)$ by summing up the V-value of the last fact.

If we replace the rule above with the following one

$$p(Y, S) \leftarrow q(X, Y, V), sum((Y), V, S)$$

then we get $p(c, 5)$ from the first and last facts, and $p(d, 4)$ from the second fact.

We now formally define the syntax of rules with the *sum* aggregate.

Definition 6.2   A *Datalog*^{sum} *rule* is of the form:

$$p(\overline{Y}, S) \leftarrow body(\overline{W}, V), sum((\overline{X}), V, S)$$

where

- $\overline{Y}$ and $\overline{W}$ are lists of terms, $\overline{X}$ is a list of variables, and $var(\overline{Y}) \subseteq \overline{X} \subseteq var(\overline{W})$;

- V is a cost variable such that $V \notin \overline{X}$ and S is a distinct variable such that $S \notin var(\overline{W})$; and

- $body(\overline{W}, V)$ is a conjunction of standard and comparison atoms whose terms are $\overline{W}$ and V.

A *Datalog*^{sum} *program* is a finite set of Datalog and Datalog^{sum} rules, where for every Datalog^{sum} rule, the predicate symbol in the head is not mutually recursive with any of the predicate symbols in the body.

Following Greco [1999a], the semantics of a Datalog^{sum} program is given in terms of a choice-most program (cf. Section 4.6) derived from the original one by replacing every Datalog^{sum} rule with two groups of rules.

More specifically, consider a Datalog^{sum} program P and a Datalog^{sum} rule $r \in P$ of the following form (i.e., as per Definition 6.2):

$$p(\overline{Y}, S) \leftarrow body(\overline{W}, V), sum((\overline{X}), V, S).$$

The first group of rules is used to partition the set of *body* tuples with respect to the values of the variables in $\overline{X}$ and define a linear order for each partition. Formally, we define $ord(r)$ as the set consisting of the following rules:

$$
\begin{aligned}
ordered_r(0, \overline{X}, root) &\leftarrow body(\overline{W}, V). \\
ordered_r(J', \overline{X}, V) &\leftarrow ordered_r(J', \overline{X}, Y), body(\overline{W}, V), J = J' + 1 \\
&\quad choice((J, \overline{X}), (\overline{W})), choice((\overline{W}), (J, \overline{X})).
\end{aligned}
$$

The second group of rules is used to compute the sum of each partition by iterating over the corresponding linear order. Formally, we define $sum(r)$ as the set consisting of the following rules:

$$
\begin{aligned}
p(\overline{Y}, S) &\leftarrow sum\_body_r(J, \overline{X}, S), choice\text{-}most((\overline{X}), J). \\
sum\_body_r(0, \overline{X}, 0) &\leftarrow ordered_r(0, \overline{X}, root). \\
sum\_body_r(J, \overline{X}, S) &\leftarrow sum\_body_r(J', \overline{X}, S'), ordered_r(J, \overline{X}, V), S = S' + V, J = J' + 1.
\end{aligned}
$$

The semantics of a Datalog^{sum} program P is given in terms of the greedy choice models of the choice-most program P' derived from P by replacing every Datalog^{sum} rule r in P with $ord(r) \cup sum(r)$.[1] Notice that P' can have multiple greedy choice models, which differ only in the atoms defining the linear orders (i.e., the $ordered_r$-atoms) and, consequently, they also differ in the sum_body_r-atoms. This is not surprising since the final result of the sum of a set of elements is independent of the order in which the elements are summed up, although the partial results can be different.

Thus, the semantics of P is given by taking all the p-atoms of any greedy choice model of P' where p is a predicate symbol appearing in P. As discussed above, we can choose any greedy choice model of P' without affecting the result, and thus the semantics of P is deterministic.

Count aggregate. The count aggregate is expressed by means of atoms of the form $count((\overline{X}), C)$, where $\overline{X}$ is a list of variables and C is a variable. The intuitive meaning is that, given a multiset T of tuples of the form $(\overline{x})$, where $\overline{x}$ is a list of constants from the Herbrand universe called the $\overline{X}$-value of the tuple, for each maximal subset T' of T of tuples having the same $\overline{X}$-value, we count the number of elements of T'. The aggregate atom yields as many values for C as the number of distinct values of $\overline{X}$ in T. An example is provided below.

Example 6.3 Consider a directed graph stored by means of facts of the form $edge(a, b)$, meaning that there is an edge in the graph from node a to node b. The following rule computes the outdegree of every node having outgoing edges (i.e., having outdegree greater than 0):

$$
outdegree(X, C) \leftarrow edge(X, Y), count((X), C).
$$

---

[1]Indeed, P' is a choice-most program where arithmetic operators are allowed.

Consider now the directed graph corresponding to the following database:

$$edge(a, b).$$
$$edge(a, c).$$
$$edge(b, c).$$
$$edge(c, a).$$
$$edge(c, d).$$
$$edge(c, b).$$

The evaluation of the rule above yields $outdegree(a, 2)$ by counting the number of facts having a as the first argument, and likewise it also yields $outdegree(b, 1)$ and $outdegree(c, 3)$.

The following rule allows us to compute the indegree of every node having ingoing edges:

$$indegree(Y, C) \leftarrow edge(X, Y), count((Y), C).$$

By evaluating this rule over the database above we get $indegree(a, 1)$, $indegree(b, 2)$, $indegree(c, 2)$, and $indegree(d, 1)$.

We now formally define the syntax of programs with the *count* aggregate.

Definition 6.4   A *Datalog^{count} rule* is of the form:

$$p(\overline{Y}, C) \leftarrow body(\overline{W}), count((\overline{X}), C),$$

where

- $\overline{Y}$ and $\overline{W}$ are lists of terms, $\overline{X}$ is a list of variables, and $var(\overline{Y}) \subseteq \overline{X} \subseteq var(\overline{W})$;

- C is a variable such that $C \notin var(\overline{W})$; and

- $body(\overline{W})$ is a conjunction of standard and comparison atoms whose terms are $\overline{W}$.

A *Datalog^{count} program* is a finite set of Datalog and Datalog^{count} rules where for every Datalog^{count} rule, the predicate symbol in the head is not mutually recursive with any of the predicate symbols in the body.

The semantics of a Datalog^{count} program P is given in terms of the semantics of a Datalog^{sum} program derived from P by replacing each Datalog^{count} rule r in P of the form

$$p(\overline{Y}, C) \leftarrow body(\overline{W}), count((\overline{X}), C)$$

with the following rules:

$$p(\overline{Y}, C) \quad \leftarrow \quad body_r(\overline{W}, V), sum((\overline{X}), V, C).$$
$$body_r(\overline{W}, 1) \quad \leftarrow \quad body(\overline{W}).$$

Thus, *count* can be reduced to the case of *sum*. Specifically, every tuple involved in the counting is given an extra argument whose values is 1 (see the second rule above), then such values are summed (see the first rule above), thereby obtaining the effect of counting.

6.3 SUMMATION

The *summation* aggregate is a useful construct for expressing optimization problems (e.g., see Examples 6.8 and 6.10 in the following). It is expressed by means of atoms of the form *summation*$((\overline{X}), V, S)$, where $\overline{X}$ is a list of variables, and V and S are variables. The intuitive meaning is that, given a multiset T of tuples of the form $(\overline{x}, v)$, where $\overline{x}$ is a list of constants from the Herbrand universe called the $\overline{X}$-value of the tuple and v is a value from N called the V-value of the tuple, for each maximal subset T' of T such that there are no two tuples in T' with the same $\overline{X}$-value, all the V-values must be added, yielding S.

In other words, if $T[\overline{X}]$ denotes the set of $\overline{X}$-values in T and, for each $\overline{x}$ in $T[\overline{X}]$, $\gamma(\overline{x})$ non-deterministically selects exactly one value v for which $(\overline{x}, v)$ is in T, then a value for S is obtained as $\sum_{\overline{x} \in T[\overline{X}]} \gamma(\overline{x})$. An example is provided below.

Example 6.5 Consider the following rule:

$$p(S) \leftarrow q(X, W, V), summation((X), V, S)$$

and the database consisting of the following facts:

$$q(a, c, 1).$$
$$q(a, c, 2).$$
$$q(b, c, 2).$$
$$q(b, d, 3).$$

The evaluation of the rule above yields the atoms $p(3)$ (using the first and third facts in the database), $p(4)$ (using the first and the fourth facts or using the second and the third ones), and $p(5)$ (using the second and the fourth facts). If we replace the rule above with the following one:

$$p(S) \leftarrow q(X, W, V), summation((W), V, S);$$

that is, variable W is used in place of variable X in the summation atom, then we get the atoms $p(4)$ (using the first and fourth facts in the database) and $p(5)$ (using the second and the fourth facts or using the third and the fourth ones).

The syntax of programs with the *summation* aggregate is defined as follows.

Definition 6.6 A *Datalog$^{\Sigma}$* rule is of the form:

$$p(S_1, \ldots, S_n) \leftarrow body(\overline{W}, \overline{X}, V_1, \ldots, V_n),$$
$$summation((\overline{X}), V_1, S_1), \ldots, summation((\overline{X}), V_n, S_n),$$

where

- $\overline{W}$ is a list of terms and $\overline{X}$ is a list of variables;

- $V_1, \ldots, V_n, S_1, \ldots, S_n$ are distinct variables none of which belongs to $\overline{W}$ or $\overline{X}$; and

- $body(\overline{W}, \overline{X}, V_1, \ldots, V_n)$ is a conjunction of standard and comparison atoms whose terms are $\overline{W}, \overline{X}, V_1, \ldots, V_n$.

A *Datalog$^\Sigma$ program* is a finite set of Datalog and Datalog$^\Sigma$ rules where for every Datalog$^\Sigma$ rule, the predicate symbol in the head is not mutually recursive with any of the predicate symbols in the body.

Observe that the body of a Datalog$^\Sigma$ rule may contain several *summation* atoms, but must satisfy the following constraints:

- all summation atoms must have the same first argument $\overline{X}$;

- variables $\overline{X}, V_1, \ldots, V_n$ must appear in the conjunction $body(\overline{W}, \overline{X}, V_1, \ldots, V_n)$;

- only variables S_i may occur in the head and they cannot appear in $body(\overline{W}, \overline{X}, V_1, \ldots, V_n)$; and

- variables $V_1, \ldots, V_n, S_1, \ldots, S_n$ take values from the domain N.

The semantics of a Datalog$^\Sigma$ program is given in terms of a choice-most program derived from P as follows. We first define a linear order on the values of the variables $\overline{X}$ by using the non-determinism of the choice construct. More specifically, consider a Datalog$^\Sigma$ program P and a Datalog$^\Sigma$ rule r in P of the form (see Definition 6.6)

$$p(S_1, \ldots, S_n) \leftarrow body(\overline{W}, \overline{X}, V_1, \ldots, V_n),$$
$$summation((\overline{X}), V_1, S_1), \ldots, summation((\overline{X}), V_n, S_n).$$

We define $ord(r)$ as the set consisting of the following rules:

$$ordered_r(0, root).$$
$$ordered_r(J, \overline{X}) \leftarrow ordered_r(J', \overline{X'}), body(\overline{W}, \overline{X}, V_1, \ldots, V_n),$$
$$choice((J), (\overline{X})), choice((\overline{X}), (J)), J = J' + 1.$$

The linear order on the values of the variables $\overline{X}$ is built by defining a bijection between the set of possible values of $\overline{X}$ and the cardinal numbers: this is enforced by the atoms $choice((J), (\overline{X}))$ and $choice((\overline{X}), (J))$ in the body of the rule above.

We now define $sum(r)$ as the set consisting of the following rules:

$$p(S_1, \ldots, S_n) \leftarrow p_r(J, S_1, \ldots, S_n), choice\text{-}most((), J).$$
$$p_r(0, 0, \ldots, 0).$$
$$p_r(J, S_1, \ldots, S_n) \leftarrow p_r(J', S'_1, \ldots, S'_n), J = J' + 1,$$
$$ordered_r(J, \overline{X}), body(\overline{W}, \overline{X}, V_1, \ldots, V_n),$$
$$S_1 = S'_1 + V_1, \ldots, S_n = S'_n + V_n,$$

where p_r is a fresh predicate symbol.

The semantics of a Datalog$^\Sigma$ program P is given in terms of the choice-most program P' derived from P by replacing every Datalog$^\Sigma$ rule r in P with $ord(r) \cup sum(r)$. Similar to Datalog^{sum} programs, P' can have multiple greedy choice models, which have the same p-atoms for every predicate symbol p appearing in P. The semantics of P is given by the set of such atoms, which is the same across all greedy choice models of P'.

Example 6.7   Consider the following Datalog$^\Sigma$ rule r:

$$p(Y, V) \leftarrow range(I, X_i), item(I, Y_i, V_i), summation((I), Y_i, Y), summation((I), V_i, V).$$

Then, $ord(r) \cup sum(r)$ consists of the following rules:

$$
\begin{aligned}
ordered_r(0, root). & \\
ordered_r(J, I) \quad \leftarrow \quad & ordered_r(J', I'), range(I, X_i), item(I, Y_i, V_i), , \\
& choice((J), (I)), choice((I), (J)), J = J' + 1. \\
p(Y, V) \quad \leftarrow \quad & p'(J, Y, V), choice\text{-}most((), J). \\
p'(0, 0, 0). & \\
p'(J, Y, V) \quad \leftarrow \quad & p'(J', Y', V'), J = J' + 1, \\
& ordered_r(J, I), range(I, X_i), item(I, Y_i, V_i) \\
& Y = Y' + Y_i, V = V' + V_i.
\end{aligned}
$$

6.4   COMBINING SUMMATION AND GREEDY CHOICE

In this section, we consider programs where the *summation* aggregate is used along with the *choice-least*/*choice-most* constructs, and show that they are well suited to express optimization problems—the former can be used to compute summations and the latter can be used to select optimal values. In particular, we will focus on the combination of *summation* and *choice-most*; the case involving *choice-least* is analogous. An example is given below.

Example 6.8   Given 1000 dollars to invest in different enterprises, we want to determine how we should allocate this amount of money in order to have maximum profit. Specifically, assume we have facts of the form $invest(e_i, x_i, p_i)$ meaning that p_i is the profit from the investment of x_i dollars on enterprise e_i, and we want to determine the exact distribution of the resources in each of the enterprises so that the global profit is maximized.

By combining *summation* and *choice-most*, the problem can be expressed as follows:

$$
\begin{aligned}
global\_profit(S) \quad \leftarrow \quad & profit(D, S), choice\text{-}most((), S). \\
profit(D, S) \quad \leftarrow \quad & invest(E, X, P), \\
& summation((E), X, D), D \leq 1000, \\
& summation((E), P, S), choice\text{-}most((D), S).
\end{aligned}
$$

The second rule above computes the maximum profit S we can get by investing D dollars, for different values of D (less than or equal to 1000). Then, the first rule selects the maximum value of S across all values derived from the second rule.

We now define the syntax of programs including *summation* and *choice-most*.

Definition 6.9   A *Datalog*$^{\Sigma,most}$ *rule* is of the form:

$$p(S_1, \ldots, S_n) \quad \leftarrow \quad body(\overline{W}, \overline{X}, V_1, \ldots, V_n),$$
$$summation(\overline{X}, V_1, S_1), \ldots, summation(\overline{X}, V_n, S_n),$$
$$choice\text{-}most((S_1, \ldots, S_{n-1}), S_n),$$

where

- $\overline{W}$ is a list of terms and $\overline{X}$ is a list of variables;

- $V_1, \ldots, V_n, S_1, \ldots, S_n$ are distinct variables none of which belongs to $\overline{W}$ or $\overline{X}$; and

- $body(\overline{W}, \overline{X}, V_1, \ldots, V_n)$ is a conjunction of standard and comparison atoms whose terms are $\overline{W}, \overline{X}, V_1, \ldots, V_n$.

A *Datalog*$^{\Sigma,most}$ *program* is a finite set of Datalog, choice-most, and Datalog$^{\Sigma,most}$ rules where, for every choice-most or Datalog$^{\Sigma,most}$ rule, the predicate symbol in the head is not mutually recursive with any of the predicate symbols in the body.

The semantics of a Datalog$^{\Sigma,most}$ program P is given in terms of a choice-most program P' obtained from P by replacing every Datalog$^{\Sigma,most}$ rule r in P by $ord(r)$ as defined in Section 6.3, plus the following set of rules:

$$p(S_1, \ldots, S_n) \quad \leftarrow \quad p_r(J, S_1, \ldots, S_n), choice\text{-}most((), J).$$
$$p_r(0, 0, \ldots, 0).$$
$$p_r(J, S_1, \ldots, S_n) \quad \leftarrow \quad p_r(J', S_1', \ldots, S_n'), J = J' + 1,$$
$$ordered_r(J, \overline{X}), body(\overline{W}, \overline{X}, V_1, \ldots, V_n),$$
$$S_1 = S_1' + V_1, \ldots, S_n = S_n' + V_n,$$
$$choice\text{-}most((J, S_1, \ldots, S_{n-1}), S_n),$$

where p_r is a fresh predicate symbol.

Recall that predicate $ordered_r$ is defined by rules in $ord(r)$ (see the previous section). Similar to the semantics discussed in the previous sections, the semantics of P is given in terms of the p-atoms of any greedy choice model of P', where p is a predicate symbol appearing in P—once again, even if P' can have multiple greedy choice models, they all agree on the p-atoms (with p being a predicate symbol that appears in P) and thus the semantics is deterministic.

Details on the evaluation of Datalog$^{\Sigma,most}$ programs (as well as Datalog$^{\Sigma,least}$ programs) can be found in Greco [1999a]. A general technique for the propagation of extrema predicates into Datalog programs has been defined in Greco et al. [1998] (see also Ganguly et al. [1991]).

Below we report another example where the *summation* aggregate is used along with the *choice-most* construct to express an optimization problem.

Example 6.10   Suppose we are given a set of facts of the form $item(i, b_i, v_i)$ meaning that there is an item i with weight b_i and value v_i. The following Datalog$^{\Sigma, most}$ program returns the maximum value of the expression $\sum_i v_i \times x_i^2$ under the constraint $\sum_i b_i \times x_i \leq 15$—here the x_i's variables can take non-negative integer values.

$$
\begin{aligned}
max\_p(V) &\leftarrow p(B, V), choice\text{-}most((), V). \\
p(B, V) &\leftarrow range(X_i), item(I, B_i, V_i), \\
&\quad B_i' = X_i \times B_i, summation((I), B_i', B), B \leq 15, \\
&\quad V_i' = X_i \times X_i \times V_i, summation((I), V_i', V), choice\text{-}most((B), V).
\end{aligned}
$$

Thus, the above program formulates a quadratic integer programming problem. Notice that we also have a fact $range(v)$ for every integer value v that a variable X_i can take.

Dynamic programming is a technique for solving optimization problems which decomposes a problem into subproblems of smaller size, solves the smaller subproblems, and uses their solutions to later solve larger subproblems up to the original problem. The technique is based on a bottom-up approach which is also the approach used by the evaluation strategy of Datalog. For instance, the resource allocation problem above can be solved with a dynamic programming approach. Greco [1999a] reports other examples showing that the summation aggregate in combination with greedy choice allows us to express many optimization problems in a declarative way.

BIBLIOGRAPHIC NOTES

The classes of programs discussed in this chapter can be easily extended to accommodate stratified negation, see Greco [1999a].

Notice also that we considered classes of programs with only one aggregate. For instance, Datalog^{sum} programs cannot contain Datalog^{count} rules. However, the generalization to classes of programs containing both Datalog^{sum} and Datalog^{count} rules is easy since the semantics of such programs can be defined by rewriting each Datalog^{sum} rule and each Datalog^{count} rule as discussed in Section 6.2. The same argument applies to other combinations of rules with aggregates belonging to the same program.

The extension of Datalog with aggregates has been widely investigated, with particular focus on the definition of a suitable semantics and the design of techniques for the efficient evaluation of such programs.

A semantics for Datalog programs with non-recursive and monotonic recursive aggregates was first proposed in Mumick et al. [1990].

The extension of the well-founded semantics to logic programs with aggregates was considered in Kemp and Stuckey [1991]. A different definition (based on the alternating fixpoint) of the well-founded semantics in the presence of aggregates was proposed in Van Gelder [1992], which was later generalized by Osorio and Jayaraman [1999]. The main shortcoming of such semantics is that they often leave too many undefined atoms, as shown by Ross and Sagiv [1997]. The latter is an alternative approach based on the definition of monotonicity conditions using lattices and which is more general than the one defined by set-containment. This semantics does not capture some important cases such as cost-monotonic programs. Yet another semantics based on the definition of a stronger partial order relation was proposed in Gelder [1993]. An extension of the well-founded semantics to programs with aggregates was proposed also in Pelov et al. [2007] and Alviano et al. [2011].

Efficient bottom-up techniques for evaluating different classes of Datalog programs with aggregates were proposed in Ganguly et al. [1991], Sudarshan and Ramakrishnan [1991], whereas a top-down method which uses extension tables was presented in Dietrich [1992]. The technique presented in Sudarshan and Ramakrishnan [1991] was also implemented in the CORAL system [Ramakrishnan et al., 1992].

The efficient evaluation of Datalog programs extended with both negation and aggregation was studied in Kemp and Ramamohanarao [1998].

Incremental techniques for efficiently evaluating programs with monotonic aggregates were proposed in Ramakrishnan et al. [1994].

Expressive power and complexity of different extensions of Datalog with aggregates were investigated in Consens and Mendelzon [1990], Mumick and Shmueli [1995].

Semantics and complexity of Datalog extended with unstratified negation, disjunction, and aggregates were investigated in Faber et al. [2011]. A discussion of various other approaches can be found in Pelov et al. [2007].

CHAPTER 7

Query Optimization

In this chapter, we discuss techniques that take advantage of the information in Datalog queries to make their evaluation more efficient.

The first technique is called *magic-sets rewriting* and consists of rewriting a Datalog query into an equivalent one which combines the advantages of the bottom-up and top-down evaluation strategies. The Datalog query obtained from the rewriting is evaluated in a bottom-up fashion, but it indeed emulates a top-down evaluation strategy of the original query.

The second technique we present applies to a special class of Datalog queries, called *chain queries*, and is based on the rewriting of the original Datalog query into a new one (containing function symbols) that emulates a pushdown automaton. Several other techniques defined in the literature (e.g., the counting method) are characterized as special cases of this technique.

7.1 MAGIC-SETS REWRITING

Magic-sets rewriting [Bancilhon et al., 1986, Beeri and Ramakrishnan, 1991] is a well-known technique for the efficient evaluation of Datalog queries. The approach consists of rewriting a Datalog query into an equivalent one whose bottom-up evaluation simulates the pushing of binding information that occurs in top-down evaluation approaches. We illustrate this aspect in the following example.

Example 7.1   Consider a database storing facts of the form $person(a)$ and $parent(a, b)$ meaning that a is a person and b is a parent of a, respectively. Consider the Datalog query $\langle P, same\text{-}generation(john, Y)\rangle$[1] asking for those people of the same generation as *john*, where P is the following Datalog program:

$$samegeneration(X, X) \leftarrow person(X).$$
$$samegeneration(X, Y) \leftarrow parent(X, X_1), samegeneration(X_1, Y_1), parent(Y, Y_1).$$

This query could be answered rather efficiently using a top-down evaluation strategy. As discussed in Chapter 3, a top-down evaluation tries to avoid the inference of atoms that are irrelevant for proving the atoms of interest—in our example, we are interested only in the people of the same generation as *john*.

---

[1]Recall that a Datalog query is a pair $\langle P, G \rangle$ where P is a Datalog program and G is an atom, called *query goal*—see Section 3.4 for further details.

In contrast, bottom-up algorithms (such as those seen in Chapter 3) would compute the entire *samegeneration* relation to eventually keep only those tuples belonging to the query answer. If there are many tuples not involving *john* in the *samegeneration* relation, then the bottom-up computation would spend time to compute them even though they are useless for the purpose of answering the query.

The previous example highlights some advantages of the top-down evaluation. However, a bottom-up computation has also different advantages over top-down strategies. In fact, a top-down evaluation strategy might get stuck in infinite loops, and even if it is possible to avoid them, detecting termination is not easy. Moreover, bottom-up evaluation strategies can make use of efficient techniques for computing joins of big relations.

Magic-sets rewriting is a technique that combines the advantages of both the top-down and the bottom-up evaluation strategies. It consists of three steps.

1. An *adornment step* which derives a new program, called *adorned program*, from the original one. In the adorned program the relationships between bound arguments in the head of a rule and the bindings in the rule body are made explicit by "adorning" predicate symbols— roughly speaking, by attaching strings (specifying if a term is expected to be free or bound) to predicate symbols.

2. A *modification step* which modifies the adorned rules obtained at the first step by introducing new atoms, called *magic atoms*, into the rule bodies.

3. A *generation step* which adds new rules, called *magic rules*, to the adorned program obtained at the second step. The magic rules define the atoms introduced in the second step and simulate the top-down evaluation scheme.

The first step in the magic-sets rewriting is to produce an adorned query. Query adornment is a formal way of depicting information flow between atoms in rules. This is done by annotating predicate symbols with strings. More precisely, an *adornment* α for a predicate symbol p of arity n is a string $\alpha_1 \ldots \alpha_n$ of length n built from the letters b (which stands for *bound*) and f (which stands for *free*). So, p^α is an *adorned predicate symbol* and $p^\alpha(t_1, \ldots, t_n)$ is an *adorned atom*, where the t_i's are terms. For instance, *parent*^{fb} is an adorned predicate symbol and *parent*$^{fb}(X, john)$ is an adorned atom.

Intuitively, an adorned atom $p^\alpha(t_1, \ldots, t_n)$ is used to express if each t_i is expected to be bound or free during the evaluation of a program. Depending on the information flow, if t_i is expected to be bound (resp. free), then α_i is set to b (resp. f).

First of all, we define how the query goal is adorned.

Definition 7.2   Given a query goal G of the form $g(t_1, \ldots, t_m)$, the *adorned version* of G is the adorned atom $g^\alpha(t_1, \ldots, t_m)$ where adornment $\alpha = \alpha_1 \ldots \alpha_m$ is defined as follows: if t_i is a constant, then $\alpha_i = b$; otherwise (t_i is a variable) $\alpha_i = f$. The adorned version of G is denoted by *adorn*(G).

Now the program of the given query has to be adorned. Adornments are generated with reference to a specific *sideways information-passing strategy* (SIPS). A sideways information passing strategy is an inherent component of any query evaluation strategy. Intuitively, for a rule of a program, a SIPS represents a decision about the order in which the atoms of the rule will be evaluated, and how values for variables are passed from atoms to other atoms during evaluation. Specifically, a SIPS describes how bindings passed to a rule's head by unification are used to evaluate the atoms in the rule's body. Thus, a SIPS describes how we evaluate a rule when a given set of head terms are bound to constants. Below is an example.

Example 7.3   Consider again the Datalog query $\langle P, samegeneration(john, Y)\rangle$ of Example 7.1. The first argument of the query goal is bound to *john* and thus, in the first rule of P, variable X is bound to *john* as well and can be used in the body to check if *john* is a person.

In the second rule, a possible SIPS is the following one. Variable X is bound to *john* and is used to retrieve *john*'s parents. The value of X_1, bound to a parent of *john*, is available for the evaluation of $samegeneration(X_1, Y_1)$. Thus, in the second rule, variable X is passed sideways from $samegeneration(X, Y)$ in the head to $parent(X, X_1)$ in the body whereas variable X_1 is passed sideways from $parent(X, X_1)$ to $samegeneration(X_1, Y_1)$.

If the query goal is $samegeneration(X, john)$, the following different strategy can be used. In the second rule, the value of Y is bound to *john* and is passed sideways to the body atom $parent(Y, Y_1)$, so that the value of Y_1 is used to retrieve *john*'s parents; the (bound) variable Y_1 is then available for the evaluation of $samegeneration(X_1, Y_1)$. Therefore, the evaluation strategy depends on SIPSs, that is, how bindings are passed though atoms.

SIPSs are associated with a rule according to the query goal form—in particular, according to the adorned version of the query goal. Different query goals usually have different SIPSs for the same program (e.g., the two different query goals in the example above, whose adorned versions are $samegeneration^{bf}(X, Y)$ and $samegeneration^{fb}(X, Y)$). However, different SIPSs can be associated with the same query form too (e.g., see Example 7.5 in the following). The choice of one SIPS over another is guided by factors such as the current and expected size of the different relations and the employed indexing mechanism.

In a given rule, two atoms A and A' are *connected* if they share a common variable or there exists an atom A'' connected to both A and A'. The notion of SIPS is formally defined as follows.

Definition 7.4   Let r be a Datalog rule, $p(t_1, \ldots, t_n)$ the atom in the head of r, and $\alpha = \alpha_1 \ldots \alpha_n$ an adornment for p. A *sideways information-passing strategy* (SIPS) for r with respect to p^α is a labeled graph satisfying the following conditions:

- each edge is of the form $N \rightarrow_{\overline{X}} s$, where $N \subseteq (body(r) \cup \{p^\alpha(t_1, \ldots, t_n)\})$, $s \in body(r)$, and $\overline{X}$ is a non-empty set of variables. Moreover,

    - each variable in $\overline{X}$ appears in s; and

- each variable in $\overline{X}$ appears either in a term t_i s.t. $\alpha_i = b$, provided that $p^\alpha(t_1, \ldots, t_n)$ is in N, or in an atom in $N - \{p^\alpha(t_1, \ldots, t_n)\}$ (or both); and

- each atom in N is connected to s.

- There exists a total order of $body(r) \cup \{p^\alpha(t_1, \ldots, t_n)\}$ s.t.

    - $p^\alpha(t_1, \ldots, t_n)$ precedes all atoms in $body(r)$;

    - every atom which does not appear in the graph follows every atom appearing in the graph; and

    - for each edge $N \to_{\overline{X}} s$ in the SIPS, every element in N precedes s.

Intuitively, an edge $N \to_{\overline{X}} s$ means that by evaluating the join of the atoms in N (with some terms possibly bound to constants), values for the variables in $\overline{X}$ are obtained, and these values are passed to atom s, and are used to restrict its computation. Clearly, we can have different SIPSs for a given rule, as shown in the following example.

Example 7.5   Consider the Datalog query $\langle P, q(1, Y) \rangle$, where P is the following program:

$$q(X, Y) \leftarrow a(X, Y, Z).$$
$$q(X, Y) \leftarrow a(X, W, Z), q(Z, T), b(T, W), q(T, Y).$$
$$q(X, Y) \leftarrow b(X, Z), p(Z, Y), c(Y).$$

Here q and p are derived predicate symbols, while a, b, and c are base predicate symbols. The adorned version of the query goal is $q^{bf}(1, Y)$.

A possible SIPS for the first rule w.r.t. q^{bf} is the one consisting of the following edge:

$$\{q^{bf}(X, Y)\} \to_{\{X\}} a(X, Y, Z).$$

A SIPS for the second rule w.r.t. q^{bf} is the one consisting of the following edges:

$$\{q^{bf}(X, Y)\} \to_{\{X\}} a(X, W, Z)$$
$$\{q^{bf}(X, Y), a(X, W, Z)\} \to_{\{Z\}} q(Z, T)$$
$$\{q^{bf}(X, Y), a(X, W, Z), q(Z, T)\} \to_{\{T, W\}} b(T, W)$$
$$\{q^{bf}(X, Y), a(X, W, Z), q(Z, T), b(T, W)\} \to_{\{T\}} q(T, Y).$$

Notice that this is a SIPS for the second rule w.r.t. q^{bf} as:

- all edges satisfy the conditions stated in the first bullet of Definition 7.4. For instance, consider the last edge above (an analogous reasoning can be applied to all other edges). The left-hand side of $\to_{\{T\}}$ contains $q^{bf}(X, Y)$ and atoms in the body of the second rule, while the right-hand side is an atom in the body of the second rule. Moreover,

    - T appears in $q(T, Y)$;

- T appears in $\{a(X, W, Z), q(Z, T), b(T, W)\}$; and
- each atom in $\{q^{bf}(X, Y), a(X, W, Z), q(Z, T), b(T, W)\}$ is connected to $q(T, Y)$. Notice that $b(T, W)$ is connected to $q(T, Y)$ because they share the same variable T. For the same reason, $q(Z, T)$ is connected to $q(T, Y)$. Then, $a(X, W, Z)$ is connected to $q(T, Y)$ because it shares variable Z with $q(Z, T)$, which is connected to $q(T, Y)$. Finally, $q^{bf}(X, Y)$ is connected to $q(T, Y)$ as they share variable Y.

• The total order $q^{bf}(X, Y), a(X, W, Z), q(Z, T), b(T, W), q(T, Y)$ satisfies the conditions in second bullet of Definition 7.4.

Another possible SIPS for the second rule w.r.t. q^{bf} might be the following:

$$\{q^{bf}(X, Y)\} \to_{\{X\}} a(X, W, Z)$$
$$\{a(X, W, Z)\} \to_{\{Z\}} q(Z, T)$$
$$\{q(Z, T)\} \to_{\{T\}} b(T, W)$$
$$\{b(T, W)\} \to_{\{T\}} q(T, Y).$$

There is a subtle difference between the two SIPSs for the second rule reported above. In the first one, the last three edges specify that each atom in the body of the rule receives some information based on the evaluation of the *conjunction* of the body atoms to its left. However, in the second SIPS, although $q(Z, T)$ passes ground values for T to $b(T, W)$ (see the third edge), the ground values for W that are generated need not be the same set of ground values for W computed by evaluating $a(X, W, Z)$ from the previous edge. It is only when all the tuples for the body atoms are joined at the end that the compatible values of W from b and a are reconciled (unified).

A possible SIPS for the third rule w.r.t. q^{bf} is the one consisting of the following edges:

$$\{q^{bf}(X, Y)\} \to_{\{X\}} b(X, Z)$$
$$\{q^{bf}(X, Y), b(X, Z)\} \to_{\{Z\}} p(Z, Y)$$
$$\{q^{bf}(X, Y), b(X, Z), p(Z, Y)\} \to_{\{Y\}} c(Y).$$

For ease of presentation, we omit explicit SIPSs and assume a default SIPS for every rule, according to which if the tail of an edge contains a body atom A, then it also includes all atoms to the left of A in the rule (including the head). We also assume that all SIPSs have been *normalized* as follows. Given n SIPS edges of the form

$$N_1 \to_{\overline{X}_1} s$$
$$N_2 \to_{\overline{X}_2} s$$
$$\vdots$$
$$N_n \to_{\overline{X}_n} s.$$

The *normalized edge* for s is

$$N_1 \cup N_2 \cup \cdots \cup N_n \to_{\cup_{i=1}^n \overline{X}_i} s.$$

Algorithm 4 Adornment

Input: A Datalog query $\langle P, g(t_1, \ldots, t_m) \rangle$ and a set S of SIPSs

Output: An (adorned) Datalog query $\langle P^\mu, g^\alpha(t_1, \ldots, t_m) \rangle$ and a set S' of SIPSs

1: $g^\alpha(t_1, \ldots, t_m) = adorn(g(t_1, \ldots, t_m))$;
2: $N = \{g^\alpha\}$;
3: $P^\mu = \emptyset; \quad D = \emptyset; \quad S' = \emptyset$;
4: **while** $N \neq \emptyset$ **do**
5:      move an adorned predicate symbol q^β from N to D;
6:      **for each** rule $r \in def(q, P)$ **do**
7:          let r' be a copy of r;
8:          let $S(r)$ be a copy of the SIPS associated with r w.r.t. q^β;
9:          replace q with q^β in the head of r';
10:          **for each** derived atom $p(v_1, \ldots, v_k)$ in the body of r' **do**
11:             $\gamma = adornment(p(v_1, \ldots, v_k), S(r))$;
12:             replace $p(v_1, \ldots, v_k)$ in both r' and $S(r)$ by $p^\gamma(v_1, \ldots, v_k)$;
13:             **if** $p^\gamma \notin D$ **then**
14:                 $N = N \cup \{p^\gamma\}$;
15:          $P^\mu = P^\mu \cup \{r'\}$;
16:          $S' = S' \cup \{S(r)\}$;
17: **return** $\langle P^\mu, g^\alpha(t_1, \ldots, t_m) \rangle$ and S';

The adornment of a Datalog query is performed by Algorithm 4. It takes as input a Datalog query $\langle P, g(t_1, \ldots, t_m) \rangle$ and a set S of SIPSs for the rules of P, and gives as output an adorned Datalog query $\langle P^\mu, g^\alpha(t_1, \ldots, t_m) \rangle$ and a set S' of SIPSs for the rules of P^μ.

Algorithm 4 maintains a set P^μ of adorned rules obtained by adorning rules of P, a set N of adorned predicate symbols not yet defined in P^μ, a set D of adorned predicate symbols defined in P^μ, and a set S' of SIPSs for the rules in P^μ. Initially, D is empty and N contains the adorned predicate symbol corresponding to the query goal. Then, the algorithm iteratively moves a predicate symbol q^β from N to D and adds to P^μ the rules defining q in P adorned with respect to β. Moreover, SIPSs from S are added to S' by replacing predicate symbols with adorned predicate symbols.

Function $adornment(p(v_1, \ldots, v_k), S(r))$ on line 11 takes a (derived) atom $p(v_1, \ldots, v_k)$ from the body of a rule r and the SIPS $S(r)$ associated with r, and returns an adornment $\gamma = \gamma_1 \ldots \gamma_k$ according to the following rule: Let $N \rightarrow_{\overline{X}} p(v_1, \ldots, v_k)$ be an edge in $S(r)$ (if such an edge does not exist, then $\overline{X}$ is assumed to be empty). If $v_i \in \overline{X}$ or v_i is a constant, then set γ_i to b, otherwise set γ_i to f, for $1 \leq i \leq k$.

Given a Datalog query $Q = \langle P, G \rangle$ and a set S of SIPSs, the *adorned version* of Q w.r.t. S, denoted $Adorn(Q, S)$, is the adorned Datalog query returned by Algorithm Adornment when called with Q and S as input.

Example 7.6 The adorned version of the Datalog query and the SIPSs of Example 7.5 (for the second rule, the first SIPS reported in Example 7.5 is considered) is $\langle P', q^{bf}(1, Y) \rangle$, where P' consists of the following rules:

$$q^{bf}(X, Y) \leftarrow a(X, Y, Z).$$
$$q^{bf}(X, Y) \leftarrow a(X, W, Z), q^{bf}(Z, T), b(T, W), q^{bf}(T, Y).$$
$$q^{bf}(X, Y) \leftarrow b(X, Z), p^{bf}(Z, Y), c(Y).$$

Notice that base atoms are not adorned as the **for each** loop in lines 10–14 considers only derived atoms. If we consider a different order for the body atoms of the third rule (and thus a different SIPS), where base atoms precede the derived atom, the adorned version of the rule is

$$q^{bf}(X, Y) \leftarrow b(X, Z), c(Y), p^{bb}(Z, Y).$$

An important property of the adornment step discussed above is that the adorned version of a Datalog query is equivalent to the original one [Balbin et al., 1991, Beeri and Ramakrishnan, 1991]. Recall that two Datalog queries are equivalent iff they give the same result for every database (cf. Section 3.4).

Thus far, we have seen how the first step of the magic-sets rewriting is performed, that is, how to derive an adorned Datalog query Q' from the original one. After Q' has been generated, the magic-sets rewriting proceeds by introducing new adorned atoms (called *magic atoms*) into the bodies of the adorned rules of Q' and introducing new rules (called *magic rules*) defining the new adorned atoms.

The new adorned atoms are related to the adorned atoms appearing in Q' as follows: if A is an adorned atom of the form $q^{\alpha_1 \cdots \alpha_n}(t_1, \ldots, t_n)$ appearing in Q', then the new adorned atom is obtained from A by replacing predicate symbol $q^{\alpha_1 \cdots \alpha_n}$ with the predicate symbol $magic\_q^{\alpha_1 \cdots \alpha_n}$ and deleting the variables t_i s.t. $\alpha_i = f$, for $1 \leq i \leq n$ (thus, the arity of $magic\_q^{\alpha_1 \cdots \alpha_n}$ is less than or equal to n). For instance, given the adorned atom $p^{bfb}(X, Y, Z)$, the magic atom is $magic\_p^{bfb}(X, Z)$, that is, the second term has been eliminated since the second symbol in the adornment is f. Given an adorned atom A, $magic(A)$ denotes the magic atom derived from A.

Algorithm 5 performs the magic-sets rewriting. It takes as input the adorned Datalog query and the set of SIPSs returned by Algorithm 4; it gives as output a new Datalog query. For Algorithm 5, initially, P' is empty. Then, for each adorned rule in P^{μ}, a modified rule and a set of magic rules (one for each edge in the associated SIPS) are added to P'. In the algorithm, for a SIPS edge $N \rightarrow_{\overline{X}} s$, we use $conj(N)$ to denote the conjunction of the atoms in N.

Consider a Datalog query Q and a set S of SIPSs, and let Q' and S' be the adorned Datalog query and the set of SIPSs returned by Adornment(Q, S). We denote by $magicRew(Q, S)$ the

---

Algorithm 5 Magic-sets

Input: An adorned query $\langle P^\mu, g^\alpha(t_1, \ldots, t_m) \rangle$ and a set S of SIPSs
Output: An adorned query $\langle P', g^\alpha(t_1, \ldots, t_m) \rangle$
  1: $P' = \emptyset$;
  2: **for each** rule $r \in P^\mu$ **do**
  3:     add the rule $head(r) \leftarrow magic(head(r)), body(r)$ to P';
  4:     **for each** edge $N \rightarrow_{\overline{X}} s$ in the SIPS associated with r **do**
  5:       **if** $head(r) \in N$ **then**
  6:         add the rule $magic(s) \leftarrow magic(head(r)), conj(N - \{head(r)\})$ to P';
  7:       **else**
  8:         add the rule $magic(s) \leftarrow conj(N)$ to P';
  9: $P' = P' \cup \{magic(g^\alpha(t_1, \ldots, t_m)).\}$;
 10: **return** $\langle P', g^\alpha(t_1, \ldots, t_m) \rangle$;

---

adorned Datalog query returned by Algorithm Magic-Set when called with Q' e S' as input. Thus, the overall magic-sets rewriting for a Datalog query Q is carried out by first calling Algorithm Adornment and then calling Algorithm Magic-sets on the output of Algorithm Adornment.

An important property of the magic-sets rewriting technique is that $magicRew(Q, S)$ is equivalent to the original Datalog query Q [Balbin et al., 1991, Beeri and Ramakrishnan, 1991].

Example 7.7   Consider the Datalog query $Q = \langle P, p(1, C) \rangle$ where P consists of the following rules:

$$
\begin{aligned}
p(X, C) &\leftarrow q(X, 2, C). \\
q(X, Y, C) &\leftarrow a(X, Y, C). \\
q(X, Y, C) &\leftarrow b(X, Y, Z, W), q(Z, W, D), c(D, C).
\end{aligned}
$$

In this program, q and p are derived predicate symbols, while a, b, and c are base predicate symbols. Assume a default SIPS for every rule where if the tail of an edge contains a body atom A, then it also includes all atoms to the left of A in the rule (including the head). Let S be the set of such SIPSs. The adorned version of Q is $\langle P^\mu, p^{bf}(1, C) \rangle$ where P^μ is as follows:

$$
\begin{aligned}
p^{bf}(X, C) &\leftarrow q^{bbf}(X, 2, C). \\
q^{bbf}(X, Y, C) &\leftarrow a(X, Y, C). \\
q^{bbf}(X, Y, C) &\leftarrow b(X, Y, Z, W), q^{bbf}(Z, W, D), c(D, C).
\end{aligned}
$$

In the third rule, predicate symbol b passes the bindings from the (bound) head variables X and Y to the variables Z and W appearing in the derived atom $q(Z, W, D)$. Then, Algorithm Magic-sets returns the query $\langle P', p^{bf}(1,C)\rangle$, where P' is as follows:

$$magic\_p^{bf}(1).$$
$$magic\_q^{bbf}(X,2) \quad \leftarrow \quad magic\_p^{bf}(X).$$
$$magic\_q^{bbf}(Z,W) \quad \leftarrow \quad magic\_q^{bbf}(X,Y), b(X,Y,Z,W).$$

$$p^{bf}(X,C) \quad \leftarrow \quad magic\_p^{bf}(X), q^{bbf}(X,2,C).$$
$$q^{bbf}(X,Y,C) \quad \leftarrow \quad magic\_q^{bbf}(X,Y), a(X,Y,C).$$
$$q^{bbf}(X,Y,C) \quad \leftarrow \quad magic\_q^{bbf}(X,Y), b(X,Y,Z,W), q^{bbf}(Z,W,D), c(D,C).$$

In the example above, notice that the conjunction $magic\_q^{bbf}(X,Y), b(X,Y,Z,W)$ appears in two rules of the final program P' and, thus, it might be computed twice during the bottom-up evaluation. The *supplementary magic-sets* technique is an improvement of the magic-sets method that computes repeated conjunctions only once. As an example, the program of Example 7.7 is rewritten by introducing a new predicate symbol (called *supplementary* predicate symbol) as follows:

$$magic\_p^{bf}(1).$$
$$magic\_q^{bbf}(X,2) \quad \leftarrow \quad magic\_p^{bf}(X).$$
$$magic\_q^{bbf}(Z,W) \quad \leftarrow \quad sup\_magic(X,Y,Z,W).$$

$$sup\_magic(X,Y,Z,W) \quad \leftarrow \quad magic\_q^{bbf}(X,Y), b(X,Y,Z,W).$$

$$p^{bf}(X,C) \quad \leftarrow \quad magic\_p^{bf}(X), q^{bbf}(X,2,C).$$
$$q^{bbf}(X,Y,C) \quad \leftarrow \quad magic\_q^{bbf}(X,Y), a(X,Y,C).$$
$$q^{bbf}(X,Y,C) \quad \leftarrow \quad sup\_magic(X,Y,Z,W), q^{bbf}(Z,W,D), c(D,C).$$

The rule defining *sup_magic* computes the conjunction $magic\_q^{bbf}(X,Y), b(X,Y,Z,W)$ only once so that its results, namely $sup\_magic(X,Y,Z,W)$, is used in place of the conjunction itself.

7.2   CHAIN QUERIES

In this section, we present a method for the optimization of *chain queries*, that is, queries where bindings are propagated from the head to the body of rules in a "chain-like" fashion [Beeri et al., 1990, Dong, 1992b, Wood, 1990]. The method, called *pushdown* method [Greco et al., 1995, 1999], is based on the fact that a chain query can be associated with a context-free language, and a pushdown automaton recognizing this language can be emulated by rewriting the query as a particular left-linear program.

The method presented in this section generalizes and unifies techniques such as the *counting* [Bancilhon et al., 1986] and *right-, left-, mixed-linear* methods [Naughton et al., 1989b]. It also succeeds in reducing many nonlinear queries to equivalent linear ones.

Using general optimization methods (e.g., the magic-sets rewriting discussed in the previous section) for chain queries does not allow us to take advantage of the chain structure, thereby resulting in inefficient query evaluation. Therefore, as chain queries are rather frequent in practice (e.g., in graph applications), there is a need for ad-hoc optimization methods. Several specialized methods for chain queries have been proposed [Afrati and Cosmadakis, 1989, Beeri et al., 1990, Dong, 1992b, Wood, 1990, Yannakakis, 1990]. These methods do not fully exploit possible bindings. One method that is particularly specialized for bound chain queries is the *counting* method [Bancilhon et al., 1986]. However, this method, although proposed in the context of general queries [Haddad and Naughton, 1991, Saccà and Zaniolo, 1987, 1988], preserves the original simplicity and efficiency [Bancilhon et al., 1986, Marchetti-Spaccamela et al., 1991, Ullman, 1989] only for a subset of chain queries whose recursive rules are linear.

The approach proposed in this section exploits the relationship between chain queries and context-free languages. We will show that classical grammar transformations can be applied to optimize queries. Moreover, the relationship between context-free languages and pushdown automata allows us to rewrite chain queries into a format that is more suitable for the bottom-up evaluation.

Besides giving an efficient execution scheme to bound chain queries and providing an extension of the counting method, another nice property of the presented method is that it introduces a unified framework for the treatment of special cases, such as the factorization of right-, left-, mixed-linear programs (see Naughton et al. [1989b]), as well as the linearization of non-linear programs. A number of specialized techniques for the above special cases are known in the literature [Ioannidis, 1992, Ioannidis and Wong, 1988, Naughton et al., 1989a,b, Saraiya, 1989, Troy et al., 1989, Wood, 1990]. Given the importance and frequency of these special situations in practical applications, novel deductive systems call for the usage of a unique method that includes all advantages of the various specialized techniques.

Before presenting the pushdown method, we introduce some notation and terminology. Given a Datalog program P, we say that a rule r in P with p as head predicate symbol is

- *recursive* if p is mutually recursive with some predicate symbol in the body of r;

- *linear* if there is at most one atom in the body of r whose predicate symbol is mutually recursive with p;

- *left-recursive* (resp. *right-recursive*) if the predicate symbol of the first (resp. last) atom in the body is mutually recursive with p.

If r is linear and left-recursive (resp. right-recursive), then it is also-called *left-linear* (resp. *right-linear*).

Example 7.8   Consider the following Datalog program:

$$sg(X_0, Y_0) \leftarrow a(X_0, Y_0).$$
$$sg(X_0, Y_2) \leftarrow b(X_0, Y_0), sg(Y_0, X_1), c(X_1, Y_1), sg(Y_1, X_2), d(X_2, Y_2).$$

The first rule is not recursive, as the only predicate symbol in the body is a, which is not mutually recursive with the head predicate symbol sg. Thus, the rule is linear. Moreover, the rule is neither left-recursive nor right-recursive.

Consider now the second rule. Notice that predicate symbol sg is mutually recursive with itself. Thus, the second rule is recursive, as sg appears in the head and in the body. The rule is not linear, as there are two atoms in the body whose predicate symbol is sg. Also, the rule is neither left-recursive nor right-recursive, as the first body atom's predicate symbol is b and the last body atom's predicate symbol is d, both of which are not mutually recursive with the head predicate symbol sg.

Given a Datalog program P and a set $\mathbf{q}$ of derived predicate symbols occurring in P, a rule r of P is a $\mathbf{q}$-*chain rule* if it is of the form:

$$p_0(\overline{X}_0, \overline{Y}_n) \leftarrow a_0(\overline{X}_0, \overline{Y}_0), q_1(\overline{Y}_0, \overline{X}_1), a_1(\overline{X}_1, \overline{Y}_1), q_2(\overline{Y}_1, \overline{X}_2), \ldots,$$
$$a_{n-1}(\overline{X}_{n-1}, \overline{Y}_{n-1}), q_{n-1}(\overline{Y}_{n-1}, \overline{X}_n), a_n(\overline{X}_n, \overline{Y}_n).$$

where $n \geq 0$, the $\overline{X}_i$'s and $\overline{Y}_i$'s are non-empty lists of distinct variables, the $a_i(\overline{X}_i, \overline{Y}_i)$'s are (possibly empty) conjunction of atoms whose predicate symbols are not in $\mathbf{q}$ and are not mutually recursive with p_0, and the q_i's are (not necessarily distinct) predicate symbols in $\mathbf{q}$. We require that the lists of variables are pairwise disjoint; moreover, for each i ($0 \leq i \leq n$), if $a_i(\overline{X}_i, \overline{Y}_i)$ is empty then $\overline{Y}_i = \overline{X}_i$, otherwise the variables occurring in the conjunction include all those in $\overline{X}_i$ and $\overline{Y}_i$ plus possibly other variables that do not occur elsewhere in the rule. For instance, the two rules of Example 7.8 above are $\{sg\}$-chain rules.

If $n = 0$, then r reduces to $p_0(\overline{X}_0, \overline{Y}_0) \leftarrow a_0(\overline{X}_0, \overline{Y}_0)$ and is called an *exit chain rule*. In all other cases (i.e., $n > 0$), r is called a *recurrence chain* rule. Observe that a chain rule is left-recursive (resp. right-recursive) iff $a_0(\overline{X}_0, \overline{Y}_0)$ (resp. $a_n(\overline{X}_n, \overline{Y}_n)$) is the empty conjunction and q_1 (resp. q_{n-1}) is mutually recursive with p_0. For instance, the first rule in Example 7.8 is an exit chain rule, while the second one is a recurrence chain rule.

A Datalog program P is a $\mathbf{q}$-*chain program* if for each predicate symbol p in $\mathbf{q}$, every rule with p in the head is a $\mathbf{q}$-chain rule and for each two atoms $p(\overline{X}, \overline{Y})$ and $p(\overline{Z}, \overline{W})$ occurring in the body or the head of $\mathbf{q}$-chain rules, $\overline{X} = \overline{Z}$ and $\overline{Y} = \overline{W}$ modulo renaming of the variables.

A $\mathbf{q}$-*bound chain Datalog query* (or simply *chain query* when $\mathbf{q}$ is clear from the context or is not relevant) Q is a Datalog query $\langle P, p(\overline{b}, \overline{Y}) \rangle$, where P is a $\mathbf{q}$-chain program, p is a predicate symbol in $\mathbf{q}$, $\overline{b}$ is a list of constants, and $\overline{Y}$ is a list of variables.

In the following we present a method which, given a $\mathbf{q}$-bound chain Datalog query $\langle P, p(\overline{b}, \overline{Y}) \rangle$, constructs an equivalent left-linear query. The obtained query can be implemented efficiently using the bottom-up fixpoint computation. In order to guarantee that the binding $\overline{b}$ is propagated through all $\mathbf{q}$-chain rules, we will assume that

- $\mathbf{q} = \{p\} \cup \mathbf{q}'$ for some $\mathbf{q}'$;

- $\mathbf{q}' \subseteq leq(p)^2$; and

---

[2]Recall that $leq(p)$ denotes the set of all predicate symbols p depends on.

- for each q in $\mathbf{q}$, every $q' \in leq(p)$ s.t. $q \leq q'$ is in $\mathbf{q}$ as well.

Moreover, in order to restrict optimization to those portions which depend on some recursion, we will also assume that for each q in $\mathbf{q}$, there exists at least one recursive predicate symbol q' in $\mathbf{q}$ s.t. $q' \leq q$.

7.2.1   THE PUSHDOWN METHOD

The *pushdown method* is based on the analogy of chain queries and context-free grammars [Ullman, 1992]. Without loss of generality we assume that each list of variables in chain rules consist of one variable and that the first argument of the query goal is a constant whereas the second one is a variable. Thus, all considered predicate symbols are binary. We start by introducing the basic idea in the following example.

Example 7.9   Consider the chain query $Q = \langle P, sg(1, Y)\rangle$, where P is the (non-linear) program of Example 7.8. A context-free language corresponding to this program is generated by the following grammar[3]

$$G(Q) = \langle V_N, V_T, \Pi, sg\rangle$$

where the set of non-terminal symbols V_N contains only sg, the set of terminal symbols V_T is $\{a, b, c, d\}$, and Π consists of the following production rules:

$$
\begin{aligned}
sg &\rightarrow a \\
sg &\rightarrow b\ sg\ c\ sg\ d
\end{aligned}
$$

Note that the production rules in Π are obtained from the rules of P by dropping the arguments of predicate symbols and reversing the arrow. The language $L(Q)$ generated by this grammar can be recognized by the automaton shown in Figure 7.1.

  This automaton can in turn be implemented by the following program $\hat{\Pi}$ (where function symbols are used)

[3]We refer the reader to Hopcroft and Ullman [1979] for a treatment of automata theory and languages.

	b	c	d	a	ϵ
(q_0, Z_0)					$(q,\ sg\ Z_0)$
(q, sg)	$(q,\ sg\ c\ sg\ d)$			$(q,\ \epsilon)$	
(q, c)		$(q,\ \epsilon)$			
(q, d)			$(q,\ \epsilon)$		

Figure 7.1: Pushdown Automaton for the query of Example 7.9.

$$q([sg]).$$
$$q(T) \leftarrow q([sg \mid T]), a.$$
$$q([sg, c, sg, d \mid T]) \leftarrow q([sg \mid T]), b.$$
$$q(T) \leftarrow q([c \mid T]), c.$$
$$q(T) \leftarrow q([d \mid T]), d.$$

We can now derive a program $\hat{P}$ by reintroducing variables into $\hat{\Pi}$—the derived program will be used as part of a query equivalent to the original one. Specifically, variables X and Y are added to the non-recursive predicate symbols. For the recursive predicate symbol, we add the variable Y to the occurrences of the predicate symbol in the head, and the variable X to the occurrences of the predicate symbol in the body. The resulting program $\hat{P}$ is:

$$q(1, [sg]).$$
$$q(Y, T) \leftarrow q(X, [sg \mid T]), a(X, Y).$$
$$q(Y, [sg, c, sg, d \mid T]) \leftarrow q(X, [sg \mid T]), b(X, Y).$$
$$q(Y, T) \leftarrow q(X, [c \mid T]), c(X, Y).$$
$$q(Y, T) \leftarrow q(X, [d \mid T]), d(X, Y).$$

The query $\langle \hat{P}, q(Y, []) \rangle$ is equivalent to the original one. Observe that the rewritten program is not a Datalog program anymore as function symbols have been used (see Chapter 5).

We now present how the technique works in general. We start by defining the context-free language associated with a **q**-chain query $Q = \langle P, p(b, Y) \rangle$. Let V be the set of all predicate symbols occurring in the **q**-chain rules. The set V_N of non-terminal symbols is **q** and the set of terminal symbols is $V_T = V - V_N$. We associate with Q the context-free language $L(Q)$ on the alphabet V_T defined by the grammar $G(Q) = \langle V_N, V_T, \Pi, p \rangle$ where the production rules in Π are defined as follows.

For each **q**-chain rule r_j of the form:

$$p_0^j(X_0, Y_n) \leftarrow a_0^j(X_0, Y_0), p_1^j(Y_0, X_1), a_1^j(X_1, Y_1), \ldots, p_{n-1}^j(Y_{n-1}, X_n), a_n^j(X_n, Y_n).$$

with $n \geq 0$, the following production rule is generated:

$$p_0^j \rightarrow a_0^j \; p_1^j \; a_1^j \; \cdots \; p_{n-1}^j \; a_n^j.$$

The language $L(Q)$ is recognized by a pushdown automaton defined as follows:

- it has two states q_0 and q, which are, respectively, the initial and the final state; and

- the transition table has one column for each symbol in V_T plus a column for the ϵ symbol, one row for the pair (q_0, Z_0), where Z_0 is the starting pushdown symbol, and one row (q, v) for each $v \in V$.

Figure 7.2 illustrates the transition table. Note that, for the sake of presentation, the pushdown alphabet is not distinct from the language alphabet. The last entry in the first row corresponds to the start up of the pushdown automaton and consists of entering the query goal predicate symbol p in the pushdown store. The remaining rows corresponds to the generic **q**-chain rule r_j shown above; specifically, we have one row for a_0^j and one row for each a_i^j, $1 \leq i \leq n$, that is not empty. Obviously, if the rule is an exit rule (i.e., $n = 0$), the entry corresponding to a_0^j is (q, ϵ).

		a_0^j	a_1^j	$\cdots$	a_n^j	ϵ
(q_0, Z_0)						$(q, p\, Z_0)$
$\cdots$						
(q, p_0^j)		$(q, p_1^j a_1^j \cdots p_{n-1}^j a_n^j)$				
(q, a_1^j)			(q, ϵ)			
$\cdots$						
(q, a_n^j)					(q, ϵ)	
$\cdots$						

Figure 7.2: Pushdown automaton recognizing $L(Q)$.

Given a string $\alpha = a_{i_1}^{k_1} a_{i_2}^{k_2} \cdots a_{i_m}^{k_m}$ in V_T^*, a *path spelling* α on P is a sequence of $m + 1$ (not necessarily distinct) constants $b_0, b_1, b_2, \ldots, b_m$ such that for each j, $1 \leq j \leq m$, $a_{i_j}^{k_j}(b_{j-1}, b_j)$ is an atom in the least model of P; if $m = 0$ then the path spells the empty string ϵ [Afrati and Cosmadakis, 1989].

It is well known that, given a database D, a ground atom $p(b, c)$ belongs to $Q(D)$ if and only if there exists a path from b to c spelling a string α of $L(Q)$ on P. Therefore, in order to compute $Q(D)$, it is sufficient to use the automaton of Figure 7.2 to recognize all paths leaving from b and spelling a string α of $L(Q)$ on P [Afrati and Cosmadakis, 1989]. This can be easily done by a logic program $\hat{P}$ which implements the automaton. In fact, $\hat{P}$ can be directly constructed using all transition rules of Figure 7.2. Specifically, we use a rule for each entry in the table. The start-up of the automaton is simulated by a fact which sets both the initial node of the path spelling a string of the language and the initial state of the pushdown store. For the chain query $Q = \langle P, p(b, Y) \rangle$, the resulting program $\hat{P}$ is as follows:

$$q(b, [p]).$$
$$\cdots$$
$$q(Y, [p_1^j, a_1^j, \ldots, p_{n-1}^j, a_n^j | T]) \quad \leftarrow \quad q(X, [p_0^j | T]), a_0^j(X, Y).$$
$$q(Y, T) \quad \leftarrow \quad q(X, [a_1^j | T]), a_1^j(X, Y).$$
$$\cdots$$
$$q(Y, T) \quad \leftarrow \quad q(X, [a_n^j | T]), a_n^j(X, Y).$$
$$\cdots$$

Program $\hat{P}$ will be called the *pushdown program* of the Datalog query Q; the query $\hat{Q} = \langle \hat{P}, q(Y, []) \rangle$ will be called the *pushdown query* of Q. The technique for constructing pushdown-queries will be called the *pushdown method*. Here one important property is that Q is equivalent to its pushdown query [Greco et al., 1999].

We point out that a naive execution of the rewritten program can sometimes be ineffi-cient or even non-terminating for cyclic databases. In Section 7.2.5 we will present a technique, based on the approach of Greco and Zaniolo [1992], where lists implementing pushdown stores are represented as pairs consisting of the head and a pointer to the tuple storing the tail of the list. In this way, each possible cyclic sequence in the pushdown store is recorded only once and termination is guaranteed.

7.2.2   RIGHT-LINEAR PROGRAMS

The pushdown method is based on constructing a particular pushdown automaton to recognize a context-free language.

Let us consider the case of a chain query Q for which every recursive chain rule is *right-linear*, that is, both right-recursive and linear. Then, the associated grammar $G(Q)$ is regular right-linear (see Hopcroft and Ullman [1979] for more details) and, therefore, the pushdown actually acts as a finite state automaton. Indeed, if the query is right-linear, then the pushdown store either is empty or contains only one symbol. Therefore, it is possible to delete the pushdown store and put the information of the pushdown store into the states.

Of course, for right-linear chain queries, it is possible to generate directly the push-down query which works as a finite state automaton. Thus, given a chain right-linear query $Q = \langle P, p(b, Y) \rangle$, the pushdown query is $\langle \hat{P}, p_F(Y) \rangle$ where $\hat{P}$ consists of:

- a fact of the form

$$q(b);$$

- a rule of the form

$$q'(Y) \leftarrow q(X), a(X, Y).$$

  for each production rule of the form $q \to a\, q'$ in $G(Q)$ with q and q' being mutually recur-sive; and

- a rule of the form

$$q_F(Y) \leftarrow q(X), a(X, Y).$$

  for each production rule of the form $q \to a$ in $G(Q)$.

The query obtained as described above is called the *finite state query* of Q.

Example 7.10   Consider the chain query $Q = \langle P, p(c, Y) \rangle$, where P is:

$$p(X, Y) \leftarrow b(X, Y).$$
$$p(X, Y) \leftarrow a(X, Z), p(Z, Y).$$

The grammar $G(Q)$ is regular right-linear and is as follows:

$$p \rightarrow b \mid a \; p.$$

The pushdown automaton recognizing $L(Q)$ is as follows

	a	b	ϵ
(q_0, Z_0)			$(q, p \, Z_0)$
(q, p)	(q, p)	(q, ϵ)	

The pushdown query of Q is $\hat{Q} = \langle \hat{P}, q(Y, [\,]) \rangle$ with $\hat{P}$ as follows:

$$
\begin{aligned}
q(c, [p]). & \\
q(Y, [p]) \;\; &\leftarrow \;\; q(X, [p]), a(X, Y). \\
q(Y, [\,]) \;\; &\leftarrow \;\; q(X, [p]), b(X, Y).
\end{aligned}
$$

By deleting the pushdown store and putting its information into the state we obtain the query $\langle \hat{P}', q(Y) \rangle$ where $\hat{P}'$ is as follows:

$$
\begin{aligned}
q_p(c). & \\
q_p(Y) \;\; &\leftarrow \;\; q_p(X), a(X, Y). \\
q(Y) \;\; &\leftarrow \;\; q_p(X), b(X, Y).
\end{aligned}
$$

Observe that the language $L(Q)$ can be recognized by a finite state automaton whose transition function is as follows:

$$
\begin{aligned}
\delta(p, a) \;\; &\rightarrow \;\; p \\
\delta(p, b) \;\; &\rightarrow \;\; p_F,
\end{aligned}
$$

where p and p_F denote the initial state and the final state, respectively. The finite state query of Q is $\langle \hat{P}'', p_F(Y) \rangle$ where $\hat{P}''$ is the following program:

$$
\begin{aligned}
p(c). & \\
p(Y) \;\; &\leftarrow \;\; p(X), a(X, Y). \\
p_F(Y) \;\; &\leftarrow \;\; p(X), b(X, Y).
\end{aligned}
$$

Thus, for right-linear queries the pushdown method does not use any pushdown store and the pushdown query of Q reduces to the finite state query of Q. Given a **q**-chain query Q such that $G(Q)$ is right-linear, the finite state query of Q is equivalent to Q [Greco et al., 1999].

7.2.3 GRAMMAR TRANSFORMATIONS TO IMPROVE PUSHDOWN

In this section, we demonstrate that the use of automata becomes more effective if the grammar of the language has a particular structure. More interestingly, we show that if the grammar does not have this structure, then the program can be rewritten so that the corresponding grammar achieves the desired structure. The rewriting is mainly done by applying known techniques for transforming grammars.

Observe that, for a Datalog query Q, if the grammar $G(Q)$ is regular left-linear, then the pushdown method does not emulate a finite state automaton, as opposed to the case where $G(Q)$ is regular right-linear, and it may become rather inefficient or even non-terminating. As shown in the following, we can overcome this problem by replacing left-recursion with right-recursion applying well-known reduction techniques for grammars.

Consider a **q**-chain query $Q = \langle P, p(b, Y) \rangle$ and suppose that a predicate symbol $s \in \mathbf{q}$ is in the head of some left-recursive chain rule—in this case, we say that s is *left-recursive*. Then, the definition $def(s, P)$ of s consists of $m > 0$ left-recursive chain rules and n chain rules that are not left-recursive, that is, $def(s, P)$ is as follows (below we assume $n > 0$ for the sake of simplicity):

$$
\begin{aligned}
s(X, Y) &\leftarrow \alpha_i(X, Y). & 1 \leq i \leq n \\
s(X, Y) &\leftarrow s'(X, Z), \beta_i(Z, Y). & 1 \leq i \leq m,
\end{aligned}
$$

where $\alpha_i(X, Y)$ and $\beta_i(Z, Y)$ are conjunctions of atoms. The production rules defining the symbol s in the grammar $G(Q)$ are:

$$
\begin{aligned}
s &\to \alpha_i & 1 \leq i \leq n \\
s &\to s' \beta_i & 1 \leq i \leq m,
\end{aligned}
$$

where α_i and β_i denote the sequences of predicate symbols appearing in $\alpha_i(X, Y)$ and $\beta_i(Z, Y)$, respectively. We can apply known transformations to remove left-recursion from the second group of production rules for all left-recursive predicate symbols s; we then write the corresponding Datalog rules accordingly. It turns out that the resulting program, which is said to be in *canonical form* and is denoted by $can(P)$, does not contain any left-recursive **q**-chain rule. Moreover, $\langle P, p(b, Y) \rangle$ is equivalent to $\langle can(P), p(b, Y) \rangle$ [Greco et al., 1999].

Example 7.11   Consider the following left-linear **q**-chain query $Q = \langle P, path(b, Y) \rangle$, where $\mathbf{q} = \{path\}$ and P contains the following two rules:

$$
\begin{aligned}
path(X, Y) &\leftarrow edge(X, Y). \\
path(X, Y) &\leftarrow path(X, Z), edge(Z, Y).
\end{aligned}
$$

Program P computes the transitive closure of the binary relation *edge* and is left-linear. The associated grammar $G(Q)$ is

$$
path \to edge \mid path\ edge
$$

and is left-recursive. To remove left-recursion, the grammar above can be rewritten into the following right-recursive grammar:

$$
\begin{aligned}
path &\to edge\ path' \\
path' &\to edge\ path' \mid \epsilon.
\end{aligned}
$$

So, the program $can(P)$ is:

$$path(X, Y) \leftarrow edge(X, Z), path'(Z, Y).$$
$$path'(X, X).$$
$$path'(X, Y) \leftarrow edge(X, Z), path'(Z, Y)$$

and is right-linear. Therefore, the pushdown query can be now solved efficiently.

Notice that the rule $path'(X, X)$ does not satisfy the safety condition for Datalog programs (cf. Section 3.1) because variable X is not limited—the reason is that the rule body is empty. However, the rule might be made safe by adding the atom $edge(Y, X)$ in the body, without altering the semantics of the query. In general, we can add suitable atoms in the body of rules in $can(P)$ specifying what are the values that the variables appearing only in the head can take.

Example 7.12 Assume now that program P of Example 7.11 is defined as the following non-linear program:

$$path(X, Y) \leftarrow edge(X, Y).$$
$$path(X, Y) \leftarrow path(X, Z), path(Z, Y).$$

This program is left-recursive and, after the first step of the procedure for removing left-recursion, is rewritten as follows:

$$r_1 : \; path(X, Y) \leftarrow edge(X, Z), path'(Z, Y).$$
$$r_2 : \; path'(X, X).$$
$$r_3 : \; path'(X, Y) \leftarrow path(X, Z), path'(Z, Y).$$

The second step removes left recursion from rule r_3 by rewriting it as follows:

$$path'(X, Y) \leftarrow edge(X, W), path'(W, Z), path'(Z, Y).$$

We now introduce a program transformation that improves the performance of the pushdown method for an interesting case of right-recursion. Suppose that there exists a predicate symbol s in P such that $def(s, P)$ consists of a single chain rule of the form $s(X, X)$ and $m > 0$ right-recursive chain rules of the form:

$$s(X, Y) \leftarrow \alpha_i(X, Z), s(Z, Y). \quad 1 \le i \le m.$$

We rewrite each recursive chain rule that is in the following format:

$$s(X, Y) \leftarrow \alpha_i(X, Z), s(Z, W), s(W, Y).$$

as follows:

$$s(X, Y) \leftarrow \alpha_i(X, Z), s(Z, Y).$$

That is, we drop one occurrence of the recursive atoms at the end of the rule. If the resulting rule has still multiple recursive atoms at the end, we repeat the transformation. The program obtained after performing the above transformations for all the predicate symbols s in P is denoted by $simple(P)$. Then, $\langle P, p(b, Y) \rangle$ is equivalent to $\langle simple(P), p(b, Y) \rangle$ [Greco et al., 1999].

Example 7.13   Consider the program $P' = can(P)$ of Example 7.12 which is reported below:

$$
\begin{aligned}
r_1 :\ & path(X, Y)\ \leftarrow\ edge(X, Z), path'(Z, Y). \\
r_2 :\ & path'(X, X). \\
r_3 :\ & path'(X, Y)\ \leftarrow\ edge(X, W), path'(W, Z), path'(Z, Y).
\end{aligned}
$$

Clearly, $def(path', P') = \{r_2, r_3\}$. Then, $simple(P')$ is as follows:

$$
\begin{aligned}
& path(X, Y)\ \leftarrow\ edge(X, Z), path'(Z, Y). \\
& path'(X, X). \\
& path'(X, Y)\ \leftarrow\ edge(X, W), path'(W, Y).
\end{aligned}
$$

Thus, we have eventually linearized the non-linear transitive closure.

We observe that the transformation $simple$ can be applied to a larger number of cases by applying further grammar rewriting. For instance, given the grammar:

$$
\begin{aligned}
s\ & \rightarrow\ a\, s' \\
s'\ & \rightarrow\ b\, s\, s' \mid \epsilon.
\end{aligned}
$$

We can modify it into:

$$
\begin{aligned}
s\ & \rightarrow\ a\, s' \\
s'\ & \rightarrow\ b\, a\, s'\, s' \mid \epsilon
\end{aligned}
$$

so that we can eventually apply the transformation $simple$.

Example 7.14   Consider the $\{path\}$-chain query $Q = \langle P, path(b, Y) \rangle$ where P is defined as follows:

$$
\begin{aligned}
path(X, Y)\ & \leftarrow\ yellow(X, Y). \\
path(X, Y)\ & \leftarrow\ path(X, U), red(U, V), path(V, W), blue(W, Z), path(Z, Y).
\end{aligned}
$$

Then, $can(P)$ is as follows:

$$
\begin{aligned}
& path(X, Y)\ \leftarrow\ yellow(X, Z), path'(Z, Y). \\
& path'(X, X). \\
& path'(X, Y)\ \leftarrow\ red(X, U), path(U, W), blue(W, Z), path(Z, T), path'(T, Y).
\end{aligned}
$$

We now replace the two occurrence of *path* in the body of the last rule with the body of the first rule and obtain the equivalent program P':

$$path(X, Y) \leftarrow yellow(X, Z), path'(Z, Y).$$
$$path'(X, X).$$
$$path'(X, Y) \leftarrow red(X, U), yellow(U, V), path'(V, W), blue(W, Z),$$
$$yellow(Z, S), path'(S, T), path'(T, Y).$$

We can now apply the transformation *simple* to *path'* and the last rule of P' becomes:

$$path'(X, Y) \leftarrow red(X, U), yellow(U, V), path'(V, W), bblue(W, Z), yellow(Z, S), path'(S, Y).$$

We now apply another transformation for the predicate symbols for which the transformation *simple* cannot be applied because of the lack of the chain rule of the form $s(X, X)$. Suppose that there exists a predicate symbol s in $\mathbf{q}$ such that $def(s, P)$ consists of $n > 0$ exit chain rules, say

$$s(X, Y) \leftarrow \beta_i(X, Y). \quad 1 \le i \le n$$

and $m > 0$ right-recursive chain rules of the form:

$$s(X, Y) \leftarrow \alpha_i(X, Z), s(Z, Y). \quad 1 \le i \le m$$

We rewrite the above rules as follows:

$$s(X, Y) \leftarrow s'(X, Z), \beta_i(Z, Y). \quad 1 \le i \le n$$
$$s'(X, X).$$
$$s'(X, Y) \leftarrow \alpha_i(X, Z), s'(Z, Y). \quad 1 \le i \le m.$$

We now replace atoms in α_i having s as predicate symbol with the bodies of the rules defining s. In this way, every rule will not have two consecutive recursive predicate symbols at the end of the body.

The program obtained after performing the above transformations for all the predicate symbols in P is denoted by $simple'(P)$. As shown in Greco et al. [1999], $\langle simple'(P), p(b, Y) \rangle$ is equivalent to the original chain query $\langle P, p(b, Y) \rangle$.

Example 7.15   Consider the $\{path\}$-chain query $Q = \langle P, path(b, Y) \rangle$ where P is defined as follows:

$$path(X, Y) \leftarrow yellow(X, Y).$$
$$path(X, Y) \leftarrow red(X, V), path(V, W), path(W, Y).$$

Then, $simple'(P)$ consists of the following rules:

$$path(X, Y) \leftarrow path'(X, Z), yellow(Z, Y).$$
$$path'(X, X).$$
$$path'(X, Y) \leftarrow red(X, V), path'(V, W), yellow(W, T), path'(T, Y).$$

As discussed in the next section, the form of *simple'(P)* is very effective for the performance not only of the pushdown method but also of the counting method.

7.2.4   WHEN PUSHDOWN REDUCES TO COUNTING

In this section, we describe some conditions under which the pushdown method reduces to the counting method [Bancilhon et al., 1986, Saccà and Zaniolo, 1988]. Actually, the counting method can be seen as a space-efficient implementation of the pushdown store. On the other hand, as the pushdown method has a larger application domain, we can conclude that the pushdown method is a powerful extension of the counting method.

We first observe that, given the pushdown program of a **q**-chain query, the pushdown store can be efficiently implemented whenever it contains strings of the form $\alpha^k (\beta)^n$, with $0 \leq k \leq 1$ and $n \geq 0$. Indeed, the store can be replaced by the counter n and the introduction of two new states q_α and q_β to record whether the top symbol is α or β, respectively. This situation arises when the program consists of a number of exit chain rules and right-linear chain rules, and a single linear non-left-recursive chain rule. The next example illustrates that the above implementation of the pushdown store corresponds to applying the counting method.

Example 7.16   Consider the Datalog query $\langle P, sg(d, Y) \rangle$ where P is the linear program below:

$$sg(X, Y) \leftarrow c(X, Y).$$
$$sg(X, Y) \leftarrow a(X, X1), sg(X1, Y1), b(Y1, Y).$$

The pushdown query is $\langle P', q(Y, [\,]) \rangle$, where P' is:

$$q(d, [sg]).$$
$$q(Y, [sg, b \,|\, T]) \leftarrow q(X, [sg \,|\, T]), a(X, Y).$$
$$q(Y, T) \leftarrow q(X, [sg \,|\, T]), c(X, Y).$$
$$q(Y, T) \leftarrow q(Y, [b \,|\, T]), b(X, Y).$$

Observe that the pushdown store contains strings of the form $sg(b)^n$ or of the form $(b)^n$, with $n \geq 0$. So, we replace the store with the counter n and the introduction of two new states q_{sg} and q_b to record whether the top symbol is sg or b, respectively. Therefore, the rules above can be rewritten as follows:

$$q_{sg}(d, 0).$$
$$q_{sg}(Y, I) \leftarrow q_{sg}(X, J), a(X, Y), I = J + 1.$$
$$q_b(Y, I) \leftarrow q_{sg}(X, I), c(X, Y).$$
$$q_b(Y, I) \leftarrow q_b(Y, J), b(X, Y), I = J - 1.$$

These rules are the same as those generated by the counting method. The query goal becomes $q_b(Y, 0)$.

We now show that the above counting implementation of the pushdown store can be done also when the pushdown strings are of the form $\alpha^k (\beta\alpha)^n$ where $0 \le k \le 1$ and $n \ge 0$. This situation arises when the query's program consists of a number of exit chain rules and right-linear chain rules, and a single bi-linear (i.e., the rule body contains two atoms whose predicate symbols are mutually recursive with the head predicate symbol) recursive chain rule that is right-recursive but not left-recursive, e.g., the rule might be of the form:

$$p(X_0, Y_2) \leftarrow a_0(X_0, Y_0), p(Y_0, X_1), a_1(X_1, Y_1), p(Y_1, Y_2).$$

Example 7.17 Consider the query $Q = \langle P, path(b, Y) \rangle$ where P is:

$$path(X, X).$$
$$path(X, Y) \leftarrow red(X, V), path(V, W), yellow(W, T), path(T, Y).$$

Using the counting implementation of the pushdown store, we obtain the following program:

$$q_{path}(b, 0).$$
$$q_{yellow}(X, I) \leftarrow q_{path}(X, I).$$
$$q_{path}(Y, I + 1) \leftarrow q_{path}(X, I), red(X, Y).$$
$$q_{path}(Y, I - 1) \leftarrow q_{yellow}(X, I), yellow(X, Y).$$

The query goal is $q_{yellow}(Y, 0)$. It is worth noting that the above program cannot be handled by the counting method.

7.2.5 IMPLEMENTATION AND TERMINATION

As pointed out in Section 7.2.1, the pushdown method could be inefficient or even non-terminating for cyclic databases. In this section, we show how the method can be implemented in order to guarantee efficiency and termination.

The basic idea is to "distribute" stores among facts and link the facts used to memorize the same store. Specifically, the store associated with a fact is memorized by means of two distinct elements: a list containing a block of elements in the top of the store and a *link* to a fact which can be used to derive the tail of the store. Thus, a fact of the form $q(x, [p_1, \ldots, p_n])$ is memorized as $q(x, [p_1, \ldots, p_k], Id)$ where $k \le n$ and Id is a link to some fact which permit to determine the tail $[p_{k+1}, \ldots, p_n]$ of the store.

We now present how the pushdown method is implemented. Let $Q = \langle P, p(a, Y) \rangle$ be a chain Datalog query and let $\hat{Q} = \langle P', q(Y, [\,]) \rangle$ be the pushdown query of Q. Recall that P' has rules of the form (see Section 7.2.1):

$$q(b, [p]).$$
$$\ldots$$
$$q(Y, [p_1^j, a_1^j, \ldots, p_{n-1}^j, a_n^j | T]) \leftarrow q(X, [p_0^j | T]), a_0^j(X, Y).$$
$$q(Y, T) \leftarrow q(X, [a_1^j | T]), a_1^j(X, Y).$$
$$\ldots$$
$$q(Y, T) \leftarrow q(X, [a_n^j | T]), a_n^j(X, Y).$$
$$\ldots$$

The *pushdown implementation query* of Q, denoted $I(\hat{Q})$, is the pushdown query $\langle P'', q(Y, [], nil) \rangle$ where P'' is derived from P' as follows.

1. A fact of the form
$$q(b, [p]).$$
is substituted by the following fact where *nil* is a new constant
$$q(b, [p], nil).$$

2. A rule r^j of the form
$$q(Y, [p_1^j, a_1^j, \ldots, p_n^j, a_n^j \mid T]) \leftarrow q(X, [p_0^j \mid T]), a_0^j(X, Y)$$
is substituted by the rule
$$q(Y, [p_1^j, a_1^j, \ldots, p_n^j, a_n^j], Id(X)) \leftarrow q(X, [p_0^j \mid T], I), a_0^j(X, Y),$$
where $Id(X)$ is a unique identifier associated with the list of ground tuples having X as first argument. In the following, for the sake of simplicity, we assume that $Id(X) = X$.

3. A rule r^j of the following form with $i < n$
$$q(Y, T) \leftarrow q(X, [a_i^j \mid T]), a_i^j(X, Y)$$
is substituted by the rule
$$q(Y, T, I) \leftarrow q(X, [a_i^j \mid T], I), a_i^j(X, Y).$$

4. A rule r^j of the form
$$q(Y, T) \leftarrow q(X, [a_n^j \mid T]), a_n^j(X, Y)$$
is substituted by the rule
$$q(Y, T, I) \leftarrow q(X, [a_n^j], Id(Z)), q(Z, [p \mid T], I), a_n^j(X, Y).$$

Recall that p is the predicate symbol of the goal of the original chain Datalog query.

The following example illustrates how the pushdown implementation query is carried out.

Example 7.18   Consider the query $Q = \langle P, sg(1, Y) \rangle$ of Example 7.9. As already discussed in Example 7.9, the pushdown query is $\langle \hat{P}, q(Y, [\,]) \rangle$, where $\hat{P}$ is as follows:

$$
\begin{aligned}
q(1, [sg]). & \\
q(Y, T) & \leftarrow q(X, [sg \mid T]), a(X, Y). \\
q(Y, [sg, c, sg, d \mid T]) & \leftarrow q(X, [sg \mid T]), b(X, Y). \\
q(Y, T) & \leftarrow q(X, [c \mid T]), c(X, Y). \\
q(Y, T) & \leftarrow q(X, [d \mid T]), d(X, Y).
\end{aligned}
$$

The pushdown implementation query $I(\hat{Q})$ is $\langle P'', sg(Y, [\,], nil) \rangle$ where P'' is as follows:

$$
\begin{aligned}
q(1, [sg], nil). & \\
q(Y, T, I) & \leftarrow q(X, [sg \mid T], I), a(X, Y). \\
q(Y, [sg, c, sg, d], X) & \leftarrow q(X, [sg \mid T], I), b(X, Y). \\
q(Y, T, I) & \leftarrow q(X, [c \mid T], I), c(X, Y). \\
q(Y, T, I) & \leftarrow q(X, [d], Z), q(Z, [sg \mid T], I), d(X, Y).
\end{aligned}
$$

As shown in Greco et al. [1999], $I(\hat{Q})$ is equivalent to the original query Q. Moreover, the implementation technique, besides efficiency, guarantees also termination of the evaluation process, that is, the bottom-up computation of $I(\hat{Q})$ always terminates [Greco et al., 1999].

The following example shows how queries are computed in the presence of cyclic databases.

Example 7.19   Let $I(\hat{Q}) = \langle P'', sg(Y, [\,], nil) \rangle$ be the pushdown query of Example 7.18. Consider the database pictured in Figure 7.3 where a fact $p(x, y)$ is represented by an edge from x to y with label p.

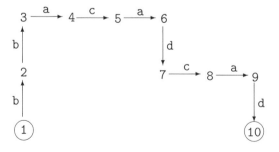

Figure 7.3: Acyclic database.

The evaluation of program P'' produces the following ground atoms: $q(1,[sg],nil)$, $q(2,[sg,c,sg,d],1)$, $q(3,[sg,c,sg,d],2)$, $q(4,[c,sg,d],2)$, $q(5,[sg,d],2)$, $q(6,[d],2)$, $q(7,[c,sg,d],1)$, $q(8,[sg,d],1)$, $q(9,[d],1)$, and $q(10,[],nil)$. Therefore, the answer is $Y = 10$.

Consider now the cyclic database pictured in Figure 7.4. The evaluation of program P'' produces the ground atoms $q(1,[sg],nil)$, $q(2,[sg,c,sg,d],1)$, $q(1,[sg,c,sg,d],2)$, $q(3,[c,sg,d],1)$, $q(4,[sg,d],1)$, $q(5,[d],1)$, $q(6,[],nil)$, $q(6,[c,sg,d],2)$, $q(7,[sg,d],2)$, $q(8,[d],2)$, $q(9,[c,sg,d],1)$, $q(10,[sg,d],1)$, $q(11,[d],1)$ and $q(10,[],nil)$. Therefore, the answers are $Y = 6$ and $Y = 12$.

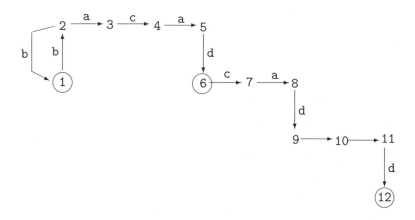

Figure 7.4: Cyclic database.

The implementation of the pushdown method can be seen as a smart implementation of the supplementary magic-sets method [Saccà and Zaniolo, 1986] (see also Beeri and Ramakrishnan [1991]). Moreover, for non-linear programs there is an important difference since the method generates less non-linear recursive rules than the supplementary magic-sets method. For instance, consider the non-linear query of Example 7.9. The program obtained by applying the supplementary magic-sets method is as follows:

$$
\begin{aligned}
m\_sg(b).\\
m\_sg(X_1) &\leftarrow s\_sg_1(Z,X_1).\\
m\_sg(Y_2) &\leftarrow s\_sg_3(Z,Y_2).\\
s\_sg_1(X,X_1) &\leftarrow m\_sg(X),b(X,X_1).\\
s\_sg_2(X,X_2) &\leftarrow s\_sg_1(X,X_1),sg(X_1,X_2).\\
s\_sg_3(X,X_3) &\leftarrow s\_sg_2(X,X_2),c(X_2,Y_2).\\
sg(X,Y) &\leftarrow m\_sg(X),a(X,Y).\\
sg(X,Y) &\leftarrow s\_sg_3(X,Y_2),sg(Y_2,Y_1),d(Y_1,Y).
\end{aligned}
$$

The rule defining predicate symbol s_sg_2 and the second rule defining predicate symbol sg are bi-linear, that is, they have two occurrences of predicate symbols mutually recursive with the head predicate symbol. The program generated by the pushdown method contains only one bi-linear rule and, therefore, its execution can be more efficient.

In the general case, given a nonlinear recursive rule having $n > 1$ occurrences of predicate symbols in its body that are mutually recursive with the head predicate symbol, the pushdown method generates only one bi-linear rule whereas the supplementary magic-sets method generates n bi-linear rules. Observe also that the space used by the pushdown method is less than that used by the supplementary magic-sets method since the pushdown method does not use *magic* predicates.

BIBLIOGRAPHIC NOTES

Magic-sets rewriting has been studied in several papers [Bancilhon and Ramakrishnan, 1988, Bancilhon et al., 1986, Beeri and Ramakrishnan, 1987, 1991, Greco and Zaniolo, 1992, 1994, Naughton et al., 1989a,b, Ramakrishnan et al., 1989, Ullman, 1989]

The analogies between chain queries and context-free languages were investigated by several authors, including [Afrati and Papadimitriou, 1987, Beeri et al., 1990, Dong, 1992a,b, Pereira and Warren, 1980, Ullman, 1992, Ullman and Van Gelder, 1986]. In particular, the use of automata to compute general logic queries was first proposed by Lang [1988]. Lang's method is based on pushing facts from the database onto the stack for later use in reverse order in the proof of a goal. As the method applies to general queries, it is not very effective for chain queries; besides, it does not exploit possible bindings.

Vieille [1989] independently proposed an extension of SLD-resolution which avoids replicated computations in the evaluation of general logic queries using stacks to perform a set-oriented computation. Also this method does not take advantage of a possible chain structure but it does exploit possible bindings.

The first proposal of a method that is both specialized for chain queries and based on the properties of context-free language is due to Yannakakis [1990], who proposed a dynamic programming technique implementing the method of Cocke-Younger and Kasami to recognize strings of general context-free languages. This technique turns out to be efficient for unbound queries but it does not support any mechanism to reduce the search space when bindings are available.

Strategies for processing and optimizing Datalog queries are discussed also in Abiteboul et al. [1995], Bancilhon and Ramakrishnan [1986], Ceri et al. [1989], Green et al. [2013], Ullman [1989].

Several extensions of the magic-sets technique have been proposed to deal with Datalog extended with stratified negation [Behrend, 2003], a restricted form of negation called modular stratification [Ross, 1994], unstratified negation [Faber et al., 2007], disjunction [Cumbo et al.,

2004], disjunction and stratified negation [Alviano et al., 2012, Greco, 1998b, 1999b, 2003], and disjunction and constraints [Greco et al., 2005].

CHAPTER 8

Applications

Recently, there has been a great deal of interest in applying Datalog in several domains [Huang et al., 2011] such as declarative networking [Loo et al., 2005a,b, 2006], network monitoring [Abiteboul et al., 2005], program analysis [Bravenboer and Smaragdakis, 2009], security [Marczak et al., 2010, Zhou et al., 2009], cloud computing [Alvaro et al., 2010], information extraction [Gottlob et al., 2004, Shen et al., 2007], P2P deductive databases [Caroprese et al., 2006], and social network analysis [Seo et al., 2013]. Specifically, these works extend the Datalog language and its implementation techniques with constructs that are particularly useful for a specific domain.

The arguments in favor of Datalog-like languages is the declarative nature of the resulting languages, which eases the problem formulation for the user and allows powerful performance optimizations on the part of the system.

In this chapter, we briefly discuss different domains where Datalog or Datalog-like languages have been recently applied.

8.1 SECURITY

The *Binder* language [DeTreville, 2002] is a Datalog-based language for access control in distributed systems.

A "principal" in Binder refers to a component in a distributed environment. Each principal has its own local context where its rules reside. Binder assumes an untrusted network, where different components can serve different roles running distinct sets of rules. Because of the lack of trust among nodes, a component does not have control over rule execution at other nodes. Instead, Binder allows separate programs to interoperate correctly and securely via the export and import of rules and derived tuples across contexts

Example 8.1 Binder has a distinguished operator *says*. The says operator implements a common logical construct in authentication, where "*p says s*" means that principal *p* supports statement *s*. For instance, in Binder we can write:

$$access(P, O, read) \leftarrow good(P).$$
$$access(P, O, read) \leftarrow bob \, says \, access(P, O, read).$$

The rules above state that any principal *P* may access any object *O* in read mode if *P* is good or if *bob* says that *P* may do so. The says operator abstracts from the details of authentication.

8.2 NETWORKING

Network Datalog (NDlog) [Loo et al., 2006] is a Datalog-like language used for querying network graphs, allowing one to implement a variety of routing protocols and overlay networks.

Example 8.2   The following NDlog programs finds all pairs of reachable vertices over a graph stored by means of *link*-facts representing the graph edges.

$$reachable(@S, D) \leftarrow link(@S, D).$$
$$reachable(@S, D) \leftarrow link(@S, Z), reachable(@Z, D).$$

The rules above specify a distributed transitive closure computation. NDlog supports a location specifier in each predicate, expressed with @ symbol followed by an attribute. This attribute is used to denote the source location of each corresponding tuple. For example, all reachable and link tuples are stored based on the @S address field.

The *Secure Network Datalog* (SeNDlog) language [Zhou et al., 2009] unifies Binder and NDlog. *SecureBlox* [Marczak et al., 2010] is a declarative system that unifies a distributed query processor with a security policy framework. SecureBlox decouples security concerns from system specification allowing easy reconfiguration of a system's security properties to suit a given execution environment.

8.3 WEB DATA MANAGEMENT

Webdamlog [Abiteboul et al., 2011] is a language to support the distribution of both data and knowledge (i.e., programs) over a network of autonomous peers communicating in an asynchronous way. The language supports updates, distribution, negation, and the novel feature of delegation, that is, the ability for a peer to communicate a program to another peer.

The following example illustrates the main aspects of the language—for a formal definition we refer the reader to Abiteboul et al. [2011].

Example 8.3   [Abiteboul et al., 2011] Consider a relation *birthday* at a peer named *myIphone* storing information on friends' birthdays and how to wish them a happy birthday (i.e., on which servers and with which messages). Facts of this kind can be express as follows:

$$birthday@myIphone(\text{``Alice,''} \ sendmail, \ inria.fr, \ 08/08)$$
$$birthday@myIphone(\text{``Bob,''} \ sms, \ BobIphone, \ 01/12),$$

where, for instance, the first fact says that Alice's birthdays is August 8th and wishes should be sent by email to server *inria.fr*.

A rule of the following form can be used to send birthday messages:

$$\$message@\$peer(\$name, \text{``Happy birthday''}) \ :- $$
$$today@myIphone(\$d),$$
$$birthday@myIphone(\$name, \$message, \$peer, \$d)$$

An identifier starting with the symbol $ is a variable. While the two facts above represent pieces of local knowledge of *myIphone*, the fact

$$sendmail@inria.fr(Alice, ``Happy\ birthday")$$

describes a message that is sent from *myIphone* to *inria.fr*.

The semantics of the global system is defined based on local semantics and the exchange of messages and rules. Intuitively, a given peer chooses how to move to another state based on its local state (a set of local facts and messages received from other peers) and its program. A move consists in (1) consuming the local facts, (2) deriving new local facts, which define the next state, (3) deriving nonlocal facts, i.e., messages sent to other peers, and (4) modifying their programs via "delegations."

Example 8.3 showed the derivation of local facts and messages sent to other peers. The following example illustrates delegation, one of the main features of Webdamlog.

Example 8.4 [Abiteboul et al., 2011] Consider the following rule, installed at peer p:

$$at\ p:\ m@q()\ :\ -m_1@p(\$x),\ m_2@p'(\$x).$$

Suppose that $m_1@p(a_1)$ holds, for some value a_1. Then, the effect of the rule is to install at p' the following rule:

$$at\ p':\ m@q()\ :\ -m_2@p'(a1).$$

The action of installing a rule at some other peer is called *delegation*.

When p' runs, if $m_2@p'(a_1)$ holds, it will send the message $m@q()$ to q. The basic idea of the delegation from p to p' is that there is some knowledge from p' that is needed to perform the task specified by the rule above. So, to perform that task, p delegates the remainder of the rule to p'.

8.4 PROGRAM ANALYSIS

The *Doop* framework has been proposed in Bravenboer and Smaragdakis [2009] for points-to analysis of Java programs. Points-to analysis concerns the problem of determining which objects a program variable can point to. The approach of Bravenboer and Smaragdakis [2009] relies on Datalog for specifying program analyses and proposes optimizations to speed-up such analyses.

Example 8.5 For the purpose of performing points-to analysis the following two base relations can be used:

- a binary relation *AssignHeapAllocation* storing facts of the form *AssignHeapAllocation*(v, o), where v is a Java variable and o identifies a heap object (pointed to by v)—such facts can be derived from a Java program by introducing one fact for each instruction a = new A() in the Java program, that is, when a heap object is allocated and assigned to a Java variable; and

- a binary relation *Assign* storing facts of the form *Assign(from, to)*, where *from* and *to* are Java variables—the *Assign* relation has one fact for each assignment between two Java (reference) variables, that is, when a Java assignment `to = from` is found.

Given the *AssignHeapAllocation* and *Assign* relations of a given Java program, a simple points-to analysis can be easily expressed in Datalog as follows:

$$varPointsTo(V, O) \leftarrow AssignHeapAllocation(V, O).$$
$$varPointsTo(To, O) \leftarrow Assign(From, To), varPointsTo(From, O).$$

The declarative nature of Datalog and its ability of expressing recursive relations makes Datalog suitable for expressing complex program analysis algorithms. For instance, Example 8.5 showed how a simple points-to analysis can be succinctly expressed in Datalog leveraging recursion.

As another example, recursion can be exploited to easily express a Datalog program checking whether a method m_1 is reachable from a method m_2, provided that we have points-to information, so that the target objects of a virtual method call are known.

8.5   MODULE COMPOSITION

A Datalog language for automatic service composition has been proposed in Albanese et al. [2013]. Composition comes into play when a user's request cannot be fulfilled by a single software module, but the composition of multiple modules can provide the requested services.

The general framework of Albanese et al. [2013] allows users to express QoS and security attributes associated with services and take them into account in the composition process. In addition, it is possible to express both hard and soft requirements for the QoS and security attributes that should come with the requested services. The adopted language is Datalog augmented with disjunction, negation, strong and weak constraints [Buccafurri et al., 2000].

The following example illustrates some of the basic features of the language.

Example 8.6   Suppose we are given a set of modules, where each of them provides services to other modules and possibly requires services from other modules in order to deliver those offered. Modules and their required/provided services can be expressed by means of facts of the following form.

- A fact *module(m)* means that m is a module.

- A fact *requires(m, r)* means that r is a service required by module m.

- A fact *provides(m, p)* means that p is a service provided by module m.

- A fact of the form *compatible(m$_1$, p, m$_2$, r)* means that service p provided by module m_1 can fulfill service r required by module m_2. Facts of this kind can be computed by means of Datalog rules expressing specific compatibility criteria.

The following Datalog rules can be used to guess a set of modules and determine the services that can be delivered through their composition:

$$
\begin{aligned}
taken(M) \vee not\_taken(M) \quad &\leftarrow \quad module(M). \\
fulfilled(M2, R) \quad &\leftarrow \quad taken(M2), requires(M2, R), \\
&\qquad delivers(M1, P), compatible(M1, P, M2, R). \\
delivers(M, I) \quad &\leftarrow \quad taken(M), provides(M, I), \neg cannot\_deliver(M). \\
cannot\_deliver(M) \quad &\leftarrow \quad requires(M, I), \neg fulfilled(M, I).
\end{aligned}
$$

The first rule above is used to guess a subset of the available modules, say S. The second rule says that $fulfilled(\langle M2, R)$ is derived if R is a service required by module $M2$ and there is a module $M1$ in S delivering a service P that fulfils R. The third rule allows us to derive $delivers(M, I)$ if module M can deliver service I. The fourth rule allows us to derive $cannot\_deliver(M)$ if M is a module whose provided services cannot be delivered because at least one of its required services cannot be matched with a service delivered by a taken module.

Bibliography

Serge Abiteboul and Victor Vianu. Datalog extensions for database queries and updates. *J. Comp. and System Sci.*, 43(1):62–124, 1991. DOI: 10.1016/0022-0000(91)90032-Z. 59, 60

Serge Abiteboul, Richard Hull, and Victor Vianu. *Foundations of Databases*. Addison-Wesley, 1995. 11, 12, 13, 15, 26, 32, 38, 59, 126

Serge Abiteboul, Zoë Abrams, Stefan Haar, and Tova Milo. Diagnosis of asynchronous discrete event systems: datalog to the rescue! In *Proc. 24th ACM SIGACT-SIGMOD-SIGART Symp. on Principles of Database Systems*, pages 358–367, 2005. DOI: 10.1145/1065167.1065214. 129

Serge Abiteboul, Meghyn Bienvenu, Alban Galland, and Emilien Antoine. A rule-based language for web data management. In *Proc. 30th ACM SIGACT-SIGMOD-SIGART Symp. on Principles of Database Systems*, pages 293–304, 2011. DOI: 10.1145/1989284.1989320. 130, 131

Foto N. Afrati and Stavros S. Cosmadakis. Expressiveness of restricted recursive queries (extended abstract). In *Proc. 21st Annual ACM Symp. on Theory of Computing*, pages 113–126, 1989. DOI: 10.1145/73007.73018. 110, 114

Foto N. Afrati and Christos H. Papadimitriou. The parallel complexity of simple chain queries. In *Proc. 6th ACM SIGACT-SIGMOD-SIGART Symp. on Principles of Database Systems*, pages 210–213, 1987. DOI: 10.1145/28659.28682. 126

Foto N. Afrati, Stavros S. Cosmadakis, and Mihalis Yannakakis. On datalog vs. polynomial time. *J. Comp. and System Sci.*, 51(2):177–196, 1995. DOI: 10.1006/jcss.1995.1060. 31, 33

Alfred V. Aho and Jeffrey D. Ullman. The universality of data retrieval languages. In *Proc. 16th ACM SIGACT-SIGPLAN Symp. on Principles of Programming Languages*, pages 110–120, 1979. DOI: 10.1145/567752.567763. 18, 31

Massimiliano Albanese, Sushil Jajodia, and Cristian Molinaro. A logic framework for flexible and security-aware service composition. In *Proc. IEEE International Conference on Autonomic and Trusted Computing*, pages 337–346, 2013. DOI: 10.1109/UIC-ATC.2013.11. 132

Peter Alvaro, Tyson Condie, Neil Conway, Khaled Elmeleegy, Joseph M. Hellerstein, and Russell Sears. Boom analytics: exploring data-centric, declarative programming for the cloud. In *Proc. European Conference on Computer Systems*, pages 223–236, 2010. DOI: 10.1145/1755913.1755937. 129

Mario Alviano, Wolfgang Faber, and Nicola Leone. Disjunctive asp with functions: Decidable queries and effective computation. *Theory & Practice of Logic Program.*, 10(4-6):497–512, 2010. DOI: 10.1017/S1471068410000244. 86

Mario Alviano, Francesco Calimeri, Wolfgang Faber, Nicola Leone, and Simona Perri. Unfounded sets and well-founded semantics of answer set programs with aggregates. *J. Artificial Intel. Res.*, 42:487–527, 2011. DOI: 10.1613/jair.3432. 99

Mario Alviano, Wolfgang Faber, Gianluigi Greco, and Nicola Leone. Magic sets for disjunctive datalog programs. *Artificial Intell.*, 187:156–192, 2012. DOI: 10.1016/j.artint.2012.04.008. 127

Krzysztof R. Apt. *Logic Programming*, pages 493–574. Handbook of Theoretical Computer Science. Elsevier, 1991. 15, 22

Krzysztof R. Apt and Maarten H. van Emden. Contributions to the theory of logic programming. *J. ACM*, 29(3):841–862, 1982. DOI: 10.1145/322326.322339. 32

Krzysztof R. Apt, Howard A. Blair, and Adrian Walker. Towards a theory of declarative knowledge. In *Foundations of Deductive Databases and Logic Programming.*, pages 89–148. Morgan Kaufmann, 1988. 36, 38

Molham Aref, Balder ten Cate, Todd J. Green, Benny Kimelfeld, Dan Olteanu, Emir Pasalic, Todd L. Veldhuizen, and Geoffrey Washburn. Design and implementation of the logicblox system. In *Proc. ACM SIGMOD Int. Conf. on Management of Data*, pages 1371–1382, 2015. DOI: 10.1145/2723372.2742796. 60

Thomas Arts and Jürgen Giesl. Termination of term rewriting using dependency pairs. *Theor. Comp. Sci.*, 236(1-2):133–178, 2000. DOI: 10.1016/S0304-3975(99)00207-8. 86

Isaac Balbin and Kotagiri Ramamohanarao. A generalization of the differential approach to recursive query evaluation. *J. Logic Program.*, 4(3):259–262, 1987. DOI: 10.1016/0743-1066(87)90004-5. 32

Isaac Balbin, Graeme S. Port, Kotagiri Ramamohanarao, and Krishnamurthy Meenakshi. Efficient bottom-up computation of queries on stratified databases. *J. Logic Program.*, 11(3&4): 295–344, 1991. DOI: 10.1016/0743-1066(91)90030-S. 107, 108

François Bancilhon and Raghu Ramakrishnan. Performance evaluation of data intensive logic programs. In *Foundations of Deductive Databases and Logic Program.* Morgan Kaufmann, 1988. DOI: 10.1016/B978-0-934613-40-8.50016-6. 126

François Bancilhon, David Maier, Yehoshua Sagiv, and Jeffrey D. Ullman. Magic sets and other strange ways to implement logic programs. In *Proc. 5th ACM SIGACT-SIGMOD Symp. on*

Principles of Database Systems, pages 1–15, 1986. DOI: 10.1145/6012.15399. 101, 109, 110, 121, 126

François Bancilhon and Raghu Ramakrishnan. An amateur's introduction to recursive query processing strategies. In *Proc. ACM SIGMOD Int. Conf. on Management of Data*, pages 16–52, 1986. DOI: 10.1145/16856.16859. 32, 126

Sabrina Baselice, Piero A. Bonatti, and Giovanni Criscuolo. On finitely recursive programs. *Theory & Practice of Logic Program.*, 9(2):213–238, 2009. DOI: 10.1017/S147106840900372X. 86

Catriel Beeri and Raghu Ramakrishnan. On the power of magic. In *Proc. 6th ACM SIGACT-SIGMOD-SIGART Symp. on Principles of Database Systems*, pages 269–284, 1987. DOI: 10.1145/28659.28689. 126

Catriel Beeri and Raghu Ramakrishnan. On the power of magic. *J. Logic Program.*, 10(3&4): 255–299, 1991. DOI: 10.1016/0743-1066(91)90038-Q. 101, 107, 108, 125, 126

Catriel Beeri, Paris C. Kanellakis, François Bancilhon, and Raghu Ramakrishnan. Bounds on the propagation of selection into logic programs. *J. Comp. and System Sci.*, 41(2):157–180, 1990. DOI: 10.1016/0022-0000(90)90035-J. 109, 110, 126

Andreas Behrend. Soft stratification for magic set based query evaluation in deductive databases. In *Proc. 22nd ACM SIGACT-SIGMOD-SIGART Symp. on Principles of Database Systems*, pages 102–110, 2003. DOI: 10.1145/773153.773164. 126

Nicole Bidoit and Richard Hull. Positivism vs. minimalism in deductive databases. In *Proc. 5th ACM SIGACT-SIGMOD Symp. on Principles of Database Systems*, pages 123–132, 1986. DOI: 10.1145/6012.15409. 59

Piero A. Bonatti. Reasoning with infinite stable models. *Artificial Intell.*, 156(1):75–111, 2004. DOI: 10.1016/j.artint.2004.02.001. 86

Martin Bravenboer and Yannis Smaragdakis. Strictly declarative specification of sophisticated points-to analyses. In *Proc. 24th ACM SIGPLAN Conf. on Object-Oriented Programming Systems, Languages & Applications*, pages 243–262, 2009. DOI: 10.1145/1639949.1640108. 129, 131

Maurice Bruynooghe, Michael Codish, John P. Gallagher, Samir Genaim, and Wim Vanhoof. Termination analysis of logic programs through combination of type-based norms. *ACM Trans. Prog. Lang. and Syst.*, 29(2), 2007. DOI: 10.1145/1216374.1216378. 86

Francesco Buccafurri, Sergio Greco, and Domenico Saccà. The expressive power of unique total stable model semantics. In *24th Int. Colloquium on Automata, Languages, and Programming*, pages 849–859, 1997. DOI: 10.1007/3-540-63165-8_237. 59

Francesco Buccafurri, Nicola Leone, and Pasquale Rullo. Enhancing disjunctive datalog by constraints. *IEEE Trans. Knowl. and Data Eng.*, 12(5):845–860, 2000. DOI: 10.1109/69.877512. 132

Marco Cadoli and Luigi Palopoli. Circumscribing datalog: Expressive power and complexity. *Theor. Comp. Sci.*, 193(1-2):215–244, 1998. DOI: 10.1016/S0304-3975(97)00108-4. 59

M. Calautti, S. Greco, F. Spezzano, and I. Trubitsyna. Checking termination of bottom-up evaluation of logic programs with function symbols. *Theory & Practice of Logic Program.*, 2015a. DOI: 10.1017/S1471068414000623. 86

Marco Calautti, Sergio Greco, and Irina Trubitsyna. Detecting decidable classes of finitely ground logic programs with function symbols. In *Proc. International Symposium on Principles and Practice of Declarative Programming*, pages 239–250, 2013. DOI: 10.1145/2505879.2505883. 86

Marco Calautti, Sergio Greco, Cristian Molinaro, and Irina Trubitsyna. Checking termination of logic programs with function symbols through linear constraints. In *Proc. International Web Rule Symposium*, pages 97–111, 2014. DOI: 10.1007/978-3-319-09870-8_7. 86

Marco Calautti, Sergio Greco, Cristian Molinaro, and Irina Trubitsyna. Logic program termination analysis using atom sizes. In *Proc. 24th Int. Joint Conf. on AI*, pages 2833–2839, 2015b. 86

Marco Calautti, Sergio Greco, Cristian Molinaro, and Irina Trubitsyna. Checking termination of datalog with function symbols through linear constraints. In *Proc. 23rd Italian Symposium on Advanced Database Systems*, 2015c. 86

Marco Calautti, Sergio Greco, Cristian Molinaro, and Irina Trubitsyna. Using linear constraints for logic program termination analysis. *Theory & Practice of Logic Program.*, 2016. 86

Andrea Calì, Georg Gottlob, and Thomas Lukasiewicz. A general datalog-based framework for tractable query answering over ontologies. In *Proc. 28th ACM SIGACT-SIGMOD-SIGART Symp. on Principles of Database Systems*, pages 77–86, 2009. DOI: 10.1016/j.websem.2012.03.001. 12

Andrea Calì, Georg Gottlob, and Thomas Lukasiewicz. Datalog$^{\pm}$: a unified approach to ontologies and integrity constraints. In *Proc. 12th Int. Conf. on Database Theory*, pages 14–30, 2009. DOI: 10.1145/1514894.1514897. 12

Francesco Calimeri, Susanna Cozza, Giovambattista Ianni, and Nicola Leone. Computable functions in asp: Theory and implementation. In *Proc. 24th Int. Conf. Logic Programming*, pages 407–424, 2008. DOI: 10.1007/978-3-540-89982-2_37. 64, 86

Francesco Calimeri, Susanna Cozza, Giovambattista Ianni, and Nicola Leone. Enhancing ASP by functions: Decidable classes and implementation techniques. In *Proc. 24th National Conf. on Artificial Intelligence*, 2010. 86

Luciano Caroprese, Cristian Molinaro, and Ester Zumpano. Integrating and querying P2P deductive databases. In *Proc. 10th International Database Engineering and Applications Symposium (IDEAS)*, pages 285–290, 2006. DOI: 10.1109/IDEAS.2006.28. 129

Stefano Ceri, Georg Gottlob, and Letizia Tanca. What you always wanted to know about datalog (and never dared to ask). *IEEE Trans. Knowl. and Data Eng.*, 1(1):146–166, 1989. DOI: 10.1109/69.43410. 126

Stefano Ceri, Georg Gottlob, and Letizia Tanca. *Logic Programming and Databases*. Springer, 1990. DOI: 10.1007/978-3-642-83952-8. 32

Ashok K. Chandra and David Harel. Structure and complexity of relational queries. *J. Comp. and System Sci.*, 25(1):99–128, 1982. DOI: 10.1016/0022-0000(82)90012-5. 32

Ashok K. Chandra and David Harel. Horn clauses queries and generalizations. *J. Logic Program.*, 2(1):1–15, 1985. DOI: 10.1016/0743-1066(85)90002-0. 36

Ashok K. Chandra and Philip M. Merlin. Optimal implementation of conjunctive queries in relational data bases. In *Proc. 9th Annual ACM Symp. on Theory of Computing*, pages 77–90, 1977. DOI: 10.1145/800105.803397. 12

Peter Cholak and Howard A. Blair. The complexity of local stratification. *Fundam. Inform.*, 21 (4):333–344, 1994. DOI: 10.3233/FI-1994-2144. 59

E. F. Codd. Relational completeness of data base sublanguages. In: R. Rustin (ed.): Database Systems: 65-98, Prentice Hall and IBM Research Report RJ 987, San Jose, California, 1972. 15

Edgar F. Codd. A relational model of data for large shared data banks. *Commun. ACM*, 13(6): 377–387, 1970. DOI: 10.1145/362384.362685. 3, 15

Michael Codish, Vitaly Lagoon, and Peter J. Stuckey. Testing for termination with monotonicity constraints. In *Proc. 21st Int. Conf. Logic Programming*, pages 326–340, 2005. DOI: 10.1007/11562931_25. 86

Mariano P. Consens and Alberto O. Mendelzon. Low complexity aggregation in graphlog and datalog. In *Proc. 3rd Int. Conf. on Database Theory*, pages 379–394, 1990. DOI: 10.1007/3-540-53507-1_90. 99

Chiara Cumbo, Wolfgang Faber, Gianluigi Greco, and Nicola Leone. Enhancing the magic-set method for disjunctive datalog programs. In *Proc. 20th Int. Conf. Logic Programming*, pages 371–385, 2004. DOI: 10.1007/978-3-540-27775-0_26. 126

Evgeny Dantsin, Thomas Eiter, Georg Gottlob, and Andrei Voronkov. Complexity and expressive power of logic programming. In *IEEE Conference on Computational Complexity*, pages 82–101, 1997. DOI: 10.1109/CCC.1997.612304. 32

Evgeny Dantsin, Thomas Eiter, Georg Gottlob, and Andrei Voronkov. Complexity and expressive power of logic programming. *ACM Comput. Surv.*, 33(3):374–425, 2001. DOI: 10.1145/502807.502810. 32, 43, 47, 59

Chris J. Date. *An Introduction to Database Systems (7th ed.)*. Addison-Wesley-Longman, 2000. 15

Danny De Schreye and Stefaan Decorte. Termination of logic programs: The never-ending story. *J. Logic Program.*, 19/20:199–260, 1994. DOI: 10.1016/0743-1066(94)90027-2. 86

John DeTreville. Binder, a logic-based security language. In *Proc. IEEE Symposium on Security and Privacy*, pages 105–113, 2002. DOI: 10.1109/SECPRI.2002.1004365. 129

Alin Deutsch, Alan Nash, and Jeffrey B. Remmel. The chase revisited. In *Proc. 27th ACM SIGACT-SIGMOD-SIGART Symp. on Principles of Database Systems*, pages 149–158, 2008. DOI: 10.1145/1376916.1376938. 86

Suzanne W. Dietrich. Shortest path by approximation in logic programs. *ACM Lett. on Program. Lang. and Syst.*, 1(2):119–137, 1992. DOI: 10.1145/151333.151377. 99

Guozhu Dong. Datalog expressiveness of chain queries: Grammar tools and characterizations. In *Proc. 11th ACM SIGACT-SIGMOD-SIGART Symp. on Principles of Database Systems*, pages 81–90, 1992a. DOI: 10.1145/137097.137113. 126

Guozhu Dong. On datalog linearization of chain queries. In *Theoretical Studies in Computer Science*, pages 181–206, 1992b. 109, 110, 126

Sergey Dudakov. On the complexity of perfect models of logic programs. *Fundam. Inform.*, 39 (3):249–258, 1999. DOI: 10.3233/FI-1999-39302. 59

Thomas Eiter, Georg Gottlob, and Heikki Mannila. Disjunctive datalog. *ACM Trans. Database Syst.*, 22(3):364–418, 1997a. DOI: 10.1145/261124.261126. 59, 60

Thomas Eiter, Nicola Leone, and Domenico Saccà. On the partial semantics for disjunctive deductive databases. *Ann. of Math. and Artificial Intell.*, 19(1-2):59–96, 1997b. DOI: 10.1023/A:1018947420290. 59

Thomas Eiter, Nicola Leone, and Domenico Saccà. Expressive power and complexity of partial models for disjunctive deductive databases. *Theor. Comp. Sci.*, 206(1-2):181–218, 1998. DOI: 10.1016/S0304-3975(97)00129-1. 59

Ramez Elmasri and Shamkant B. Navathe. *Fundamentals of Database Systems, 3rd ed.* Addison-Wesley-Longman, 2000. 15

Jörg Endrullis, Johannes Waldmann, and Hans Zantema. Matrix interpretations for proving termination of term rewriting. *J. of Automated Reason.*, 40(2-3):195–220, 2008. DOI: 10.1007/s10817-007-9087-9. 86

Wolfgang Faber, Gianluigi Greco, and Nicola Leone. Magic sets and their application to data integration. *J. Comp. and System Sci.*, 73(4):584–609, 2007. DOI: 10.1016/j.jcss.2006.10.012. 126

Wolfgang Faber, Gerald Pfeifer, and Nicola Leone. Semantics and complexity of recursive aggregates in answer set programming. *Artificial Intell.*, 175(1):278–298, 2011. DOI: 10.1016/j.artint.2010.04.002. 99

Ronald Fagin, Phokion G. Kolaitis, Renée J. Miller, and Lucian Popa. Data exchange: semantics and query answering. *Theor. Comp. Sci.*, 336(1):89–124, 2005. DOI: 10.1016/j.tcs.2004.10.033. 12, 86

Maria C. F. Ferreira and Hans Zantema. Total termination of term rewriting. *Applic. Algebra in Eng., Commun. and Comput.*, 7(2):133–162, 1996. DOI: 10.1007/BF01191381. 86

Amelia C. Fong and Jeffrey D. Ullman. Induction variables in very high level languages. In *Proc. 3rd ACM SIGACT-SIGPLAN Symp. on Principles of Programming Languages*, pages 104–112, 1976. DOI: 10.1145/800168.811544. 32

Filippo Furfaro, Sergio Greco, and Cristian Molinaro. A three-valued semantics for querying and repairing inconsistent databases. *Ann. of Math. and Artificial Intell.*, 51(2-4):167–193, 2007. DOI: 10.1007/s10472-008-9088-3. 59

Hervé Gallaire and Jack Minker, editors. *Logic and Data Bases, Symposium on Logic and Data Bases, Centre d'études et de recherches de Toulouse, 1977*, Advances in Data Base Theory, 1978. Plemum Press. 32

Hervé Gallaire, Jack Minker, and Jean-Marie Nicolas. Logic and databases: A deductive approach. *ACM Comput. Surv.*, 16(2):153–185, 1984. DOI: 10.1145/356924.356929. 32

Sumit Ganguly, Sergio Greco, and Carlo Zaniolo. Minimum and maximum predicates in logic programming. In *Proc. 10th ACM SIGACT-SIGMOD-SIGART Symp. on Principles of Database Systems*, pages 154–163, 1991. DOI: 10.1145/113413.113427. 97, 99

Hector Garcia-Molina, Jeffrey D. Ullman, and Jennifer Widom. *Database Systems - The Complete Book (2nd ed.)*. Pearson Education, 2009. 15

Martin Gebser, Torsten Schaub, and Sven Thiele. Gringo: A new grounder for answer set programming. In *Proc. 9th Int. Conf. Logic Programming and Nonmonotonic Reasoning*, pages 266–271, 2007. DOI: 10.1007/978-3-540-72200-7_24. 63, 86

Martin Gebser, Benjamin Kaufmann, and Torsten Schaub. Conflict-driven answer set solving: From theory to practice. *Artificial Intell.*, 187-188:52–89, 2012. DOI: 10.1016/j.artint.2012.04.001. 60

Allen Van Gelder. Foundations of aggregation in deductive databases. In *Proc. 3rd Int. Conf. on Deductive and Object-Oriented Databases*, pages 13–34, 1993. DOI: 10.1007/3-540-57530-8_2. 99

Michael Gelfond and Vladimir Lifschitz. The stable model semantics for logic programming. In *Proc. 5th Int. Conf. Logic Programming*, pages 1070–1080, 1988. 41

Michael Gelfond and Vladimir Lifschitz. Classical negation in logic programs and disjunctive databases. *New Generation Comput.*, 9(3/4):365–386, 1991. DOI: 10.1007/BF03037169. 59

Fosca Giannotti and Dino Pedreschi. Datalog with non-deterministic choice computers ndb-ptime. *J. Logic Program.*, 35(1):79–101, 1998. DOI: 10.1016/S0743-1066(97)10004-8. 60

Fosca Giannotti, Dino Pedreschi, Domenico Saccà, and Carlo Zaniolo. Non-determinism in deductive databases. In *Proc. 2nd Int. Conf. on Deductive and Object-Oriented Databases*, pages 129–146, 1991. DOI: 10.1007/3-540-55015-1_7. 47, 53, 54, 55, 60

Fosca Giannotti, Dino Pedreschi, and Carlo Zaniolo. Semantics and expressive power of nondeterministic constructs in deductive databases. *J. Comp. and Syst. Sci.*, 62(1):15–42, 2001. DOI: 10.1006/jcss.1999.1699. 47, 50, 60

Georg Gottlob, Christoph Koch, Robert Baumgartner, Marcus Herzog, and Sergio Flesca. The lixto data extraction project - back and forth between theory and practice. In *Proc. 23rd ACM SIGACT-SIGMOD-SIGART Symp. on Principles of Database Systems*, pages 1–12, 2004. DOI: 10.1145/1055558.1055560. 129

Bernardo Cuenca Grau, Ian Horrocks, Markus Krötzsch, Clemens Kupke, Despoina Magka, Boris Motik, and Zhe Wang. Acyclicity notions for existential rules and their application to query answering in ontologies. *J. Artificial Intell. Res.*, 47:741–808, 2013. DOI: 10.1613/jair.3949. 86

Gianluigi Greco, Sergio Greco, Irina Trubitsyna, and Ester Zumpano. Optimization of bound disjunctive queries with constraints. *Theory & Practice of Logic Program.*, 5(6):713–745, 2005. DOI: 10.1017/S1471068404002273. 127

Sergio Greco.   Extending datalog with choice and weak constraints.   In *Proc. Joint Conf. on Declarative Programming, APPIA-GULP-PRODE*, pages 329–340, 1996. DOI: 10.1007/BF03037430. 60

Sergio Greco. Non-determinism and weak constraints in datalog. *New Generation Comput.*, 16 (4):373–396, 1998a. DOI: 10.1007/BF03037430. 60

Sergio Greco. Binding propagation in disjunctive databases. In *Proc. 24th Int. Conf. on Very Large Data Bases*, pages 287–298, 1998b. DOI: 10.1109/TKDE.2003.1185840. 127

Sergio Greco. Dynamic programming in datalog with aggregates. *IEEE Trans. Knowl. and Data Eng.*, 11(2):265–283, 1999a. DOI: 10.1109/69.761663. 89, 90, 91, 97, 98

Sergio Greco. Optimization of disjunctive queries. In *Proc. 16th Int. Conf. Logic Programming*, pages 441–455, 1999b. DOI: 10.1109/69.842265. 127

Sergio Greco.   Binding propagation techniques for the optimization of bound disjunctive queries.   *IEEE Trans. on Knowl. and Data Eng.*, 15(2):368–385, 2003. DOI: 10.1109/TKDE.2003.1185840. 127

Sergio Greco and Domenico Saccà.   The expressive power of "possible-is-certain" semantics (extended abstract). In *Proc. Asian Computing Science Conference*, pages 33–42, 1996. DOI: 10.1007/BFb0027777. 59

Sergio Greco and Domenico Saccà. Deterministic semantics for datalog¬: Complexity and expressive power. In *Proc. 5th Int. Conf. on Deductive and Object-Oriented Databases*, pages 337–350, 1997a. DOI: 10.1007/3-540-63792-3_24. 60

Sergio Greco and Domenico Saccà. "possible is certain" is desirable and can be expressive. *Ann. of Math. and Artificial Intell.*, 19(1-2):147–168, 1997b. DOI: 10.1023/A:1018903705269. 60

Sergio Greco and Domenico Saccà. Complexity and expressive power of deterministic semantics for datalog¬. *Inform. and Comput.*, 153(1):81–98, 1999. DOI: 10.1006/inco.1999.2800. 60

Sergio Greco and Francesca Spezzano. Chase termination: A constraints rewriting approach. *Proc. VLDB Endowment*, 3(1):93–104, 2010. DOI: 10.14778/1920841.1920858. 86

Sergio Greco and Carlo Zaniolo. Optimization of linear logic programs using counting methods. In *Advances in Database Technology, Proc. 3rd Int. Conf. on Extending Database Technology*, pages 72–87, 1992. DOI: 10.1007/BFb0032424. 115, 126

Sergio Greco and Carlo Zaniolo. Efficient execution of recursive queries through controlled binding propagation. In *Proc. 8th Int. Symposium on Methodologies for Intelligent Systems*, pages 193–202, 1994. DOI: 10.1007/3-540-58495-1_20. 126

Sergio Greco and Carlo Zaniolo. Greedy algorithms in datalog with choice and negation. In *Proc. 15th Int. Conf. Logic Programming*, pages 294–309, 1998. 54, 57

Sergio Greco and Carlo Zaniolo. Greedy algorithms in datalog. *Theory & Practice of Logic Program.*, 1(4):381–407, 2001. DOI: 10.1017/S1471068401001090. 48, 54

Sergio Greco, Carlo Zaniolo, and Sumit Ganguly. Greedy by choice. In *Proc. 11th ACM SIGACT-SIGMOD-SIGART Symp. on Principles of Database Systems*, pages 105–113, 1992. DOI: 10.1145/137097.137836. 54

Sergio Greco, Domenico Saccà, and Carlo Zaniolo. Datalog queries with stratified negation and choice: from p to d^P. In *Proc. 5th Int. Conf. on Database Theory*, pages 82–96, 1995. DOI: 10.1007/3-540-58907-4_8. 60, 109

Sergio Greco, Carlo Zaniolo, and Sumit Ganguly. Optimization of logic queries with MIN and MAX predicates. In *Proc. 3rd Int. Conf. Flexible Query Answering Systems*, pages 188–202, 1998. DOI: 10.1007/BFb0056001. 97

Sergio Greco, Domenico Saccà, and Carlo Zaniolo. Grammars and automata to optimize chain logic queries. *Int. J. Found. Comput. Sci.*, 10(3):349–372, 1999. DOI: 10.1142/S0129054199000253. 109, 115, 116, 117, 119, 120, 124

Sergio Greco, Domenico Saccà, and Carlo Zaniolo. Extending stratified datalog to capture complexity classes ranging from p to qh. *Acta Informatica*, 37(10):699–725, 2001. DOI: 10.1007/PL00013306. 60

Sergio Greco, Cristian Molinaro, and Irina Trubitsyna. Implementation and experimentation of the logic language NP datalog. In *Proc. 17th Int. Conf. on Database and Expert Systems Applications*, pages 622–633, 2006. DOI: 10.1007/11827405_61. 60

Sergio Greco, Cristian Molinaro, Irina Trubitsyna, and Ester Zumpano. NP datalog: A logic language for expressing search and optimization problems. *Theory & Practice of Logic Program.*, 10(2):125–166, 2010. DOI: 10.1017/S1471068409990251. 60

Sergio Greco, Francesca Spezzano, and Irina Trubitsyna. Stratification criteria and rewriting techniques for checking chase termination. *Proc. VLDB Endowment*, 4(11):1158–1168, 2011. DOI: 10.1109/TKDE.2014.2339816. 86

Sergio Greco, Cristian Molinaro, and Francesca Spezzano. *Incomplete Data and Data Dependencies in Relational Databases*. Synthesis Lectures on Data Management. Morgan & Claypool Publishers, 2012a. DOI: 10.2200/S00435ED1V01Y201207DTM029. 12, 13, 86

Sergio Greco, Francesca Spezzano, and Irina Trubitsyna. On the termination of logic programs with function symbols. In *Proc. 28th Int. Conf. Logic Programming*, pages 323–333, 2012b. DOI: 10.4230/LIPIcs.ICLP.2012.323. 66, 68, 74, 86

Sergio Greco, Cristian Molinaro, and Irina Trubitsyna. Bounded programs: A new decidable class of logic programs with function symbols. In *Proc. 23rd Int. Joint Conf. on AI*, pages 926–932, 2013a. 70, 75, 86

Sergio Greco, Cristian Molinaro, and Irina Trubitsyna. Logic programming with function symbols: Checking termination of bottom-up evaluation through program adornments. *Theory & Practice of Logic Program.*, 13(4-5):737–752, 2013b. DOI: 10.1017/S147106841300046X. 76, 84

Todd J. Green, Shan Shan Huang, Boon Thau Loo, and Wenchao Zhou. Datalog and recursive query processing. *Found. and Trends in Databases*, 5(2):105–195, 2013. DOI: 10.1561/1900000017. 126

Ramsey W. Haddad and Jeffrey F. Naughton. A counting algorithm for a cyclic binary query. *J. Comp. and System Sci.*, 43(1):145–169, 1991. DOI: 10.1016/0022-0000(91)90034-3. 110

John E. Hopcroft and Jeffrey D. Ullman. *Introduction to Automata Theory, Languages and Computation*. Addison-Wesley, 1979. 112, 115

Shan Shan Huang, Todd Jeffrey Green, and Boon Thau Loo. Datalog and emerging applications: an interactive tutorial. In *Proc. ACM SIGMOD Int. Conf. on Management of Data*, pages 1213–1216, 2011. DOI: 10.1145/1989323.1989456. 129

Yannis E. Ioannidis. Commutativity and its role in the processing of linear recursion. *J. Logic Program.*, 14(3&4):223–252, 1992. DOI: 10.1016/0743-1066(92)90012-R. 110

Yannis E. Ioannidis and Eugene Wong. Transforming nonlinear recursion into linear recursion. In *Expert Database Conf.*, pages 401–421, 1988. 110

David S. Johnson. A catalog of complexity classes. In *Handbook of Theoretical Computer Science, Volume A: Algorithms and Complexity (A)*, pages 67–161. 1990. 14, 15

David B. Kemp and Kotagiri Ramamohanarao. Efficient recursive aggregation and negation in deductive databases. *IEEE Trans. Knowl. and Data Eng.*, 10(5):727–745, 1998. DOI: 10.1109/69.729729. 99

David B. Kemp and Peter J. Stuckey. Semantics of logic programs with aggregates. In *International Symposium on Logic Programming*, pages 387–401, 1991. 98

Michael Kifer, Raghu Ramakrishnan, and Abraham Silberschatz. An axiomatic approach to deciding query safety in deductive databases. In *Proc. 7th ACM SIGACT-SIGMOD-SIGART Symp. on Principles of Database Systems*, pages 52–60, 1988. DOI: 10.1145/308386.308412. 32

Phokion G. Kolaitis. The expressive power of stratified programs. *Inform. and Comput.*, 90(1): 50–66, 1991. DOI: 10.1016/0890-5401(91)90059-B. 60

Phokion G. Kolaitis and Christos H. Papadimitriou. Why not negation by fixpoint? *J. Comp. and Syst. Sci.*, 43(1):125–144, 1991. DOI: 10.1016/0022-0000(91)90033-2. 43, 59

Phokion G. Kolaitis and Moshe Y. Vardi. On the expressive power of datalog: Tools and a case study. *J. Comp. and Syst. Sci.*, 51(1):110–134, 1995. DOI: 10.1006/jcss.1995.1055. 60

Robert Kowalski. *Logic for Problem-solving*. North-Holland Publishing Co., 1986. DOI: 10.1145/1005937.1005947. 32

Robert A. Kowalski. Predicate logic as programming language. In *IFIP Congress*, pages 569–574, 1974. 32

Ravi Krishnamurthy and Shamim A. Naqvi. Non-deterministic choice in datalog. In *Proc. 3rd International Conference on Data and Knowledge Bases*, pages 416–424, 1988. 47, 60

Ravi Krishnamurthy, Raghu Ramakrishnan, and Oded Shmueli. A framework for testing safety and effective computability of extended datalog (extended abstract). In *Proc. ACM SIGMOD Int. Conf. on Management of Data*, pages 154–163, 1988. DOI: 10.1145/971701.50219. 32

Markus Krötzsch and Sebastian Rudolph. Extending decidable existential rules by joining acyclicity and guardedness. In *Proc. 22nd Int. Joint Conf. on AI*, pages 963–968, 2011. DOI: 10.5591/978-1-57735-516-8/IJCAI11-166. 86

Bernard Lang. Datalog automata. In *Proc. 3rd International Conference on Data and Knowledge Bases*, pages 389–404, 1988. 126

Maurizio Lenzerini. Data integration: A theoretical perspective. In *Proc. 21st ACM SIGACT-SIGMOD-SIGART Symp. on Principles of Database Systems*, pages 233–246, 2002. DOI: 10.1145/543613.543644. 12

Nicola Leone, Gerald Pfeifer, Wolfgang Faber, Thomas Eiter, Georg Gottlob, Simona Perri, and Francesco Scarcello. The dlv system for knowledge representation and reasoning. *ACM Trans. Comput. Log.* DOI: 10.1145/1149114.1149117. 60

Yuliya Lierler and Vladimir Lifschitz. One more decidable class of finitely ground programs. In *International Conference on Logic Programming*, pages 489–493, 2009. DOI: 10.1007/978-3-642-02846-5_40. 66, 86

Vladimir Lifschitz. On the declarative semantics of logic programs with negation. In *Foundations of Deductive Databases and Logic Programming.*, pages 177–192. Morgan Kaufmann, 1988. 36

John W. Lloyd. *Foundations of Logic Programming, 2nd ed.* Springer-Verlag, 1987. DOI: 10.1007/978-3-642-83189-8. 15, 22

Jorge Lobo, Jack Minker, and Arcot Rajasekar. *Foundations of Disjunctive Logic Programming*. Logic Programming. MIT Press, 1992. 60

Boon Thau Loo, Tyson Condie, Joseph M. Hellerstein, Petros Maniatis, Timothy Roscoe, and Ion Stoica. Implementing declarative overlays. In *Proc. 20th ACM Symp. on Operating System Principles*, pages 75–90, 2005a. DOI: 10.1145/1095809.1095818. 129

Boon Thau Loo, Joseph M. Hellerstein, Ion Stoica, and Raghu Ramakrishnan. Declarative routing: extensible routing with declarative queries. In *Proc. 2005 Conf. on Applications, Technologies, Architectures, and Protocols for Computer Communication*, pages 289–300, 2005b. DOI: 10.1145/1080091.1080126. 129

Boon Thau Loo, Tyson Condie, Minos N. Garofalakis, David E. Gay, Joseph M. Hellerstein, Petros Maniatis, Raghu Ramakrishnan, Timothy Roscoe, and Ion Stoica. Declarative networking: language, execution and optimization. In *Proc. ACM SIGMOD Int. Conf. on Management of Data*, 2006. DOI: 10.1145/1142473.1142485. 129, 130

David Maier. *The Theory of Relational Databases*. Computer Science Press, 1983. 15

Alberto Marchetti-Spaccamela, Antonella Pelaggi, and Domenico Saccà. Comparison of methods for logic-query implementation. *J. Logic Program.*, 10(3&4):333–360, 1991. DOI: 10.1016/0743-1066(91)90040-V. 110

Massimo Marchiori. Proving existential termination of normal logic programs. In *Algebraic Methodology and Software Technology*, pages 375–390, 1996. DOI: 10.1007/BFb0014328. 86

William R. Marczak, Shan Shan Huang, Martin Bravenboer, Micah Sherr, Boon Thau Loo, and Molham Aref. Secureblox: customizable secure distributed data processing. In *Proc. ACM SIGMOD Int. Conf. on Management of Data*, 2010. DOI: 10.1145/1807167.1807246. 129, 130

V. Wiktor Marek and Miroslaw Truszczynski. Autoepistemic logic. *J. ACM*, 38(3):588–619, 1991. DOI: 10.1145/116825.116836. 43, 54

Bruno Marnette. Generalized schema-mappings: from termination to tractability. In *Proc. 28th ACM SIGACT-SIGMOD-SIGART Symp. on Principles of Database Systems*, pages 13–22, 2009a. DOI: 10.1145/1559795.1559799. 87

Bruno Marnette. Generalized schema-mappings: from termination to tractability. In *Proc. 28th ACM SIGACT-SIGMOD-SIGART Symp. on Principles of Database Systems*, pages 13–22, 2009b. DOI: 10.1145/1559795.1559799. 86

Mirjana Mazuran, Edoardo Serra, and Carlo Zaniolo. A declarative extension of horn clauses, and its significance for datalog and its applications. *Theory & Practice of Logic Program.*, 13 (4-5):609–623, 2013. DOI: 10.1017/S1471068413000380. 60

Michael Meier. *On the Termination of the Chase Algorithm*. Albert-Ludwigs-Universitat Freiburg (Germany), 2010. 87

Michael Meier, Michael Schmidt, and Georg Lausen. On chase termination beyond stratification. *Proc. VLDB Endowment*, 2(1):970–981, 2009. DOI: 10.14778/1687627.1687737. 86

Jack Minker, editor. *Foundations of Deductive Databases and Logic Programming*. Morgan Kaufmann, 1988. 32

Jack Minker. Overview of disjunctive logic programming. *Ann. of Math. and Artificial Intell.*, 12 (1-2):1–24, 1994. DOI: 10.1007/BF01530759. 60

Jack Minker and Dietmar Seipel. Disjunctive logic programming: A survey and assessment. In *Computational Logic: Logic Programming and Beyond, Essays in Honour of Robert A. Kowalski, Part I*, pages 472–511, 2002. DOI: 10.1007/3-540-45628-7_18. 60

Jack Minker, Dietmar Seipel, and Carlo Zaniolo. Logic and databases: A history of deductive databases. In *Computational Logic*, pages 571–627. 2014. DOI: 10.1016/B978-0-444-51624-4.50013-7. 32

Inderpal Singh Mumick and Oded Shmueli. How expressive is statified aggregation? *Ann. of Math. and Artificial Intell.*, 15(3-4):407–434, 1995. DOI: 10.1007/BF01536403. 99

Inderpal Singh Mumick, Hamid Pirahesh, and Raghu Ramakrishnan. The magic of duplicates and aggregates. In *Proc. 16th Int. Conf. on Very Large Data Bases*, pages 264–277, 1990. 90, 98

Shamim A. Naqvi and Shalom Tsur. *A Logical Language for Data and Knowledge Bases*. Computer Science Press, 1989. 47

Jeffrey F. Naughton, Raghu Ramakrishnan, Yehoshua Sagiv, and Jeffrey D. Ullman. Argument reduction by factoring. In *Proc. 15th Int. Conf. on Very Large Data Bases*, pages 173–182, 1989a. DOI: 10.1016/0304-3975(94)00186-M. 110, 126

Jeffrey F. Naughton, Raghu Ramakrishnan, Yehoshua Sagiv, and Jeffrey D. Ullman. Efficient evaluation of right-, left-, and mult-linear rules. In *Proc. ACM SIGMOD Int. Conf. on Management of Data*, pages 235–242, 1989b. DOI: 10.1145/66926.66948. 109, 110, 126

Manh Thang Nguyen, Jürgen Giesl, Peter Schneider-Kamp, and Danny De Schreye. Termination analysis of logic programs based on dependency graphs. In *Proc. International Symposium on Logic-based Program Synthesis and Transformation*, pages 8–22, 2007. DOI: 10.1007/978-3-540-78769-3_2. 86

Naoki Nishida and Germán Vidal. Termination of narrowing via termination of rewriting. *Applic. Algebra in Eng., Commun. and Comput.*, 21(3):177–225, 2010. DOI: 10.1007/s00200-010-0122-4. 86

Enno Ohlebusch. Termination of logic programs: Transformational methods revisited. *Applic. Algebra in Eng., Communic. and Comput.*, 12(1/2):73–116, 2001. DOI: 10.1007/s002000100064. 86

Adrian Onet. The chase procedure and its applications in data exchange. In *Data Exchange, Integration, and Streams*, pages 1–37. 2013. DOI: 10.4230/DFU.Vol5.10452.1. 87

Mauricio Osorio and Bharat Jayaraman. Aggregation and negation-as-failure. *New Generation Comput.*, 17(3):255–284, 1999. DOI: 10.1007/BF03037222. 99

Robert Paige and Jacob T. Schwartz. Reduction in strength of high level operations. In *Proc. 4th ACM SIGACT-SIGPLAN Symp. on Principles of Programming Languages*, pages 58–71, 1977. 32

Luigi Palopoli. Testing logic programs for local stratification. *Theor. Comp. Sci.*, 103(2):205–234, 1992. DOI: 10.1016/0304-3975(92)90013-6. 60

Christos H. Papadimitriou. *Computational Complexity*. Addison-Wesley, 1994. ISBN 978-0-201-53082-7. 14, 15

Christos H. Papadimitriou and Kenneth Steiglitz. *Combinatorial Optimization: Algorithms and Complexity*. Prentice-Hall, 1982. 57

Nikolay Pelov, Marc Denecker, and Maurice Bruynooghe. Well-founded and stable semantics of logic programs with aggregates. *Theory & Practice of Logic Program.*, 7(3):301–353, 2007. DOI: 10.1017/S1471068406002973. 99

Fernando C. N. Pereira and David H. D. Warren. Definite clause grammars for language analysis - a survey of the formalism and a comparison with augmented transition networks. *Artificial Intell.*, 13(3):231–278, 1980. DOI: 10.1016/0004-3702(80)90003-X. 126

Halina Przymusinska and Teodor C. Przymusinski. Weakly perfect model semantics for logic programs. In *Proc. 5th Int. Conf. Logic Programming*, pages 1106–1120, 1988. 59

Teodor C. Przymusinski. On the declarative semantics of deductive databases and logic programs. In *Foundations of Deductive Databases and Logic Programming*, pages 193–216. Morgan Kaufmann, 1988. 39, 41, 59

Teodor C. Przymusinski. On the declarative and procedural semantics of logic programs. *J. Autom. Reasoning*, 5(2):167–205, 1989. DOI: 10.1007/BF00243002. 41

Teodor C. Przymusinski. Stable semantics for disjunctive programs. *New Generation Comput.*, 9 (3/4):401–424, 1991. DOI: 10.1007/BF03037171. 59

Raghu Ramakrishnan and Johannes Gehrke. *Database Management Systems (3rd ed.)*. McGraw-Hill, 2003. 15

Raghu Ramakrishnan, François Bancilhon, and Abraham Silberschatz. Safety of recursive horn clauses with infinite relations. In *Proc. 6th ACM SIGACT-SIGMOD-SIGART Symp. on Principles of Database Systems*, pages 328–339, 1987. DOI: 10.1145/28659.28694. 32

Raghu Ramakrishnan, Yehoshua Sagiv, Jeffrey D. Ullman, and Moshe Y. Vardi. Proof-tree transformation theorems and their applications. In *Proc. 8th ACM SIGACT-SIGMOD-SIGART Symp. on Principles of Database Systems*, pages 172–181, 1989. DOI: 10.1145/73721.73739. 126

Raghu Ramakrishnan, Divesh Srivastava, and S. Sudarshan. CORAL - control, relations and logic. In *Proc. 18th Int. Conf. on Very Large Data Bases*, pages 238–250, 1992. 99

Raghu Ramakrishnan, Kenneth A. Ross, Divesh Srivastava, and S. Sudarshan. Efficient incremental evaluation of queries with aggregation. In *International Symposium on Logic Programming*, pages 204–218, 1994. 99

Fabrizio Riguzzi and Terrance Swift. Terminating evaluation of logic programs with finite three-valued models. *ACM Trans. Comput. Log.*, 15(4):32:1–32:38, 2014. DOI: 10.1145/2629337. 86

John Alan Robinson. A machine-oriented logic based on the resolution principle. *J. ACM*, 12 (1):23–41, 1965. DOI: 10.1145/321250.321253. 32

Kenneth A. Ross. Modular stratification and magic sets for datalog programs with negation. *J. ACM*, 41(6):1216–1266, 1994. DOI: 10.1145/195613.195646. 126

Kenneth A. Ross and Yehoshua Sagiv. Monotonic aggregation in deductive database. *J. Comp. and System Sci.*, 54(1):79–97, 1997. DOI: 10.1006/jcss.1997.1453. 99

Domenico Saccà. Deterministic and non-deterministic stable model semantics for unbound datalog queries. In *Proc. 5th Int. Conf. on Database Theory*, pages 353–367, 1995. DOI: 10.1007/3-540-58907-4_27. 59

Domenico Saccà. The expressive powers of stable models for bound and unbound datalog queries. *J. Comp. and System Sci.*, 54(3):441–464, 1997. DOI: 10.1006/jcss.1997.1446. 60

Domenico Saccà and Carlo Zaniolo. On the implementation of a simple class of logic queries for databases. In *Proc. 5th ACM SIGACT-SIGMOD Symp. on Principles of Database Systems*, pages 16–23, 1986. DOI: 10.1145/6012.6013. 125

Domenico Saccà and Carlo Zaniolo. Magic counting methods. In *Proc. ACM SIGMOD Int. Conf. on Management of Data*, pages 49–59, 1987. DOI: 10.1145/38714.38725. 110

Domenico Saccà and Carlo Zaniolo. The generalized counting method for recursive logic queries. *Theor. Comp. Sci.*, 62(1-2):187–220, 1988. DOI: 10.1007/3-540-17187-8_28. 110, 121

Domenico Saccà and Carlo Zaniolo. Stable models and non-determinism in logic programs with negation. In *Proc. 9th ACM SIGACT-SIGMOD-SIGART Symp. on Principles of Database Systems*, pages 205–217, 1990. DOI: 10.1145/298514.298572. 47

Domenico Saccà and Carlo Zaniolo. Partial models and three-valued models in logic programs with negation. In *Proc. 1st Int. Conf. Logic Programming and Nonmonotonic Reasoning*, pages 87–101, 1991. 59

Domenico Saccà and Carlo Zaniolo. Deterministic and non-deterministic stable models. *J. of Logic and Comput.*, 7(5):555–579, 1997. DOI: 10.1093/logcom/7.5.555. 59

Yehoshua Sagiv and Moshe Y. Vardi. Safety of datalog queries over infinite databases. In *Proc. 8th ACM SIGACT-SIGMOD-SIGART Symp. on Principles of Database Systems*, pages 160–171, 1989. DOI: 10.1145/73721.73738. 32

Yatin P. Saraiya. Linearizing nonlinear recursions in polynomial time. In *Proc. 8th ACM SIGACT-SIGMOD-SIGART Symp. on Principles of Database Systems*, pages 182–189, 1989. DOI: 10.1145/73721.73740. 110

John S. Schlipf. The expressive powers of the logic programming semantics. *J. Comp. and Syst. Sci.*, 51(1):64–86, 1995. DOI: 10.1006/jcss.1995.1053. 43, 59

Peter Schneider-Kamp, Jürgen Giesl, and Manh Thang Nguyen. The dependency triple framework for termination of logic programs. In *Proc. International Symposium on Logic-based Program Synthesis and Transformation*, pages 37–51, 2009a. DOI: 10.1007/978-3-642-12592-8_4. 86

Peter Schneider-Kamp, Jürgen Giesl, Alexander Serebrenik, and René Thiemann. Automated termination proofs for logic programs by term rewriting. *ACM Trans. Comput. Log.*, 11(1), 2009b. DOI: 10.1145/1614431.1614433. 86

Peter Schneider-Kamp, Jürgen Giesl, Thomas Ströder, Alexander Serebrenik, and René Thiemann. Automated termination analysis for logic programs with cut. *Theory & Practice of Logic Program.*, 10(4-6):365–381, 2010. DOI: 10.1017/S1471068410000165. 86

Jiwon Seo, Stephen Guo, and Monica S. Lam. Socialite: Datalog extensions for efficient social network analysis. In *Proc. 29th Int. Conf. on Data Engineering*, 2013. DOI: 10.1109/ICDE.2013.6544832. 129

Alexander Serebrenik and Danny De Schreye. On termination of meta-programs. *Theory & Practice of Logic Program.*, 5(3):355–390, 2005. DOI: 10.1017/S1471068404002248. 86

Warren Shen, AnHai Doan, Jeffrey F. Naughton, and Raghu Ramakrishnan. Declarative information extraction using datalog with embedded extraction predicates. In *Proc. 33rd Int. Conf. on Very Large Data Bases*, pages 1033–1044, 2007. 129

Alexander Shkapsky, Mohan Yang, and Carlo Zaniolo. Optimizing recursive queries with monotonic aggregates in deals. In *Proc. 31st Int. Conf. on Data Engineering*, pages 867–878, 2015. DOI: 10.1007/BFb0056001. 60

Abraham Silberschatz, Henry F. Korth, and S. Sudarshan. *Database System Concepts, 6th ed.* McGraw-Hill Book Company, 2010. 15

Patrik Simons, Ilkka Niemelä, and Timo Soininen. Extending and implementing the stable model semantics. *Artificial Intell.*, 138(1-2):181–234, 2002. DOI: 10.1016/S0004-3702(02)00187-X. 60

Christian Sternagel and Aart Middeldorp. Root-labeling. In *Rewriting Techniques and Applications*, pages 336–350, 2008. DOI: 10.1007/978-3-540-70590-1_23. 86

S. Sudarshan and Raghu Ramakrishnan. Aggregation and relevance in deductive databases. In *Proc. 17th Int. Conf. on Very Large Data Bases*, pages 501–511, 1991. DOI: 10.1006/jcss.1997.1453. 99

Tommi Syrjänen. Omega-restricted logic programs. In *Proc. 6th Int. Conf. Logic Programming and Nonmonotonic Reasoning*, pages 267–279, 2001. DOI: 10.1007/3-540-45402-0_20. 86

Daniel Troy, Clement T. Yu, and Weining Zhang. Linearization of nonlinear recursive rules. *IEEE Trans. Software Eng.*, 15(9):1109–1119, 1989. DOI: 10.1109/32.31368. 110

Jeffrey D. Ullman. *Principles of Database and Knowledge-Base Systems, Volume I.* Computer Science Press, 1988. 11, 15, 26, 32

Jeffrey D. Ullman. *Principles of Database and Knowledge-Base Systems, Volume II.* Computer Science Press, 1989. 110, 126

Jeffrey D. Ullman. The interface between language theory and database theory. In *Theoretical Studies in Computer Science*, pages 133–151, 1992. 112, 126

Jeffrey D. Ullman and Allen Van Gelder. Parallel complexity of logical query programs. In *Proc. 27th Annual Symp. on Foundations of Computer Science*, pages 438–454, 1986. DOI: 10.1109/SFCS.1986.40. 126

Maarten H. van Emden and Robert A. Kowalski. The semantics of predicate logic as a programming language. *J. ACM*, 23(4):733–742, 1976. DOI: 10.1145/321978.321991. 32

Allen Van Gelder. Negation as failure using tight derivations for general logic programs. *J. Logic Program.*, 6(1&2):109–133, 1989. DOI: 10.1016/0743-1066(89)90032-0. 36

Allen Van Gelder. The well-founded semantics of aggregation. In *Proc. 11th ACM SIGACT-SIGMOD-SIGART Symp. on Principles of Database Systems*, pages 127–138, 1992. DOI: 10.1145/137097.137854. 99

Allen Van Gelder, Kenneth A. Ross, and John S. Schlipf. Unfounded sets and well-founded semantics for general logic programs. In *Proc. 7th ACM SIGACT-SIGMOD-SIGART Symp. on Principles of Database Systems*, pages 221–230, 1988. DOI: 10.1145/308386.308444. 43

Allen Van Gelder, Kenneth A. Ross, and John S. Schlipf. The well-founded semantics for general logic programs. *J. ACM*, 38(3):620–650, 1991. DOI: 10.1145/116825.116838. 43, 45, 46, 47

Sofie Verbaeten, Danny De Schreye, and Konstantinos F. Sagonas. Termination proofs for logic programs with tabling. *ACM Trans. Comput. Log.*, 2(1):57–92, 2001. DOI: 10.1145/371282.371357. 86

Laurent Vieille. Recursive query processing: The power of logic. *Theor. Comp. Sci.*, 69(1):1–53, 1989. DOI: 10.1016/0304-3975(89)90088-1. 126

Dean Voets and Danny De Schreye. Non-termination analysis of logic programs with integer arithmetics. *Theory & Practice of Logic Program.*, 11(4-5):521–536, 2011. DOI: 10.1017/S1471068411000159. 86

Peter T. Wood. Factoring augmented regular chain programs. In *Proc. 16th Int. Conf. on Very Large Data Bases*, pages 255–263, 1990. 109, 110

Mihalis Yannakakis. Graph-theoretic methods in database theory. In *Proc. 9th ACM SIGACT-SIGMOD-SIGART Symp. on Principles of Database Systems*, pages 230–242, 1990. DOI: 10.1145/298514.298576. 110, 126

Jia-Huai You and Li-Yan Yuan. On the equivalence of semantics for normal logic programs. *J. Logic Program.*, 22(3):211–222, 1995. DOI: 10.1016/0743-1066(94)00023-Y. 59

Carlo Zaniolo. Safety and compilation of non-recursive horn clauses. In *Proc. 1st International Conference on Expert Database Systems*, pages 237–252, 1986. DOI: 10.1016/0304-3975(86)90015-0. 32

Hans Zantema. Termination of term rewriting: Interpretation and type elimination. *J. of Symbol. Comput.*, 17(1):23–50, 1994. DOI: 10.1006/jsco.1994.1003. 86

Hans Zantema. Termination of term rewriting by semantic labelling. *Fundamenta Informaticae*, 24(1/2):89–105, 1995. DOI: 10.3233/FI-1995-24124. 86

Wenchao Zhou, Yun Mao, Boon Thau Loo, and Martín Abadi. Unified declarative platform for secure netwoked information systems. In *Proc. 25th Int. Conf. on Data Engineering*, pages 150–161, 2009. DOI: 10.1109/ICDE.2009.58. 129, 130

Authors' Biographies

SERGIO GRECO

Sergio Greco is a Full Professor and Chair of the DIMES Department at the University of Calabria (Italy). Before that he was Assistant Professor (1989-1998) and Associate Professor (1998-2000) at the University of Calabria and visiting researcher at the Microelectronics and Computer Corporation of Austin (1990-1991) and at the of University of California at Los Angeles (1996 and 1998). Prof. Greco's research interests include database theory, data integration, inconsistent data, data mining, knowledge representation, logic programming, and computational logic.

CRISTIAN MOLINARO

Cristian Molinaro received his Ph.D. degree in Computer Science Engineering from the University of Calabria, Italy. He was a Visiting Scholar at the Department of Computer Science and Engineering of the State University of New York at Buffalo. He was a Faculty Research Assistant at the University of Maryland Institute for Advanced Computer Studies (2009-2011). Currently, he is an Assistant Professor at the University of Calabria, Italy. His research interests include database theory and logic programming.

Printed in the United States
by Baker & Taylor Publisher Services